Holistic Approach to Quantum Cryptography in Cyber Security

This new book discusses the concepts while also highlighting the challenges in the field of quantum cryptography and also covering cryptographic techniques and cyber security techniques, in a single volume.

It comprehensively covers important topics in the field of quantum cryptography with applications, including quantum key distribution, position-based quantum cryptography, quantum teleportation, quantum e-commerce, quantum cloning, cyber security techniques' architectures and design, cyber security techniques management, software-defined networks, and cyber security techniques for 5G communication. The text also discusses the security of practical quantum key distribution systems, applications and algorithms developed for quantum cryptography, as well as cyber security through quantum computing and quantum cryptography.

The text will be beneficial for graduate students, academic researchers, and professionals working in the fields of electrical engineering, electronics and communications engineering, computer science, and information technology.

Holistic Approach to Quantum Cryptography in Cyber Security

Edited by
Shashi Bhushan
Manoj Kumar
Pramod Kumar
Renjith V. Ravi
Anuj Kumar Singh

CRC Press
Taylor & Francis Group
Boca Raton London New York

CRC Press is an imprint of the
Taylor & Francis Group, an **informa** business

First edition published 2023
by CRC Press
6000 Broken Sound Parkway NW, Suite 300, Boca Raton, FL 33487-2742

and by CRC Press
2 Park Square, Milton Park, Abingdon, Oxon, OX14 4RN

Library of Congress Cataloging-in-Publication Data

Names: Shashi Bhushan, 1928- editor.
Title: Holistic approach to quantum cryptography in cyber security / edited
   Shashi Bhushan, Manoj Kumar, Pramod Kumar, Renjith V. Ravi, Anuj Kumar
   Singh.
Description: First edition. | Boca Raton : CRC Press, 2022. | Includes
   bibliographical references and index.
Identifiers: LCCN 2022003085 (print) | LCCN 2022003086 (ebook) | ISBN
   9781032253923 (hbk) | ISBN 9781032282701 (pbk) | ISBN 9781003296034
   (ebk)
Subjects: LCSH: Data encryption (Computer science) | Computer
   networks--Security measures. | Quantum cryptography.
Classification: LCC QA76.9.D335 H65 2022 (print) | LCC QA76.9.D335
   (ebook) | DDC 005.8/24--dc23/eng/20220419
LC record available at https://lccn.loc.gov/2022003085
LC ebook record available at https://lccn.loc.gov/2022003086

ISBN: 9781032253923 (hbk)
ISBN: 9781032282701 (pbk)
ISBN: 9781003296034 (ebk)

DOI: 10.1201/9781003296034

Typeset in Times
by Deanta Global Publishing Services, Chennai, India

Contents

Preface

Quantum cryptography utilizes the subtle properties of quantum mechanics, for example, the quantum no-cloning hypothesis and the Heisenberg uncertainty principle. In contrast to conventional cryptography, whose security is regularly based on unproven computational assumptions, quantum cryptography has a significant advantage in that its security is frequently based on the laws of physics. Thus far, the proposed applications of quantum cryptography include quantum key distribution (QKD) and quantum bit commitment.

Many of us are already using wireless sensor devices in our day-to-day life, but security in those devices or applications using those devices is very important. Comprehensive analysis of practical quantum cryptography systems implemented in actual physical environments via either free-space or fiber-optic cable quantum channels is also observed. Quantum secret sharing is one of the important parts of quantum cryptography.

Apart from these, security and privacy are vital to modern blockchain technology since they can exist without an authorized third party, which means that there may not be a trusted responsible person or organization in charge of systems. Security of the current systems is based on computational hardness assumptions, and many of the standard cryptography systems are known to be vulnerable to the advent of full-fledged quantum computers. On the other hand, it is possible to make a blockchain more secure by quantum information technology. So these are some of the main reasons for writing about quantum cryptography and its applications.

Editors

Shashi Bhushan is Assistant Professor at the University of Petroleum and Energy Studies. He earned a BE from the University of Rajasthan, India, an MTech degree in Computer Science from the Amity University Rajasthan in 2013, and a PhD degree in Computer Science and Engineering.

He has 10 years of university-level teaching experience in Computer Science. He has several patents in the area of the internet of things (IoT). He has published many articles in IEEE, Springer, and other reputed journals and conferences. As a technical member and Publicity Chair, he has organized several international conferences. His areas of research include wireless sensor networks and the internet of things.

Manoj Kumar earned his PhD in Computer Science from the Northcap University, Gurugram, Haryana. He earned an MSc (Information Security and Forensics) degree from ITB, Dublin, and MTech from ITM University, Gurugram, Haryana, India. He did his BTech in Computer Science at Kurukshetra University. Dr Kumar has more than 9.5 years of experience in research and academics. He has published over 45 papers in reputed journals and conferences. Presently, Dr Kumar is an Assistant Professor (SG) at the University of Petroleum and Energy Studies, Dehradun. He is a member of various professional bodies and has reviewed many reputed international journals.

Pramod Kumar has been a Professor, Head (CSE) and Dean (CSE and IT) in Krishna Engineering College (KIET Group), Ghaziabad, since January 2018. He has also served as Director of the Tula's Institute, Dehradun, Uttarakhand. He has more than 23 years of experience in academics. He completed his PhD in Computer Science and Engineering (CSE) in 2011 and MTech (CSE) in 2006. He is a senior member of IEEE (SMIEEE) and Joint Secretary of IEEE UP Section. He has published widely his research findings related to computer networks, the internet of things (IoT), and machine learning in international journals and conferences. He has authored/co-authored more than 50 research papers and several chapters in edited books. He has supervised and co-supervised several MTech and PhD students. He has organized more than 12 IEEE International Conferences in India and abroad, and all the research papers of these conferences are now available in IEEE Explore. He is the editor of two books. He has published three patents and has conducted more than 15 Faculty Development Programs (FDP) in collaboration with EICT, IIT Roorkee, EICT, IIT Kanpur, and AKTU. Funding for the FDP, conference/seminar is from AICTE/UGC/AKTU, and departmental funding of various student projects is from DST and MEITY. He conducted the IEEE National Workshop on Research Paper writing on March 27, 2017 and the IEEE Women Symposium on February 21, 2016.

Dr. Anuj Kumar Singh is an Assistant Professor at Krishna Engineering College, Ghaziabad. He received a BTech degree in Computer Science and Engineering from Punjab Technical University, India, an MTech degree in Computer Science and Engineering from the Uttrakhand Technical University, and a PhD degree in Computer Science and Engineering. He has 12 years of university-level teaching experience in computer science. He has several patents in the area of IoT and Machine Learning. He has had many published articles in IEEE, Springer, and other reputed journals and conferences. He is a member of various professional bodies and has reviewed for many reputed international journals. Areas of research include wireless sensor networks, internet of things, and Machine Learning.

Dr. Renjith V. Ravi is an Associate Professor and Head of the Department of Electronics and Communication Engineering and Coordinator of Post Graduate Programmes conducted at MEA Engineering College, Kerala, India. He graduated with a BTech degree in Electronics and Communication Engineering in 2007, ME degree in Embedded System Technology in 2011, and PhD in Electronics and Communication Engineering in 2019. He has published several research articles in SCIE and Scopus indexed journals, edited books, and IEEE International Conferences. He has served as a reviewer for SCIE and Scopus indexed journals from Springer, Elsevier, Inderscience, and IGI Global. He has edited two books from renowned international publishers. Dr Ravi has been granted one patent, one industrial design, and two copyrights. He had been awarded several outstanding achievements and service awards, and several best paper awards from IEEE International Conferences. He is a member of ISTE, IACSIT, IAENG, and SDIWC, and a senior member of SCIEI and SAISE. He has served as the Program Committee member, Session Chair, and reviewer of several national and international conferences conducted in India and abroad. His research areas include image cryptography, image processing, machine learning, and the internet of things. He is currently focusing his research on the area of secure image communication using image cryptography.

Contributors List

Monika Agrawal, Assistant Professor, Department of CSE, Sanjivani College of Engineering Kopargaon, Maharashtra, India.

Sharmila Arun, Department of Computer Science & Engineering, Krishna Engineering College, Ghaziabad, Uttar Pradesh, India.

Supriyo Banerjee, Department of Computer Science and Engineering, Kalyani Government Engineering College, Kalyani, West Bengal, India.

Shashi Bhushan, School of Computer Science, University of Petroleum and Energy Studies, Dehradun, Uttarakhand, India.

Chindiyababy, Department of Computing Technologies, School of Computing, SRM Institute of Science and Technology, Kattankulathur, Chennai, Tamil Nadu, India.

Meetali Chauhan, Assistant Professor, Department of Computer Science and Engineering, Gulzar Institute of Engineering and Technology (Affiliated To I.K.G. Punjab Technical University, Kapurthala) Gulzar Group of Institutions, Khanna (Ludhiana) Punjab, India 141401.

Sushopti Gawade, Pillai HOC College of Engineering and Technology, Navi Mumbai, Maharashtra, India.

Sagarika Ghosh, Faculty of Computer Science, Dalhousie University, Canada.

Swati Goel, Assistant Professor, Department of CSE, Krishna Engineering College, Ghaziabad, Uttar Pradesh, India.

Akshita Gupta, School of Electronics and Communication Engineering, Shri Mata Vaishno Devi University, Kakryal-182320, Katra, Jammu & Kashmir, India.

Sachin Kumar Gupta, School of Electronics and Communication Engineering, Shri Mata Vaishno Devi University, Kakryal-182320, Katra, Jammu & Kashmir, India.

Shaurya Gupta, School of Computer Science, UPES Dehradun, Uttarakhand, India.

Ramkumar Jayaraman, Department of Computing Technologies, School of Computing, SRM Institute of Science and Technology, Kattankulathur, Chennai, Tamil Nadu, India.

Aman Kataria, Project Associate, CSIR-CSIO, Chandigarh, India 160030.

Manoj Kumar, School of Computer Science, University of Petroleum and Energy Studies, Uttarakhand, India.

Pramod Kumar, Krishna Engineering College, Uttar Pradesh, India.

Biswajit Maiti, Department of Physics, Maulana Azad College, West Bengal, India.

Sita Rani, Professor, Department of Computer Science and Engineering, Gulzar Institute of Engineering and Technology, (Affiliated To I.K.G. Punjab Technical University, Kapurthala), Gulzar Group of Institutions, Khanna (Ludhiana), Punjab, India 141401.

Renjith V. Ravi, Department of Electronics and Communication Engineering, MEA Engineering College, Kerala, India.

Banani Saha, Department of Computer Science and Engineering, University of Calcutta, West Bengal, India.

Srinivas Sampalli, Faculty of Computer Science, Dalhousie University, Canada.

Gaurav Sharma, Pillai HOC College of Engineering and Technology, Navi Mumbai, Maharashtra, India.

Manjula Sharma, School of Electronics and Communication Engineering, Shri Mata Vaishno Devi University, Kakryal-182320, Katra, Jammu & Kashmir, India.

Meenu Shukla, Department of Computer Science & Engineering, Krishna Engineering College, Ghaziabad, Uttar Pradesh, India.

Vinod Kumar Shukla, Department of Engineering and Architecture, Amity University, Dubai, UAE.

Suraj Pal Singh, Department of Computer Science and Engineering, Krishna Engineering College, Ghaziabad, Uttar Pradesh, India.

Marzia Zaman, Research and Development, Cistel Technology, Canada.

Fatima Ziya, Department of Computer Science and Engineering, Krishna Engineering College, Ghaziabad, India.

1 Toward Security in Software-Defined Networks with Trust and Monitoring

Gaurav Sharma and Sushopti Gawade

CONTENTS

1.1 INTRODUCTION

Software-defined network (SDN) has emerged as a new paradigm in networking which has introduced programmability in networking. The Control Plane and Data Plane are separated in a software-defined network, allowing for greater network management stability [1]. This separation also enables a single controller in the Control Plane to control several data-forwarding devices, such as switches. SDN controllers at the Control Plane, which are servers on which programs can be deployed, can also be configured. The SDN controller and its applications can communicate using application programming interfaces (APIs). RESTful APIs, as well as other types of APIs such as Java, Python, and others, are provided by all available controllers [2].

DOI: 10.1201/9781003296034-1

Figure 1.1 illustrates the concept of separation planes introduced in SDN compared to traditional networks. The separation of planes happens in the network devices and helps in having flexible management and control of the network devices and, hence, the network.

1.1.1 SDN ARCHITECTURE

The basic SDN architecture, with the functionality of the SDN separated in the Application Plane, Control Plane, and Data Plane, is presented in Figure 1.2.

a. **Control Plane**

In SDN, the Control Plane's job is to provide various network-related functions. The controller is located at the Control Plane and interacts with the applications and switches through the North-Bound and South-Bound APIs, respectively. The controller sends forwarding rules (flows) to Data Plane devices and sends data, statistics, and an interface to the applications to manage the network.

b. **Data Plane**

The Data Plane's role in the network is to provide forwarding. Forwarding devices like OpenFlow switches are used at the Data Plane. It saves the flow rules that the controller receives from the South-Bound API, such as the OpenFlow protocol. If there are no rules for a certain flow, it requests the flow rule from the controller.

c. **Application Plane**

The Application Plane is where the applications are incorporated with the network through the North-Bound APIs of the controller. To allow communication between the application and the controller, RESTful, Java, Python, and other APIs may be used.

SDN has many advantages, including dynamic network programmability, network virtualization, and much more effective and centralized network management. It has opened the way for innovative network functions while also necessitating the

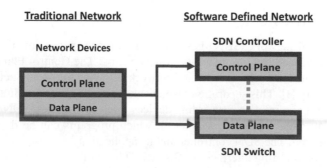

FIGURE 1.1   Separation of planes.

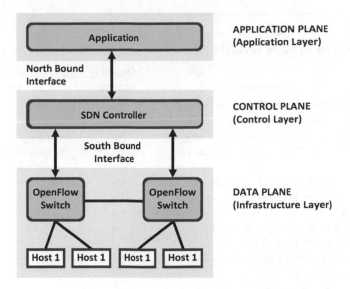

FIGURE 1.2   SDN architecture [1].

creation of new protocols and methods for implementing them. Because of its benefits, SDN is expected to replace existing traditional networks.

For all of the benefits that SDN provides, it also introduces a new series of security threats. The division of network operations in the Control Plane and Data Plane introduces new vulnerabilities into the SDN architecture.

SDN is still developing and lacks security mechanisms at different levels. So there is a strong need for external security mechanisms that can overcome such vulnerabilities in the SDN architecture.

1.2   SECURITY CHALLENGES IN SOFTWARE-DEFINED NETWORKS

SDN, with network programmability, provides several new features such as traffic programmability, agility, and the ability to establish policy-driven network supervision and network automation. However, in addition to these benefits, SDN introduces a new range of security challenges. The division of network functions in the Control Plane and Data Plane introduces new flaws into the SDN architecture.

1.2.1   THREATS TO SDN

Kreutz *et al.* [3] have identified the threat vectors in SDN security. Table 1.1 provides the details of each threat vector identified in [3] and the layer/plane in SDN architecture which may be targeted.

Yoon *et al.* [4] provide a detailed review and categorization of the vectors for possible abuse or attack in SDN. The authors have identified 22 attack vectors, which include Control Plane, Control Channel, and Data Plane attacks.

TABLE 1.1

Threat Vectors in SDN Security [3]

Threat Vector	Description	Specific to SDN	Target
1	Forged or faked traffic flows by malicious users or faulty end devices.	No	Data Plane
2	Attacks on vulnerabilities in switches	No	Data Plane
3	Attacks on Control Plane communication	Yes	North-Bound and South-Bound Communication
4	Attacks on and vulnerabilities in controllers	Yes	Control Plane
5	Lack of mechanisms to ensure trust between the controller and management applications	Yes	North-Bound Communication
6	Attacks on and vulnerabilities in administrative stations	No	Application Plane
7	Lack of trusted resources for forensics and remediation	No	All planes

Scott-Hayward *et al.* [5] also present a detailed comparison of the research work at different SDN layers/interfaces. It categorizes the potential attacks to which the SDN architecture is vulnerable as:

- Unauthorized access
- Data leakage
- Data modification
- Malicious/compromised applications
- Denial of service
- Configuration issues
- System-level SDN security

Akhunzada *et al.* [6] developed a modern layered or interface taxonomy of identified SDN security vulnerabilities, attacks, and challenges to explain the key categories of security implications of each SDN layer/interface. They have also compared the leading security solutions proposed by various researchers. Figure 1.3 presents the taxonomy of the SDN security vulnerabilities, attacks, and challenges identified by Akhunzada *et al.* [6].

Li *et al.* [7] have focused on the security challenges and countermeasures for OpenFlow-based SDN. They have considered the attacks on the SDN's confidentiality, integrity, and availability and classified the security challenges as follows:

a. Switch-related security challenges
b. Controller-related security challenges
c. Channel-related security challenges

Shaghaghi *et al.* [8] have examined recent advancements in SDNs, identified the most frequent vulnerabilities, and presented a new SDN attack taxonomy. They have

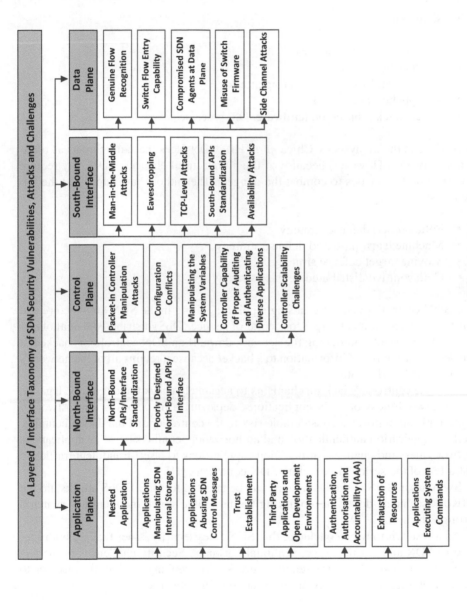

FIGURE 1.3 Taxonomy of identified SDN security vulnerabilities, attacks, and challenges [6].

also provided a detailed analysis of the challenges in protecting the SDN Data Plane and Control Plane, as well as recommended solutions for the same.

Recently, Yurekten *et al.* [9] have presented the threat categorization for SDN based on threat intelligence. It categorizes the threats, in the study, as:

- Scanning attacks
- Spoofing attacks
- Network-level DoS attacks
- Sniffing attacks
- Malware and social engineering attacks
- Web application attacks
- Other attacks (based on hardware, OS, processes)

According to the analysis by Chica *et al.* [10], SDN faces the same threats as traditional networks. However, because of the architectural changes, SDN may require new or modified tactics to combat the dangers. The authors have suggested the following strategies:

- Policy-based defense strategy
- Machine learning-based defense strategy
- Moving target defense strategy:
- Collaborative/distributed defense strategy

The SDN controller can act as a single point of failure in the SDN architecture and can become a prominent target for denial of service (DoS)/distributed denial of service (DDoS) attacks, knocking the network down. If an SDN controller is hacked, it can serve as a source of information to a hacker because it retains all of the network's topology and traffic data.

Because controllers lack mechanisms to accurately check the eligibility, legality, and trustworthiness of SDN applications, deploying a malicious or untrustworthy SDN application poses a considerable risk to the controller and the data it contains. Lack of application authentication and authorization, conflicts between applications on flow rules, and chances for malicious applications to insert fraudulent traffic are just a few of the serious issues with SDN controllers [11].

Switches in SDN at the Data Plane can be targeted for DoS/DDoS attacks, taking network segments down, or modifying the flow table stored in OpenFlow switches through the hosts.

As a result, it may be concluded that SDN faces security issues that are both specific to SDN and similar to conventional networks. Security challenges in the five focus areas can also be addressed to secure SDN, depending on all of the research to identify prospective difficulty areas in the SDN architecture:

- Application Plane (application security)
- North-Bound Interface (NBI; secure communication using APIs—RESTful, Java, Python)

- Control Plane (SDN controller security)
- South-Bound Interface (SBI; secure communication using protocols—OpenFlow, Netconf, etc.)
- Data Plane (switch and end-device security)

1.3 LITERATURE REVIEW—DIFFERENT APPROACHES TO SDN SECURITY

In recent years, many researchers have presented security solutions for SDN utilizing a variety of techniques. The following are some of the most well-known proposals for securing SDN using various techniques.

Chowdhary et al. [12] have presented a dynamic game-based security framework for SDN in the cloud. To protect SDN from DDoS attacks, it employs dynamic game theory based on reward and punishment in network bandwidth consumption. The attacker's network bandwidth is dynamically decreased for a set length of time as a punishment. The bandwidth of the player is restored (rewarded) once it starts cooperating.

In recent years, many machine learning-based approaches have been proposed to deal with security in SDN.

Elsayed et al. [13] have given an analysis of malicious traffic detection in SDN using publicly available datasets and existing machine learning algorithms. They have uncovered the flaws in traditional machine learning techniques to provide a more secure SDN security framework in the future.

Sultana et al. [14] have studied a variety of intrusion detection techniques that used machine learning and deep learning. They have also explored the difficulties in deploying such strategies in real-world networks to detect traffic problems and monitor networks.

Bawany et al. [15] have given an in-depth analysis of DDoS attack detection and mitigation approaches using SDN. They have also analyzed and classified those techniques based on entropy-based detection mechanisms, machine learning, traffic pattern analysis, connection-rate-based anomaly detection, and intrusion detection system (IDS) integration with OpenFlow. The authors have also proposed a proactive DDoS Defense Framework (ProDefense) for smart city data centers based on SDN, which allows application-specific needs for DDoS attack detection and mitigation to be implemented.

Banse et al. [16], to achieve security, have presented a taxonomy-based policy framework for SDN North-Bound Interfaces. A taxonomic relationship expresses rules that clearly define the relationships of users, switches, ports, and hosts. The rules are written using first-order logic (FOL), which does not use fixed identifiers. A policy specifies which resources a certain user has access to. It is extremely desirable in dynamic network topologies with new SDN applications possibly joining and leaving the network at any time because security regulations cannot be defined using static identifiers such as certificates or names.

Niemiec et al. [17] have proposed—Risk Assessment and Management approach to SEcure SDN (RAMSES). It investigates the reputations of external programs that deliver requests to the SDN controller and monitors their possible impact on network performance using a risk-aware methodology. The impact on the SDN network (impact) and the provider's reputation are used to assess the risk posed by an external application (likelihood).

1.3.1 TRUST-BASED APPROACHES

Yao *et al.* [11] have proposed a Trust Management Framework (TMF) for SDN applications in which the trust value of an application is evaluated and is also dynamically updated based on its performance which is continuously monitored by the Network Performance Monitor (NPM) module with the help of Trusted Platform Module (TPM). The proposed TMF can also detect and solve the flow rule conflicts between applications. It can also detect malicious applications.

Duy *et al.* [18] have proposed "Trust Trident," a trust-based authentication framework, which manages secure communication between the applications and the controller. The proposed framework works like a plug-in that intercepts the requests from applications, opens them for analysis and evaluation of their privileges, and, if found correct, forwards them to the controller. It authenticates the application by the authentication module, and the authorization module checks for the permissions of the application to consume network resources.

Chowdhary *et al.* [19] have proposed "TRUFL," a distributed Trust Management Framework. The authors have identified threat vectors—Rogue Insider Attack and Compromised Switch Attack. The framework uses Public Key Infrastructure (PKI) to establish trust between only legitimate devices to communicate between different planes. It works over OpenStack and is developed to be deployed in a cloud environment.

Pisharody *et al.* [20] have proposed a security policy analysis framework to check the vulnerability of flow rules in SDN-based cloud environments. The authors have introduced a framework that monitors and maintains a conflict-free environment, including strategies to automatically resolve conflicts. They have classified and described the possible conflicts among flow rules in SDN's forwarding table that can cause information leakage. The framework detects flow rule conflicts in multiple SDN controllers and works to avoid them.

Aliyu *et al.* [21] have proposed a trust management mechanism enabling network applications to connect with the SDN controller securely. It achieves trust by authenticating the network applications and setting authorization rules, or privileges, that determine network resources that the application can use.

Betgé-Brezetz *et al.* [22] have proposed an intermediary layer between the controller and the switch called Trusted Oriented Controller Proxy (ToCP). It compares the flow rules from different redundant controllers and installs the most trusted one on the switch. Every controller participates in configuring the paths and has a confidence level. The path is configured only if the cumulative trust level is more than the threshold.

Banse *et al.* [23] have presented a web-based, secure, independent North-Bound Interface to the controller which supports the deployment of external applications.

The SDN applications and the controller communicate with each other through an encrypted channel. The framework contains an integrated trust manager that enables the restriction of the interface to only authenticated and trusted applications. A configurable permission system allows the enforcement of authorization or permissions to the applications.

Isong *et al.* [24] have proposed a trust model to protect the controller by allowing only the applications that meet a minimum trust level to communicate with the controller and consume network resources. The researchers have proposed a trust establishment model between the application and the controller and used a trust matrix of applications corresponding to their identity for effective resources management in SDN. It uses direct trust which is based on the observation of activities performed by SDN applications when requesting network resources and also on previous interactions between the controller and applications that were either successful (s) or a failure (f).

Burikova *et al.* [25] have proposed a Trust Management Framework that establishes and manages the trust between the application and the controller for the SDN-based internet of things (IoT) platform. It includes authentication of the applications by the controller and their authorization (verifying permissions). Applications are also categorized as security applications (highest priority) and non-security applications (lowest priority) and get permissions accordingly. Trust is calculated based on factors such as reputation, operational risk, information risk, and privacy level.

Cui *et al.* [26] have proposed an approach to protect the North-Bound Interface by introducing the application authentication system, which addresses the key challenges of resolving conflicts between untrusted applications and requests. The authentication process includes permission checks to verify the access permission of the application.

Scott-Hayward *et al.* [27] have presented an approach to secure the North-Bound Interface by introducing a permission-based trust management mechanism for SDN—OperationCheckpoint. It ensures that controller operations are available to trusted applications only. However, it has limitations that cannot change the rights of the application dynamically to prevent their malicious behaviors.

Shin *et al.* [28] introduced FRESCO, an OpenFlow security application development framework that makes it easier to design and build OF-enabled detection and mitigation modules quickly and modularly. To enforce flow constraints to defend the network against threats, the authors have introduced the security enforcement kernel [28, 29].

Lamb *et al.* [30] outline the constraints of trust within SDN. It discusses the different requirements for communication between different network entities. Sood *et al.* [31] conducted a theoretical study of policy-based security management or architecture, which dynamically manages the network.

The trust-based approaches discussed above are limited to a single plane. Mostly, the focus is on introducing trust between the controller and the applications, in the North-Bound Interface (NBI).

A trust evaluation method for the Data Plane nodes based on direct, indirect, and historical trust values has been presented by Zhao *et al.* [32]. The method stores the trust scores using blockchain; hence, they have named it TrustBlock. It considers the security (identity authentication) and reliability (forwarding status) for trust calculation.

Table 1.2 summarizes several popular trust-based security approaches proposed for protecting the SDN. It also describes the layer of SDN architecture and the interface at which they work.

1.3.2 SDN MONITORING

Monitoring network behavior is one approach to network security. This has traditionally been used in conventional networks to track and then prevent security incidents. Many researchers have used this approach to improve SDN security. This method is ideal for tracking the behavior of Data Plane devices, such as switches, as well as their communication with the controller.

Giotis *et al.* [33] and Zaalouk *et al.* [34] have used and explored traditional monitoring protocols such as NetFlow/IPFIX and sFlow with the SDN protocol, OpenFlow, to monitor the SDN network.

Yu *et al.* [35] have proposed FlowSense, which uses a push-based approach to receive flow statistics from the switches. In this approach, instead of monitoring the switches by polling actively, their performance is measured by passively capturing and analyzing control messages between the switches and the centralized controller.

Phan *et al.* [36] have proposed an SDN monitoring framework that separates the monitoring logic from the forwarding logic called SDN-Mon. This approach provides

TABLE 1.2

Prominent Trust-based Security Methods Proposed for SDN

Sr.	Research Work	SDN Layer/Interface	Comment
1	Betgé-Brezetz *et al.* [22], 2015	SBI, Data Plane	Uses polling method to get a cumulative trust score of the network. Redundant controllers will add to cost and complexity
2	Aliyu *et al.* [21], 2017	Application Plane, NBI	Uses authentication and authorization to evaluate trust of applications
3	Yao *et al.* [27], 2018	Application Plane, NBI	Requires a hardware chip—Trusted Platform Module (TPM)
4	Duy *et al.* [18], 2019	Application Plane, NBI	Uses authentication and authorization of applications via a separate Trust Trident REST API
5	Chowdhary *et al.* [19], 2019	Data Plane, Control Plane, SBI	Uses PKI-based mechanism to establish trust between the controller and the switches
6	Burikova *et al.* [25], 2019	Application Plane, NBI	Uses the factors—reputation and risk for trust calculation of applications by monitoring their behavior

a very fine-grained and efficient way of monitoring which is independent of the forwarding function, making it more flexible for various management applications.

Fawcett *et al.* [37] have introduced Tennison, a multi-level distributed monitoring and remediation framework for SDN. It brings in the concept of a separate Tennison coordinator which works along with the SDN controller. It can be used to detect DoS/DDoS attacks, scanning attacks, and intrusions and can protect against them. The Tennison coordinator also uses traditional network monitoring techniques like IPFIX and sFlow for monitoring.

Tsai *et al.* [38] present an overview of SDN monitoring solutions identifying the challenges and open issues. It provides a comprehensive review of monitoring SDN. It also compares traditional network monitoring with SDN monitoring in terms of collection, pre-processing, transmission, analysis, and presentation of traffic over the networks.

Traditional network monitoring methods have been used for SDN monitoring; however, real-time SDN monitoring to generate trust values for network entities such as the SDN controller, switches, and applications, as well as conventional networking devices, has not been thoroughly investigated.

1.4 CRITICAL ANALYSIS

A lot of work has been done in implementing security in SDN based on trust. But, almost all of them have focused on only a single plane. In [33], the overall trust is calculated using direct, indirect, and historical trust values. These trust values are based on parameters based on the forwarding performance of the Data Plane switches.

Performance metrics are as follows:

- Degradation in performance due to an attack, or any other factor
- Detection of flooding of messages and DoS/DDoS attack
- Detection of suspicious behavior
- Signs of intrusion through the compromised switch or node connected to the switch

These performance metrics can also be considered to contribute to the overall trust value of the Data Plane devices.

In [24], the researchers have focused on calculating direct trust for the applications based on a Trust Access Matrix, which is used to verify, which application can access which network resource through the controller. Thus, the concept of Authentication (verification of identity, authorization (restricting access to network resources), and accounting (monitoring of applications based on their behavior) can be used.

Also, there is a need for a solution, which can be deployed in the current setting, using a hybrid SDN. A hybrid network also uses traditional, or legacy, network devices. To propose a multiple-plane trust-based security architecture, it is important to understand how hybrid SDN works and is deployed [39, 40].

It is also essential to have a good understanding of the available SDN controllers and the features they provide. Ahmad *et al.* [41] have presented an extensive survey of the SDN controllers.

1.5 NETWORK MONITORING FOR TRUST IN SDN—A CONCEPT

SDN is still evolving and a lot of research is going on in the field of SDN security. The challenges are different in SDN compared to traditional networks; hence, the proposed solution may evolve as the research work progresses.

1.5.1 PROPOSED SECURITY CONCEPT

The proposed security architecture aims to use trust scores to monitor, permit, or restrict network entities over the network. The motivation behind a trust-based framework is to come up with a security solution that can monitor different parameters at different planes and will compute a trust score.

Figure 1.4 illustrates an initial concept of the proposed security architecture. A Trust Evaluator (TE) component is conceptualized with two modules—North-Bound Interface Trust Module (NBI-TM) and South-Bound Interface Trust Module (SBI-TM). The functions of NBI-TM and SBI-TM will be to calculate trust values for applications and the switches (and the flows) connected to the controller, respectively.

NBI-TM can use mechanisms like application authentication to verify that the application is registered and allowed to be connected to the controller. It may also perform the authorization function and check the permissions that the application

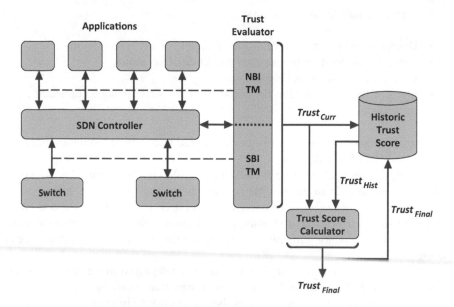

FIGURE 1.4 Proposed security architecture based on trust.

has, like, only getting the network statistics (read rights), or updating the flow rules (write rights). Additionally, it can also monitor the application behavior and keep a track of periodic updates and vulnerability patches. Based on these tasks performed on the applications regularly, NBI-TM can compute direct trust value for the application.

SBI-TM can use network monitoring tools and techniques to gather about the performance of the connected network devices. Both, techniques used for SDN and traditional networks, can be used to assess the security (authentication, vulnerabilities, incidents) and reliability (performance, task completion, data forwarding) of the Data Plane devices.

The trust score, $Trust_{Curr}$ for each network entity (applications, controllers, switches) is calculated by the Trust Evaluator (TE) module. This score is the current trust score calculated in real time. It is also stored in the Historic Trust Score (HTS) database and will be used for the final trust score calculation later. For every network entity, only one trust score entry exists in the HTS database and gets updated periodically. This trust score is $Trust_{Hist}$.

The Trust Score Calculator (TSC) module will calculate the final trust score for each network entity, $Trust_{Final}$. This score is the final trust score generated, which is based on the $Trust_{Curr}$ and $Trust_{Hist}$ scores.

$$Trust_{Final} = W_1 * Trust_{Curr} + W_2 * Trust_{Hist}$$

The security monitoring team can set the weight W_1 and W_2 for the $Trust_{Curr}$ and $Trust_{Hist}$ scores, respectively, and customize the system as per the enterprise monitoring requirements.

The final trust score, $Trust_{Final}$, is updated by the TSC module to the HTS database for future trust score calculation.

Figure 1.5 presents the tasks to be performed at each layer and the interface of the SDN architecture. The existing authentication, authorization, and accounting (AAA) processes may be used to authenticate and authorize network entities. This reduces the time, complexity, and additional skills needed to set up a security solution based on trust across multiple planes of the SDN architecture.

SDN monitoring-based approach may be deployed with less overhead in terms of new technologies and skills as the existing network monitoring tools can be used such as NetFlow/IPFIX and sFlow. Security data from already installed tools and techniques such as intrusion detection systems, firewalls, and other security protocols,

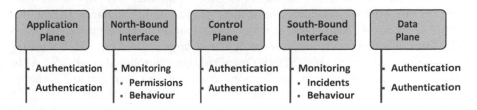

FIGURE 1.5 Tasks performed at each SDN layer and interface.

such as security incidents and anomalous activities, can also be used to calculate the trust score for network entities.

1.5.2 OBJECTIVES OF THE PROPOSED CONCEPT

As discussed earlier, many security mechanisms for SDN have been proposed to secure SDN; however, there is a lot of scope to work in this direction as there is still a lack of a trust-based security framework that can work with the SDN architecture across different planes.

The following are some areas that are not yet completely explored:

- No security framework has been proposed for a hybrid SDN setup that contains SDN and traditional network elements. Many organizations prefer to go with hybrid SDN as either they are deploying SDN gradually in a phase-wise manner or they do not intend to completely replace their traditional network with SDN.
- No single security framework has been proposed for the security of the entire SDN architecture across multiple planes.
- No security framework has been proposed that uses preventive as well as reactive strategies at the entire SDN architecture level.

The objectives that can be achieved by a trust-based security framework for SDN are:

- To have a trust management mechanism that uses monitoring, policies, and the behavior of the network entities to compute trust values
- To assess the security of different entities in SDN, working along with the traditional network
- The proposed trust-based security mechanism will present the security monitoring team with a trust score that will give the team quick information about the health of the network in real time

1.6 EXPERIMENTAL SETUP—A CASE STUDY

For the initial implementation of a test bed and deployment of an SDN with multiple nodes, OpenDayLight SDN controller with Mininet was used.

OpenDayLight controller is an open SDN controller that offers software components with well-defined application programming interfaces (APIs) that enable developers to easily build new network management and control applications [42]. Mininet is a network emulator for deploying large networks quickly for testing software-defined networking (SDN). OpenDayLight controller also provides APIs, which can be used by external applications to interact with controller and exchange data. Figure 1.6 presents the APIs provided by the OpenDayLight controller.

The APIs can be used by the applications to get, post, or update network data in the XML format as shown in Figure 1.7.

FIGURE 1.6 OpenDayLight APIs.

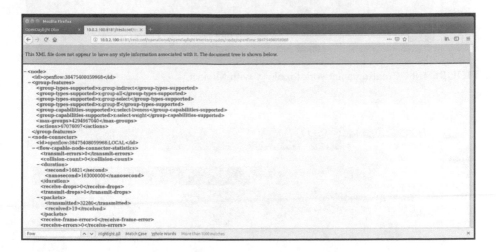

FIGURE 1.7 OpenDayLight data from APIs in XML format.

Mininet is one of the most popular network emulators for SDNs [43]. For testing the implementation, it may be used. Creating an SDN test bed with virtual machines has limitations of computing resources and may not scale beyond a certain limit. But a network emulator/simulator can be used to test the implementation on a larger network.

Figure 1.8 displays a basic topology created using Mininet. Mininet runs OpenvSwitch and has a basic controller. But Mininet can also be connected with external controllers.

The topology created using Mininet can be viewed in the connected OpenDayLight controller as shown in Figure 1.9.

FIGURE 1.8 Creating a network topology with Mininet.

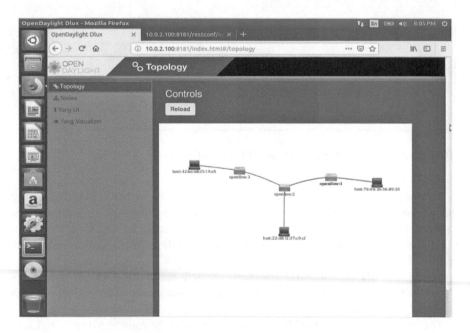

FIGURE 1.9 OpenDayLight connected to Mininet.

1.6.1   TELEMETRY DATA

Telemetry data or network monitoring data is collected using different existing tools. For example, sFlow data can be collected using sFlow-RT. Figure 1.10 presents the sFlow-RT dashboard.

The data collected can be processed and converted to formats like JSON for further processing. *sflowtool* is an example for converting sFlow data into a JSON format, which can be processed using programs to generate the required trust score based on different considerations set by the security team.

Figure 1.11 presents a flowchart for obtaining trust scores from the telemetry data. sFlow has been used as an example, but data from any, and multiple, network monitoring tool can be used. The use of standard existing monitoring techniques will ensure that the proposed mechanism will work with any SDN controller and also work with the traditional networking devices.

1.6.2   AUTHENTICATION, AUTHORIZATION, AND ACCOUNTING DATA

The already existing authentication, authorization, and accounting mechanisms can be used for authenticating the identity of the SDN applications and the various network entities. Permissions and the behavior of the apps and the network entities can be monitored for anomalies and provided to the proposed system. For this, the input can be gathered from the AAA Server, IDS, Firewalls, etc., and processed to get the trust score in real time. Any security incident or a breach can also impact the trust score.

Some SDN controllers have the AAA service embedded in them. This enables them to identify and verify the SDN applications (NBI) and the switches (SBI). This prevents spoofing of the applications and the switches.

FIGURE 1.10   OpenDayLight corrected to Mininet.

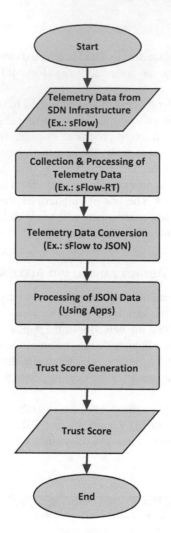

FIGURE 1.11   Trust Score using telemetry data.

Arbettu *et al.* [44] have presented a study on four leading open-source SDN controllers—OpenDaylight, ONOS, Rosemary, and Ryu. OpenDayLight controller supports AAA services for both NBI and SBI.

The network entity, app, or an entire network segment, which is more vulnerable and/or experiences more frequent attacks or failures, will over the period have a lower trust score. This will also be an indicator to the security team to quickly identify such more vulnerable sections of the network.

1.7   CONCLUSION

There is a need for a single framework that identifies the trustworthiness of all the entities in a network. Such a solution is required to simplify the identification of network entities in a network with low trust and will restrict them from accessing the network as per the policies. This will further become complex in an SDN environment with traditional network elements being used at the same time. Thus, traditional network elements and techniques also need to be considered by the framework.

The proposed mechanism is based on the existing concept of network monitoring and will use the existing techniques for the generation of trust scores for each network entity. This will help the security team to identify the low trust network entities, and also network segments, quickly and to detect and further investigate the issues in depth. This will help the team to monitor and manage the network and also in tasks like traffic engineering. As this mechanism can work with traditional and SDN devices, hybrid SDN network deployments can also use this method. The mechanism is also flexible to adapt to the changes in the network.

Thus, the proposed mechanism aims to present a comprehensive multiple-plane security framework that will overcome the shortcomings of the prior proposed methods and present a holistic solution to secure the SDN architecture.

REFERENCES

1. "Software-Defined Networking: The New Norm for Networks", https://opennetworking.org/sdn-resources/whitepapers/software-defined-networking-the-new-norm-for-networks/, Accessed: March 2021.
2. "Using HTTP Methods for RESTful Services", https://www.restapitutorial.com/lessons/httpmethods.html, Accessed: March 2021.
3. Diego Kreutz, Fernando M.V. Ramos, Paulo Verissimo, "Towards Secure and Dependable Software-defined Networks", Proceedings of the Second ACM SIGCOMM Workshop on Hot Topics in Software Defined Networking (HotSDN'13), pp. 55–60, August 2013.
4. Changhoon Yoon, Seungsoo Lee, Heedo Kang, Taejune Park, Seungwon Shin, Vinod Yegneswaran, Phillip Porras, Guofei Gu, "Flow Wars: Systemizing the Attack Surface and Defenses in Software-Defined Networks", *IEEE/ACM Transactions on Networking*, vol. 25, no. 6, pp. 3514–3530, December 2017.
5. Sandra Scott-Hayward, Sriram Natarajan, and Sakir Sezer, "A Survey of Security in Software Defined Networks", *IEEE Communication Surveys and Tutorials*, vol. 18, no. 1, First Quarter 2016.
6. Adnan Akhunzada, Abdullah Gani, Nor Badrul Anuar, Ahmed Abdelaziz, Muhammad Khurram Khan, Amir Hayat, Samee U. Khan, "Secure and Dependable Software Defined Networks", *Journal of Network and Computer Applications*, Elsevier, vol. 61, pp. 199–221, February 2016.
7. Wenjuan Li, Weizhi Meng, Lam For Kwok, "A Survey on OpenFlow-based Software Defined Networks: Security Challenges and Countermeasures", *Journal of Network and Computer Applications*, Elsevier, vol. 68, pp. 126–139, June 2016.
8. M. A. Shaghaghi, R. Kaafar, S. J. Buyya "Software-defined network (SDN) data plane security: Issues solutions and future directions", *Handbook of Computer Networks and Cyber Security, Springer*, pp. 341–387, 2020.
9. O. Yurekten and M. Demirci, "SDN-based Cyber Defense: A Survey", *Elsevier Journal: Future Generation Computer Systems*, vol. 115, pp. 126–149, February 2021.
10. J. C. C. Chica, J. C. Imbachi, and J. F. Botero, "Security in SDN: A Comprehensive Survey", *Journal of Network and Computer Applications*, vol. 159, 102595, 2020.
11. Zhen Yao, Zheng Yan, "A Trust Management Framework for Software-defined Network Applications", *Concurrency and Computation: Practice and Experience*, vol. 32, no. 16, p. e4518, March 2018.

12. Ankur Chowdhary, Sandeep Pisharody, Adel Saeed Alshamrani, Dijiang Huang, "Dynamic Game based Security framework in SDN-enabled Cloud Networking Environments", Proceedings of the ACM International Workshop on Security in Software Defined Networks & Network Function Virtualization (SDN-NFVSec '17), pp. 53–58, March 2017, Scottsdale, USA.

13. Mahmoud Said Elsayed, Nhien-An Le-Khac, Soumyabrata Dev, Anca Delia Jurcut, "Machine-Learning Techniques for Detecting Attacks in SDN", Proceedings of the IEEE 7th International Conference on Computer Science and Network Technology (ICCSNT), October 2019, Dalian, China.

14. Nasrin Sultana, Naveen Chilamkurti, Wei Peng, Rabei Alhadad, "Survey on SDN based Network Intrusion Detection System using Machine Learning Approaches", *Peer-to-Peer Networking and Applications, Springer*, vol. 12, no. 2, pp. 493–501, March 2019.

15. Narmeen Zakaria Bawany, Jawwad A. Shamsi, Khaled Salah, "DDoS Attack Detection and Mitigation Using SDN: Methods, Practices, and Solutions", *Arabian Journal for Science and Engineering*, Springer, pp. 425–441, February 2017.

16. Christian Banse, Julian Schuette, "A Taxonomy-based Approach for Security in Software-Defined Networking", *Proceedings of the IEEE International Conference on Communications (ICC)*, May 2017, Paris, France.

17. Marcin Niemiec, Piotr Jaglarz, Marcin Jekot, Piotr Chołda, and Piotr Boryło, "Risk Assessment Approach to Secure Northbound Interface of SDN Networks", *Proceedings of the International Conference on Computing, Networking and Communications (ICNC)*, April 2019, Honolulu, USA.

18. Phan The Duy, Do Thi Thu Hien, Nguyen Van Vuong, Nguyen Ngoc Hai A, Van-Hau Pham, "Toward a Trust-Based Authentication Framework of Northbound Interface in Software Defined Networking", *International Conference on Industrial Networks and Intelligent Systems (INISCOM 2019). Lecture Notes of the Institute for Computer Sciences, Social Informatics and Telecommunications Engineering*, vol. 293, pp 269–282, Springer, Cham, August 2019.

19. Ankur Chowdhary, Dijiang Huang, Adel Alshamrani, Myong Kang, Anya Kim, Alexander Velazquez, "TRUFL: Distributed Trust Management Framework in SDN", Proceedings of the IEEE International Conference on Communications (ICC), July 2019, Shanghai, China.

20. Sandeep Pisharody, Janakarajan Natarajan, Ankur Chowdhary, Abdullah Alshalan, Dijiang Huang, "Brew: A Security Policy Analysis Framework for Distributed SDN-Based Cloud Environments", *IEEE Transactions on Dependable and Secure Computing*, July 2017.

21. Aliyu Lawal Aliyu, Adel Aneiba, Mohammad Patwary, Peter Bull, "A Trust Management Framework for Software Defined Network (SDN) Controller and Network Applications", *Computer Networks, Elsevier*, vol. 181, 107421, July 2020.

22. Stéphane Betgé-Brezetz, Guy-Bertrand Kamga, Monsef Tazi, "Trust Support for SDN Controllers and Virtualized Network Applications", Proceedings of the 1st IEEE Conference on Network Softwarization (NetSoft), April 2015, London, UK.

23. Christian Banse and Sathyanarayanan Rangarajan, "A Secure Northbound Interface for SDN Applications", Proceedings of the IEEE International Conference on Trust, Security and Privacy in Computing and Communications (TrustCom), August 2015, Helsinki, Finland.

24. Bassey Isong, Tebogo Kgogo, Francis Lugayizi, Bennett Kankuzi, "Trust Establishment Framework between SDN Controller and Applications", Proceedings of the 18th IEEE/ACIS International Conference on Software Engineering, Artificial Intelligence, Networking and Parallel/Distributed Computing (SNPD), June 2017, Kanazawa, Japan.

25. Svetlana Burikova, JooYoung Lee, Rasheed Hussain, Iuliia Sharafitdinova, Roman Dzheriev, Fatima Hussain, Salah Sharieh, Alexander Ferworn, "A Trust Management Framework for Software Defined Networks-based Internet of Things", Proceedings of the IEEE 10th Annual Information Technology, Electronics and Mobile Communication Conference (IEMCON), October 2019, Vancouver, Canada.

26. Hongyan Cui, Zunming Chen, Longfei Yu, Kun Xie, Zongguo Xia, "Authentication Mechanism for Network Applications in SDN Environments", Proceedings of the 20th International Symposium on Wireless Personal Multimedia Communications (WPMC2017), December 2017, Bali, Indonesia.

27. Sandra Scott-Hayward, Christopher Kane and Sakir Sezer, "OperationCheckpoint: SDN Application Control", Proceedings of the IEEE 22nd International Conference on Network Protocols, October 2014, Raleigh, USA.

28. Seugwon Shin, Phillip Porras, Vinod Yegneswaran, Martin Fong, Guofei Gu, and Mabry Tyson, "FRESCO: Modular Composable Security Services for Software-Defined Networks", Proceedings of the Internet Society (ISOC) 20th Annual Network and Distributed System Security Symposium (NDSS), February 2013.

29. Phillip Porras, Seungwon Shin, Vinod Yegneswaran, Martin Fong, Mabry Tyson, Guofei Gu, "A Security Enforcement Kernel for OpenFlow Networks", Proceedings of the First Workshop on Hot Topics in Software Defined Networks (HotSDN '12), pp. 121–126, August 2012.

30. Christopher C. Lamb, Gregory L. Heileman, "Towards Robust Trust in Software Defined Networks", Proceedings of IEEE Globecom Workshops (GC Wkshps), December 2014, Austin, USA.

31. Keshav Sood, Kallol Krishna Karmakar, Vijay Varadharajan, Uday Tupakula, Shui Yu, "Analysis of Policy-Based Security Management System in Software-Defined Networks", IEEE Communications Letters, vol. 23, no. 4, pp. 612–615, April 2019.

32. B. Zhao, Y. Liu, X. Li, J. Li, and J. Zou, "TrustBlock: An Adaptive Trust Evaluation of SDN Network Nodes Based on Double-Layer Blockchain", PloS One, vol. 15, no. 3, article e0228844, 2020.

33. K. Giotis, C. Argyropoulos, G. Androulidakis, D. Kalogeras, and V. Maglaris, "Combining OpenFlow and sFlow for an Effective and Scalable Anomaly Detection and Mitigation Mechanism on SDN Environments", Computer Networks, vol. 62, pp. 122–136, 2014.

34. R. Zaalouk, R. M. Khondoker, and K. Bayarou, "Orchsec: An Orchestrator-based Architecture for Enhancing Network-Security Using Network Monitoring and SDN Control Functions", Proceeding of the Network Operations and Management Symposium (NOMS), IEEE, pp. 1–9, 2014.

35. C. Lumezanu Yu, Y. Zhang, V. Singh, G. Jiang, and H. V. Madhyastha, "Flowsense: Monitoring Network Utilization with Zero Measurement Cost", Proceedings of the International Conference on Passive and Active Network Measurement, Springer, pp. 31–41, 2013.

36. X. T. Phan and K. Fukuda, "SDN-Mon: Fine-grained Traffic Monitoring Framework in Software-Defined Networks", Journal of Information Processing, vol. 25, pp. 182–190, 2017.

37. L. Fawcett, S. Scott-Hayward, M. Broadbent, A. Wright, and N. Race, "Tennison: A Distributed SDN Framework for Scalable Network Security", IEEE Journal on Selected Areas in Communications, vol. 36, no. 12, pp. 2805–2818, December 2018.

38. P. Tsai, C. Tsai, C. Hsu and C. Yang, "Network Monitoring in Software-Defined Networking: A Review", IEEE Systems Journal, vol. 12, no. 4, pp. 3958–3969, December 2018.

39. S. Vissicchio, L. Vanbever and O. Bonaventure, "Opportunities and Research Challenges of Hybrid Software Defined Networks", *ACM SIGCOMM Computer Communication Review*, vol. 44, no. 2, pp. 70–75, April 2014.

40. S. Rathee, Y. Sinha and K. Haribabu, "A Survey: Hybrid SDN", *Journal of Network and Computer Applications*, vol. 100, pp. 35–55, December 2017.

41. S. Ahmad, M. A. Hussain, "Scalability, Consistency, Reliability and Security in SDN Controllers: A Survey of Diverse SDN Controllers", *Journal of Network and Systems Management*, vol. 29, no. 9, 2020.

42. "Installing OpenDayLight", https://docs.opendaylight.org/en/stable-aluminium/getting-started-guide/installing_opendaylight.html, Accessed: January 2021.

43. "Mininet Documentation", https://github.com/mininet/mininet/wiki/Documentation, Accessed: January 2021.

44. R. K. Arbettu, R. Khondoker, K. Bayarou, F. Weber, "Security Analysis of OpenDaylight, ONOS, Rosemary and Ryu SDN Controllers", Proceedings of the 17th International Telecommunications Network Strategy and Planning Symposium (Networks), pp. 37–44, Montreal, QC, Canada, 2016.

2 Quantum Key Generation and Distribution Using Decoy State

Supriyo Banerjee, Biswajit Maiti, and Banani Saha

CONTENTS

DOI: 10.1201/9781003296034-2

2.1 INTRODUCTION

With rapid advancements in electronic communication, the secure transfer between legitimate users has become extremely important against cyber-theft. Over the past two decades, several protocols have come up in both the classical and the quantum cryptography to combat this problem and to ensure unconditional security [1–5]. Starting from the first one, the BB84 protocol, several improvements are going on day by day on the security aspects against eavesdropping and information loss [6].

Quantum key distribution (QKD) is a procedure in which the sender, Alice, prepares a secret key and shares the secret key to the receiver, Bob, using an insecure communication channel. Using this secret key, the sender and the receiver can exchange the data. In this approach, it has been assumed that in Alice's laboratory she prepares the required quantum single-photon state completely secure and she prepares this single photon correctly. However, in a practical scenario, it is different as the attacker, Eve, can steal the information during the preparation phase of single-photon states. These types of attacks are commonly known as attacks on the source part.

The most common attacks at source are photon-number-splitting (PNS) attack, phase-remapping attack, and nonrandom phase attack. All these types of attacks have been performed during single photon or ancilla preparation.

To overcome this problem, physicists use decoy state which has similar characteristics such as wavelength and timing information with single state which makes it harder for Eve to segregate the single state from the mixture of single and decoy states. Moreover, the current hardware is sufficient for performing these experiments, which is an added advantage.

However, the main concern is to maximize the key generation rate for long-distance fiber optical or free-space communication. But due to less correlation between the legitimate users, some losses will occur. Very low-intensity optical pulses can be used to minimize these losses. Some more data may be lost further for performing privacy amplification that ensures better security. As a result of these huge losses, the key generation rate will be lower.

The physicists are trying to improve secrecy with high key generation rate by using a higher correlation between the data sent by the sender, Alice, and received by the receiver, Bob [7, 8].

Theoretically, an infinite number of decoy states can be used to achieve a better security, but in practice, two (one weak + one vacuum) or less number of decoy states are sufficient to achieve the security [9].

Some recent types of physical realization [10–14] show that over more than 100 km secure communication can be achieved using the weak decoy state proposal with two-decoy states (without any signal or vacuum and a weak decoy state of strength ν). But in practice, true vacuum creation is a challenging problem which initiates the two nonvacuum decoy state protocols for secure communication.

This protocol can be used as open-space QKD which can be operated from ground to ground as well as from ground to satellite [15].

This chapter is organized as follows: In Section 2.2, the difference between single and decoy states and their preparations have been described. The three important attacks—(a) photon-number-splitting attack, (b) phase-remapping attack, and (c) nonrandom phase attack—at the source end has been described for analyzing the existing decoy state protocol in Section 2.3. Theoretic as well as practical implementation of decoy state protocol has been analyzed in Sections 2.4 and 2.5, respectively. Three important parameters for analyzing the secrecy of data using decoy state protocols such as quantum bit error rate (QBER) analysis, gain analysis, and key generation rate have been described in Section 2.6. Comparative studies between existing protocols in secrecy and key generation rate have been analyzed in Section 2.7, and the chapter ends with a future scope and conclusion mentioned in Section 2.8.

2.2 DECOY STATE

In practical QKD systems, the sender uses attenuated laser pulses or weak coherent sources that occasionally generate multiphotons. The decoy state method can be implemented by both active and passive ways. In the active ways, Alice generates signals using different intensities that can be used to change the probability distributions of each photon number. Figure 2.1 shows the schematic diagram of an active decoy state method. In this method, an amplitude modulator (AM) is used to signal the amplitude of each weak coherent pulse to modulate the intensities. After creating the different levels of intensities, polarization modulation is used for encoding each data. Optical filter F is used to transmit light of the same wavelengths so that it will be more difficult for Eve to distinguish. Optical isolator "I" is used to propagate in one direction.

2.3 ATTACKS ON SOURCE

In the theoretic approach, it has been assumed that the both sender and receiver's laboratory is completely secure. But in practical situation, the sender's laboratory is not secure and it is susceptible to different kinds of sophisticated attacks such as Trojan horse attack [15], phase-remapping attack [16], nonrandom phase attack [17], and photon-number-splitting attack.

2.3.1 Trojan Horse Attack

In this attack, Eve sends bright Trojan horse pulses to Alice to know the basis selection or phase modulation process. Alice's device emits the back-reflected pulses which will give information to Eve. The insertion loss and the back-reflection level

FIGURE 2.1 Schematic diagram of decoy state method.

can be estimated by calculating the onward and reverse paths which may not be necessarily the same. Using this double pass, Eve can determine the total attenuation which provides the knowledge for the estimation of the number of photons. As a result, Eve steals the information without revealing her presence to the legitimate users. In 2006, Gisin *et al.* first proposed this attack [18]. In 2014, this kind of attack was experimentally demonstrated by Jain *et al.* [15]. In 2020, Molotkov shows that the decoy state method can be helpful to protect the data from Trojan horse attack [15]. Figure 2.2 shows the schematic diagram of a basic Trojan horse attack [19].

2.3.2 PHASE-REMAPPING ATTACK

The popular commercially used "plug-and-play" QKD structure has some practical limitations as in case of long-distance communication using a fiber optical channel. It generates phase and polarization instabilities which initiate the development of bidirectional QKD schemes. In this bidirectional QKD system, Bob initiates the session by sending signal pulse and reference pulse to Alice. The reference pulse is used to activate her phase modulator for synchronizing the signal. Then the sender performs the phase encoding of the signal pulse. Then Alice reduces the intensity of these two pulses up to single-photon level and sends them back to the receiver. In the receiver's end, Bob randomly chooses basis by phase modulation of the returning reference pulse. Since Alice allows Eve's signal to enter into her measuring device, the system is susceptible to eavesdropping which is known as phase-remapping attack [16]. Figure 2.3 shows the timing diagram of a phase-remapping attack.

2.3.3 NONRANDOM PHASE ATTACK

In this attack, Eve uses some external source to illuminate a semiconductor laser diode, which generates seed photons and creates an open door for her. Seed photons consist of emitted single photons and some parts from external sources. Both may

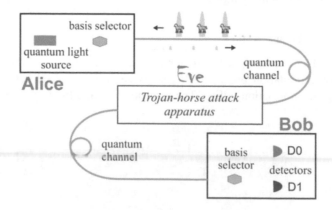

FIGURE 2.2 The schematic diagram of basic Trojan horse attack [19].

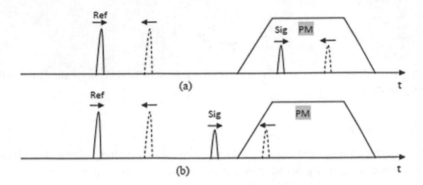

FIGURE 2.3 Timing diagram of phase-remapping attack. Sig, signal pulse; Ref, reference pulse; PM, phase modulation signal. (a) Normal QKD operation; (b) phase-remapping attack.

produce an impact on the phase of the resulting photons. If the number of photons from external sources is more than the emitted single photons, then the resultant phase largely depends on the behavior of the external device. If Eve is able to inject some photons using an external source, then she can control the resulting phase of the photons.

2.3.4 PHOTON-NUMBER-SPLITTING ATTACK

In practical QKD systems, Alice uses weak coherent laser pulses. Due to imperfection of the single-photon emitter which occasionally generates multiphotons, an open door was created for Eve to steal the information using PNS attack. In these attacks, Eve can block all the single photons generated by Alice. Then she splits the multiphotons and sends one part of the multiphotons to the receiver Bob and keeps another part in her possession for further calculation. During the phase reconciliation process, Eve can easily get the information using these multiphotons.

2.4 DECOY STATE METHOD

In the general decoy state method, a fiber-based setup model has been used widely. In this setup, the three major components are the source, the channel, and a detector. Although the decoy state has been prepared in the source end, the channel characteristics, receiver end's detector, the yield of channel, and the process play their crucial roles for secure communication in the presence of Eve.

2.4.1 SOURCE

The weak coherent laser source is used to prepare the state. During phase encoding, true random function has been applied to make this phase purely random from each other. Alice prepares the photons with the photon number μ for each pulse using the Poisson distribution. Thus, the density matrix of the emitted state will be

$$\rho_A = \sum_{k=0}^{\infty} \frac{\mu_k}{k!} e^{-\mu} |k\rangle\langle k| \tag{1}$$

where $|0\rangle\langle 0|$ depicts the vacuum or without signal state and $|k\rangle\langle k|$ is the kth photon's density matrix.

2.4.2 CHANNEL

In this method, an optical fiber-based communication channel is used. The channel transmission probability between Alice and Bob t_{AB} can be expressed as

$$t_{AB} = 10^{\frac{-\alpha l}{10}} \tag{2}$$

where α is the loss coefficient for the l km fiber optic channel.

2.4.3 DETECTOR

The transmission probability at Bob's end will be

$$\eta_{Bob} = t_{Bob}\eta_D \tag{3}$$

where η_{Bob} is the transmission probability at the receiver's end, t_{Bob} is the internal transmission efficiency, and η_D is the detector efficiency.

The total transmission efficiency between Alice and Bob η is given by

$$\eta = t_{AB}\eta_{Bob} \tag{4}$$

In case of a normal channel, we can assume that behaviors of the n photons are independent of each other. The transmission efficiency for each photon signal is η. Therefore, the total transmission efficiency will be

$$\eta_n = 1 - (1-\eta)^n \tag{5}$$

2.4.4 YIELD

The decoy state protocol is a session protocol. In the beginning of the session, the most important component yield $Y_N = 1-channel\ loss$ plays a crucial role. The channel loss is required to be optimum at a certain level because beyond this threshold limit, the protocol will go into the suspended state. With the probability p_N of generation, the decoy state and signal state must be less than the yield Y_N, i.e.,

$$Y_N > p_N$$

Alice prepares n, the mixture of multiphotons with a probability $P_n(\mu) = e^{-\mu}\mu^n / n!$ with $\mu < 1$ for the signal state and $\mu \geq 1$ for the decoy state. $Y_S = \sum_n P_n(\mu)y_n$ and $Y_{S'} = \sum_n P_n(\mu')y_{S'}$ will be the yield measured by Bob at the receiver's end for the signal source and the decoy source, respectively.

On the receiving side, due to the use of imperfect photon detector devices, the following conditions can arise.

Case I: In case of without eavesdropping (where $n = 0$), the corresponding yield will be Y_0 which is due to some background rate including dark count and stray-light timing pulses.

Case II: In the presence of Eve (where $n \geq 1$), the corresponding yield Y_n for the detection of signal photons from sources η_n with the background rate Y_0 will be [17]

$$Y_n = Y_0 + \eta_n - Y_0\eta_n$$

$$\approx Y_0 + \eta_n$$

(6)

The term $Y_0\eta_n \ll 1$ is very small, so we can ignore it.

2.4.5 PROCESS

In this method, Alice prepares the decoy state and signal state with similar characteristics such as same wavelength and timing information. Then Alice sends this mixture of these two types of states using an insecure channel.

In case of one-decoy state protocol [17], the average photon number of a decoy state for preparing this mixture will be much lower than the signal state. After sending the full data string, the process will wait for classical acknowledgment from Bob's end about receipt of signals. After receiving the classical acknowledgment, Alice announces which pulses are signal states and which are decoy states. In this mixture of signal and decoy states, all characteristics are the same except photon number distribution. An eavesdropping attack is dependent on the actual photon number of each pulse. She has no knowledge about the pulse states (signal or decoy). Any kind of modification of the characteristics of decoy states and/or signal states will be detected. If Eve introduces a photon-number-dependent attenuation, then Alice and Bob can easily detect the presence of Eve by measuring the transmittance of the decoy state which will be much lower than what is expected under normal operations. In this way, decoy state QKD can enhance security by detecting the presence of Eve.

2.5 ANALYSIS OF TWO-DECOY STATE PROTOCOL

The three important parameters for analyzing the protocol are gain analysis, quantum bit error rate (QBER) analysis, and key generation rate. The higher correlation between Alice and Bob's data will enhance gain and key generation rate and reduce the QBER rate.

2.5.1 GAIN ANALYSIS

The gain is directly dependent on the two parameters—the photon sent by Alice and the conditional probability of detection of that photon at Bob's end. The gain [19] of the nth photon will be

$$Q_n = Y_n p_n(\mu) = Y_n(e^{-\mu}\mu^n / n!) \tag{7}$$

The gain for m number of decoy state protocols will be

$$Q_{v1} = \sum_{i=0}^{\infty} Y_i \frac{v_1^{i}}{i!} e^{-v_1}$$

$$Q_{v2} = \sum_{i=0}^{\infty} Y_i \frac{v_2^{i}}{i!} e^{-v_2}$$

$$\cdots$$

$$Q_{v_m} = \sum_{i=0}^{\infty} Y_i \frac{v_m^{i}}{i!} e^{-v_m} \tag{8}$$

where $v_1, v_2, ..., v_m$ are m number of decoy state's photon number.

2.5.2 QBER ANALYSIS

In the QKD-based system, a cryptographic key is prepared by Alice using proper encoding which is a series of correlated photons and then transmitting the same correlated photons through an insecure communication channel. At the receiver end, only those data which have same basis with the Alice's acknowledgment are used for the preparation of the key. Besides the environmental noises, some errors have been introduced due to Eve's wrong basis selection. The percentage of erroneous data within the received key is known as quantum bit error rate (QBER), the determining factor for any kind of efficient protocol.

The quantum bit error rate (QBER) of the nth photon states is defined as [19]

$$e_n = \frac{e_0 Y_0 + e_{detector} \eta_n}{Y_n} \tag{9}$$

where $e_{detector}$ signifies the receiver's end error due to the impaction of detector.

The error rate for m number of decoy state protocols will be

$$E_{v_1} Q_{v_1} e^{v_1} = \sum_{i=0}^{\infty} e_i Y_i \frac{v_1^{i}}{i!}$$

$$E_{v_2} Q_{v_2} e^{v_2} = \sum_{i=0}^{\infty} e_i Y_i \frac{v_2^i}{i!}$$

$$\cdots$$

$$E_{v_m} Q_{v_m} e^{v_m} = \sum_{i=0}^{\infty} e_i Y_i \frac{v_m^i}{i!} \tag{10}$$

2.5.3 Analysis of Key Generation Rate

The secret key generation rate can be defined as a rate in which the data can be correlated between two legitimate users Alice and Bob [19]. In the existing QKD protocols, some data will be discarded due to mismatch as a result of the choice of wrong basis by Bob and some used in privacy amplification for achieving better secrecy. Therefore, the resultant key will be comparatively shortened. The key generation rate will be lower. So the physicists are trying to minimize the occurrence of error due to wrong basis selection by Bob. A highly correlated datawill give a better key generation rate.

In the paper [19] by Gottesman *et al.*, the key generation rate for the BB84 protocol has been analyzed

$$R \geq q\{-Q_\mu f(E_\mu) H_2(E_\mu) + Q_1[1 - H_2(e_1)]\} \tag{11}$$

where q is the probabilistic factor for detecting the correct value in Bob's end. In case of classical BB84 protocol, the guessing is always 50% so $q = 1/2$ for correct guessing in modified BB84 protocol $q = 1$. E_μ is the overall quantum bit error rate (QBER), e_1 is the QBER for the single-photon state. Q_μ is the overall gain, and Q_1 is the gain for the single-photon state. $f(x)$ is the bidirectional error correction efficiency, normally $f(x) \geq 1$ with Shannon limit $f(x) = 1$. H_1 and H_2 are binary entropy functions and depend on the protocol design.

$$H_2(x) = -x \log_2(x) - (1-x) \log_2(1-x) \tag{12}$$

With the intensities of the signal state μ and the non-trivial decoy state μ', Wang derived a useful upper bound for Δ, the proportion of the tagged state in the sifted key in GLLP protocol [9] [20]:

$$\Delta \leq \frac{\mu}{\mu' - \mu} \left(\frac{\mu e^{-\mu} Q_{\mu'}}{\mu' e^{-\mu'} Q_\mu} - 1 \right) + \frac{\mu e^{-\mu} Y_0}{\mu' Q_\mu} \tag{13}$$

The resultant key generation rate will be

$$R \geq q Q_\mu \{-H_2(E_\mu) + (1 - \Delta)[1 - H_2(\frac{E_\mu}{1 - \Delta})]\} \tag{14}$$

Using this method, we can avoid the estimation of QBER of single photon e_1. So, the estimation process is much simple. However, this method suffers due to the lower values of the key generation rates and distances [9].

2.6 PRACTICAL IMPLICATION OF DECOY STATE PROTOCOL

In this section, decoy state protocol has been analyzed with experimental realization. In this experiment, one-decoy pulse with a pure vacuum state is used to implement decoy state protocol. With the principles of four states, the BB84 protocol has been used here. In this method, single-photon input has been designated by $|0\rangle$ or $|1\rangle$ and vacuum is $|0\rangle$. A set of two mutually orthogonal bases $\frac{1}{\sqrt{2}}\left(\theta|1\rangle|0\rangle + e^{\theta\gamma}|0\rangle|1\rangle\right)$ is used to generate four states in the X basis ($\gamma = 0,\pi$) and the Y basis ($\gamma = \frac{\pi}{2}, \frac{3\pi}{2}$). Alice prepares two states $\frac{1}{2}[(e^{t\alpha} - 1)|1\rangle|0\rangle + t(e^{t\alpha} + 1)|0\rangle|1\rangle]$ with probabilities $\sin^2\left(\frac{a}{2}\right)$ and $\cos^2\left(\frac{a}{2}\right)$, respectively.

Alice can use weak coherent sources to prepare its input during the encoding process. Alice prepares the product state $\left|\frac{\sqrt{\mu}}{2}(e^{t\alpha} - 1)\right\rangle\left|\frac{t\sqrt{\mu}}{2}(e^{t\alpha} + 1)\right\rangle$ using the mean photon number pulses μ.

The two cases have been observed at receiver's end by choosing $\beta = 0$ or $\frac{\pi}{2}$

(i) In the receiving end, if Bob sets $\beta = 0$ and Alice prepares its states using $a = 0$ or $a = \pi$, then Bob detects signals at his detector in the X basis (0 or 1). But if Bob sets $\beta = 0$ and Alice sets $\alpha = \frac{\pi}{2}$ or $\frac{3\pi}{2}$, then their basis choice will be different which produces wrong or inconclusive results.

(ii) In the receiving end, if Bob sets $\beta = \frac{\pi}{2}$ and Alice prepares its states using $a = 0$ or $a = \pi$, then Bob detects signals at his detector in the Y basis (0 or 1). But if Bob sets $\beta = \frac{\pi}{2}$ and Alice sets $\alpha = \frac{\pi}{2}$ or $\frac{3\pi}{2}$, then their basis choice will be different which may produce wrong or inconclusive results.

In physical realization, Mach–Zehnder phase-encoding process has been applied for transferring the data between two legitimate users using a 20 km fiber optic communication channel. In this experiment, $\lambda = 1.55$ μm wavelength optical pulses have been used at 7 MHz frequency. Signal and decoy states with different intensities have been produced using an intensity modulator. A vacuum state is practically very complex to generate. In this experiment, Alice blocks the signal creating the vacuum state. A clock pulse with $\lambda = 1.3$ μm has been used for synchronization between the decoy state and the signal state.

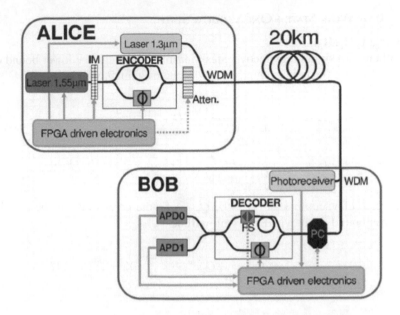

FIGURE 2.4 The system performs BB84 phase-encoding/phase-decoding process using weak + vacuum decoy states. Atten, attenuator; APD, avalanche photo diodes; FPGA, field programmable gate array; FS, fiber stretcher; IM, intensity modulator; PC, polarization controller; WDM, wavelength division multiplexer.

Figure 2.4 shows the schematic diagram of phase-encoding process in Alice's laboratory and decoding process in Bob's laboratory.

In the receiving end, Bob uses avalanche photodiode (APD) for detecting the signal. Using this APD, Bob can achieve better sensitivity. It also generates lower noise compared to PIN detectors, making it applicable with low optical power levels.

The main objective of this experiment is to maximize the key generation rate with optimal number of photons μ. The gain of single photon is directly proportional to key generation rate, i.e., if the gain will increase, then the final key length will be the maximum which will increase the key generation rate.

The ratio between the gain of the single photon and the gain of the μ number of photons, $\dfrac{Q_1}{Q_\mu}$, must be high to get a better key generation rate. But calculating the gain of single photon is a very complex task. Besides the calculation of single-photon gain, the upper bound of error rate e_1 and the lower bound of yield Y_1 need to be calculated for achieving better security. Minor errors in e_1 and Y_1 will give promising effects on the key generation rate. So the measurements of gain, error, and yield of single photon must be preciously correct.

In case of low background rate Y_0 and low transmittance $\eta \ll 1$, the key generation rate will converge to

$$R \approx -\eta\mu f(e_{\mathrm{det\,ector}})H_2(e_{\mathrm{det\,ector}}) + \eta\mu e^{-\mu}[1 - H_2(e_{\mathrm{det\,ector}})] \qquad (15)$$

2.6.1 ONE WEAK STATE + ONE VACUUM STATE

(a) **Case I (R_1+R_2)**

When both signal and decoy states measure separately, the lower bound of yield Y_1 and the upper bound of single-photon gain Q_1 will be

$$Y_1 \geq Y_1^{lower} = \frac{\mu}{\mu v - v^2} (Q_v e^v - Q_\mu e^\mu \frac{v^2}{\mu^2} - \frac{\mu^2 - v^2}{\mu^2} Y_0)$$

$$Q_1 \geq Q_1^{lower} = e^{-\mu}.Y_1 = \frac{\mu e^{-\mu}}{\mu v - v^2} (Q_v e^v - Q_\mu e^\mu \frac{v^2}{\mu^2} - \frac{\mu^2 - v^2}{\mu^2} Y_0) \tag{16}$$

In case of vacuum state $v_2 \to 0$, $Q_{v_2} \to Y_0$, the error rate will be e_0. The lower bound of the yield and gain will be

$$Y_2 \geq Y_2^{Lower} = \frac{2\mu(Q_v e^v - \frac{v^3}{\mu^3} Q_\mu e^\mu - \frac{\mu^3 - v^3}{\mu^3} Y_0 - \frac{v\mu^2 - v^3}{\mu^2} Y_1^U)}{v^2 \mu - v^3}$$

$$Q_2 \geq Q_2^{Lower} = \frac{\mu^3 e^{-\mu}(Q_v e^v - \frac{v^3}{\mu^3} Q_\mu e^\mu - \frac{\mu^3 - v^3}{\mu^3} Y_0 - \frac{v\mu^2 - v^3}{\mu^2} Y_1^U)}{v^2 \mu - v^3} \tag{17}$$

where $Y_1^U = \frac{(2Q_v e^v - 2Y_0 - Y_2^\infty v^2)}{2v}$ and Y_2^∞ is the yield derived by the theoretical infinite number of the decoy state.

(b) **Case II (R_{12})**

When both signal and decoy states measure simultaneously, then the lower bound of the yield of the double photon will be

$$(Y_1 + Y_2)^{Lower} = \frac{\mu^3 e^v Q_v - (\mu^3 - v^3)Y_0 - v^3 Q_\mu e^\mu + (v^3 \mu - \frac{1}{2} v^3 \mu^2)Y_1^L}{\mu^3 (v - \frac{1}{2} \frac{v^3}{\mu})}$$

$$Q_{12}^{Lower}(\mu) = [\frac{(Y_1 + Y_2)^{Lower}}{2} \mu^2 + (Y_1^{Lower} \mu - \frac{Y_1^{Lower} \mu^2}{2})]e^{-\mu} \tag{18}$$

2.6.2 ONE WEAK DECOY STATE

In case of one-decoy state, Bob and Alice do not know their background rate Y_0 precisely.

Upper bound of the yield will be

$$Y_0 \leq Y_0^U = \frac{E_\mu Q_\mu e^\mu}{e_0}$$

(a) **Case I (R_1+R_2)**

Using this upper bound, the lower bound of yield Y_1 and upper bound of single-photon gain Q_1 will be

$$Y_1 \ge Y_1^{\text{Lower}} = \frac{\mu}{\mu v - v^2}(Q_v e^v - Q_\mu e^\mu \frac{v^2}{\mu^2} - \frac{E_\mu Q_\mu e^\mu (\mu^2 - v^2)}{e_0 \mu^2})$$

$$Q_1 \ge Q_1^{\text{Lower}} = e^{-\mu}.Y_1 = \frac{\mu e^{-\mu}}{\mu v - v^2}(Q_v e^v - Q_\mu e^\mu \frac{v^2}{\mu^2} - \frac{E_\mu Q_\mu e^\mu (\mu^2 - v^2)}{e_0 \mu^2}) \qquad (19)$$

(b) **Case II (R_{12})**

When both signal and decoy states measure simultaneously, then the lower bound of the yield of the double photon will be

$$(Y_1 + Y_2)^{\text{Lower}} = \frac{\mu^3 e^v Q_v - (\mu^3 - v^3)\dfrac{E_\mu Q_\mu e^\mu}{e_0} - v^3 Q_\mu e^\mu + (v^3 \mu - \dfrac{1}{2} v^3 \mu^2)Y_1^L}{\mu^3 (v - \dfrac{1}{2}\dfrac{v^3}{\mu})}$$

$$Q_{12}^{\text{Lower}}(\mu) = [\frac{(Y_1 + Y_2)^{\text{Lower}}}{2}\mu^2 + (Y_1^{\text{Lower}}\mu - \frac{Y_1^{\text{Lower}}\mu^2}{2})]e^{-\mu} \qquad (20)$$

Figure 2.5 shows the comparative study. In case of infinite decoy state which is theoretically proposed, there are one weak + one vacuum decoy state, only one-decoy state, and classical single-photon device (without decoy state) method. Infinite decoy state shows the asymptotic values for decoy state methods. One weak + one vacuum decoy source can achieve a better key generation rate with maximum distance.

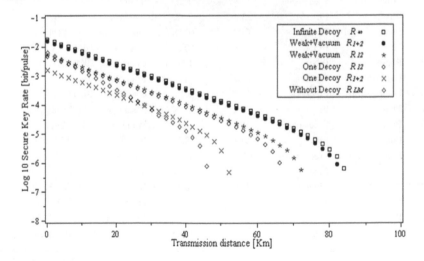

FIGURE 2.5   Key generation rate against transmission distance GYS [21].

2.7 COMPARATIVE STUDIES BETWEEN EXISTING PROTOCOLS ON SECRECY AND KEY GENERATION RATE

In the last two decades, several hacking strategies have been developed by the physicists. This shows that the security proofs are deals in ideal conditions [19]. Imperfection of source as well as receiver device leads to side-channel attacks. To combat with this kind of side-channel attacks, decoy state protocols are very much effective. But the initial phase of the decoy state protocol has been suffering with low correlation which leads to a low key generation rate.

In the last decade, the physicists have been trying to maximize the distance of communication with a higher key generation rate.

Table 2.1 shows the chronological development of the decoy state protocol for achieving the maximum distance with a higher key generation rate.

2.8 CONCLUSION

New-generation methodologies [36–41] have been adopted for achievement of user-friendly activities between two or more users. However, classical security is always getting compromised due to its inherent rigidity. The existing standard QKD protocols are mostly based on low relations between the sender and receiver, thus suffering

TABLE 2.1
Chronological Development of Decoy State-Based QKD Protocols

Year	Preparation	Medium	Distance (km)	Key Rate (bps)	References
2006	Phase	Fiber	60	422.5	Zhao et al., 2006 [22]
2007	Phase	Fiber	107	14.5	Rosenberg et al., 2007 [11]
2007	Polarization	Free space	144	12.8	Schmitt-Manderbach et al., 2007 [12]
2007	Phase	Fiber	25.3	5.5K	Yuan et al., 2007 [22]
2008	Phase	Fiber	100.8	10.1K	Dixon et al., 2008 [24]
2009	Phase	Fiber	135	0.2	Rosenberg et al., 2009 [13]
2009	Phase	Fiber	20	1.5K	Chen et al., 2009 [25]
2010	Polarization	Fiber	200	15	Liu et al., 2010 [26]
2010	Polarization	Fiber	130	0.2K	Chen et al., 2010 [27]
2011	Phase	Fiber	45	304K	Sasaki et al., 2011 [28]
2013	Polarization	Free space	96	48	Wang et al., 2013 [29]
2017	Phase	Fiber	240	8.4	Fröhlich et al., 2017 [30]
2017	Polarization	Free space	1200	1.1K	Liao et al., 2017a [14]
2018	Phase	Fiber	10	13.7M	Yuan et al., 2018 [31]
2018	Time-Bin	Fiber	421	6.5	Boaron et al., 2018 [32]
2020	Phase	Fiber	205	10^{13}	Fang Liu et al., 2020 [33]
2021	Phase	Fiber	559	10^{12}	Cong Jiang et al., 2021 [34]
2021	Polarization	Sea water	345	220.5	Cheng-Qiu Hu et al., 2021 [35]

from huge data loss. Other aspects of this data loss occur due to the imperfection of devices which compelled the physicists to derive the device-independent protocol to improve the overall system performance. In the recent past, the physicists are engaging to create a device-independent protocol to ensure high key generation rates between legitimate users. The decoy source-based method can only be useful if this data loss can be minimized at some level.

The decoy state protocol, which is based on the classical BB84, suffers data loss due to the process of privacy amplification where some data is used to ensure better secrecy. In case of BB84 protocol, the probabilistic factor $q = \dfrac{1}{2}$ for detecting the correct data at Bob's end. But if the basis can be fixed, $q \to 1$ can be achieved which can make a significant improvement in the key generation rate.

In case of man-in-the-middle attack, BB84-based decoy state protocols can deal with the presence of Eve by hiding the information about the correct basis during public discussion between Alice and Bob, two legitimate users.

Thomas Attema et al. [42] show a path for improving the better key generation rate using the same weak coherent sources. A different intensity is used to make it difficult for Eve to derive the statistics of coherent states. As a result of using the same weak devices, both legitimate users can achieve a better security.

REFERENCES

1. Bennett C.H. and Bassard G. 1984. Quantum cryptography: Public key distribution and coin tossing. *Proc. IEEE Int. Conf. Comput. Syst. Signal Process.* 175-177.
2. Bennett C.H. 1992. Quantum cryptography using any two nonorthogonal states. *Phys. Rev. Lett.* 68. 3121–3124.
3. Ekert A.K. 1991. Quantum cryptography based on Bell's theorem. *Phys. Rev. Lett.* 68. 557–559.
4. Bhatt, H., and Gautam, S. 2019. "Quantum Computing: A New Era of Computer Science," *2019 6th International Conference on Computing for Sustainable Global Development (INDIACom)*, 2019, pp. 558–561.
5. Bennett C.H, Brassard G and Mermin N.D. 1992. Quantum cryptography without Bell's theorem. *Phys. Rev. Lett.* 68(5). 557–559.
6. Hughes, R.J., Luther, G. G. Morgan, G. L., Peterson, C. G. and Simmons, C. 1996. Quantum cryptography over underground optical fibers. *Lect. Notes Comp. Sci.* 1109. 329–342.
7. Comandar L.C. et al. 2016. Quantum key distribution without detector vulnerabilities using optically seeded lasers. *Nat. Photon.* 10(5). 312–315.
8. Yin J. et al. 2017. Satellite-based entanglement distribution over 1200 kilometers. *Science.* 356. 1140–1144.
9. Ma, X. Qi, B., Zhao, Y. and Lo, H.-K. 2005. Practical decoy state for quantum key distribution. *Phys. Rev. A.* 72. 012326.
10. Peng C.-Z. et al. 2007. Experimental long-distance decoy-state quantum key distribution based on polarization encoding. *Phys. Rev. Lett.* 98. 010505.
11. Rosenberg D. et al. 2007. Long distance decoy state quantum key distribution in optical fiber. *Phys. Rev. Lett.* 98. 010503.
12. Schmitt-Manderbach T. et al. 2007. Experimental demonstration of free-space decoy-state quantum key distribution over 144 km. *Phys. Rev. Lett.* 98. 010504.

13. Rosenberg D. et al. 2009. Practical long-distance quantum key distribution system using decoy levels. *New. J. Phys.* 11. 045009.
14. Liao S.K. et al. 2017. Satellite-to-ground quantum key distribution. *Nature* 549. 43.
15. Jain N. et al. 2015. Risk analysis of Trojan-horse attacks on practical quantum key distribution systems. *IEEE J. Sel. Top. Quantum Electron.* 21. 168.
16. Xu F., Qi, B. and Lo, H.K. 2010. Experimental demonstration of phase-remapping attack in a practical quantum key distribution system. *New. J. Phys.* 12. 113026.
17. Lo H.K., Ma, X. and Chen, K. 2005. Decoy state quantum key distribution. *Phys. Rev. Lett.* 94. 230504.
18. Gisin N. et al. 2006. Trojan-horse attacks on quantum-key-distribution systems. *Phys. Rev. A* 73. 022320.
19. Teng J. et al. 2020. Twin-feld quantum key distribution with passive-decoy state. *New J. Phys.* 22. 103017.
20. Gottesman D. et al. 2004. Security of quantum key distribution with imperfect Devices. *Phys. Rev. Lett.* 94. 230504.
21. Gobby C. et al. 2004. Quantum key distribution over 122 km of standard telecom fiber. *Appl. Phys. Lett.* 84(19). 3762–3764.
22. Zhao Y. et al. 2006. Experimental quantum key distribution with Decoy States. *Phys. Rev. Lett.* 96. 070502.
23. Yuan, Z. L., Sharpe, A.W. and Shields, A.J. 2007. Unconditionally secure one-way quantum key distribution using decoy pulses. *Appl. Phys. Lett.* 90. 269901.
24. Dixon A.R et al. 2008. Gigahertz decoy quantum key distribution with 1 Mbit/s secure key rate. *Opt. Express* 16. 18790.
25. Chen T.-Y. et al. 2009. Field test of a practical secure communication network with decoy-state quantum cryptography. *Opt. Express.* 17. 6540.
26. Liu Y. et al. 2010. Decoy-state quantum key distribution with polarized photons over 200 km. *Opt. Express* 18. 8587.
27. Chen T. et al. 2010. Metropolitan all-pass and inter-city quantum communication network. *Opt. Express.* 18. 27217.
28. Sasaki M. et al. 2011. Field test of quantum key distribution in the Tokyo QKD Network. *Opt. Express.* 19. 10387.
29. Wang J.-Y. et al. 2013. Direct and full-scale experimental verifications towards ground–satellite quantum key distribution. *Nat. Photonics.* 7. 387.
30. Fröhlich B. et al. 2017. Long-distance quantum key distribution secure against coherent attacks. *Optica.* 4. 163.
31. Yuan Z. et al. 2018. 10-Mb/s quantum key distribution. *J. Lightwave Technol.* 36. 3427.
32. Boaron A. et al. 2018. Secure quantum key distribution over 421 km of optical fiber. *Physical Review Letter.* 121. 190502.
33. Liu, F. et al. 2020. Fast spin-flip enables efficient and stable organic electroluminescence from charge-transfer states. *Nat. Photonics.* 14. 422–425.
34. Jiang C. et al. 2020. Sending-or-not-sending twin-field quantum key distribution with discrete-phase-randomized weak coherent states. *Phys. Rev. A.* 101. 042330.
35. Cheng-Qiu H. et al. 2021. Multiplicity of inertial self-similar conical shapes in an electrified liquid metal. *Phys. Rev. Appl.* 15. 024060.
36. Agarwal, J. et al. 2021. Estimation of various parameters for AES, DES, and RSA. *Emerging Technologies in Data Mining and Information Security. Lecture Notes in Networks and Systems (LNNS).* SPRINGER, Singapore. 164. https://doi.org/10.100 // 978-981-15-9774-9_27.
37. Rani A. et al. 2016. Image modelling: A feature detection approach for steganalysis. *Communications in Computer and Information Science.* 721. 140–148.

38. Srivastava P. et al. 2019. A technique to detect copy-move forgery using enhanced SURF. *International Journal of Engineering and Advanced Technology.* 8(6S). 676–680. https://doi.org/ 10.35940/ijeat.F1133.0886S19.
39. Kumar M. et al. 2020. Identifying photo forgery using lighting elements. *Indian Journal of Science and Technology (IJST).* 9(48). 1–5. https://doi.org/10.17485/ijst/2016/v9i48/105748
40. Aggarwal A. et al. 2021. Image surface texture analysis and classification using deep learning. *Multimedia Tools and Applications (MTAP).* 80(1). 1289–1309. https://doi.org/ 10.1007/s11042-020-09520-2
41. Srivastava S. et al. 2021. CGP: Cluster-based gossip protocol for dynamic resource environment in cloud. *Simulation Modelling Practice and Theory.* 108. 102275. https://doi.org/10.1016/j.simpat.2021.102275
42. Attema T. et al. 2021. Optimizing the decoy-state BB84 QKD protocol parameters. *Quantum Information Processing.* 20. 154.

3 Cyber Security Techniques, Architectures, and Design

Sita Rani, Aman Kataria, and Meetali Chauhan

CONTENTS

DOI: 10.1201/9781003296034-3

3.1   INTRODUCTION

Cyber security is the potential to guard against and revive from cyberattacks (Priyadarshini 2019). In the definition proposed by the National Institute of Standards and Technology (NIST), cyber security is defined as the capacity to cushion or defend cyberspace against different types of cyberthreats (Kissel 2011, Rani *et al.* 2021). A number of networks exist in Information and Communication Systems, which are communications networks, a network of machines, the internet, and a variety of embedded systems. Consequently, cyber security is the security of all related networks. It is also related to the security of the infrastructure, applications, and cloud services; advanced technologies like the internet of things (IoT) (as shown in Figure 3.1); and all the other concerned spheres where every security is a critical issue, which are discussed below:

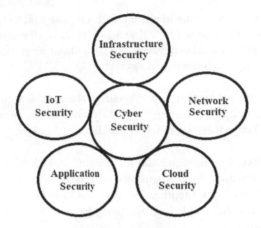

FIGURE 3.1   Cyber security: a conflux of domains.

- **Infrastructure Security**: The main areas under consideration for the security of the infrastructure are cyber-physical systems and their stationing in real-world applications. Different application areas like power grids, healthcare, industry, traffic management systems, etc., are all prone to security attacks in cyberspace. Various types of cyberattacks which are major threats to these domains are denial-of-service attack, eavesdropping, man-in-the-middle attack, etc. (Wang *et al.* 2010).
- **Network Security**: To ensure the security of data in any information system, network security plays a very vital role. It ensures the integrity of the system by protecting it from any kind of unauthorized access. Cyberattacks to breach the security of networks may fall into either the active or passive category. Denial-of-service attack, phishing, and cross-site scripting are active attacks, whereas wire tapping and port scanning fall in the category of passive attacks.
- **Cloud Security**: A number of techniques and mechanisms are used to ensure the security of cloud data and applications. As the cloud is communal among a number of stakeholders, cyberattacks may cause data loss and theft, applications, technology, and system vulnerabilities. Phishing, denial-of-service attack, and account hijacking are some of the prominent attacks which put the security of the cloud environment at stake.
- **Application Security**: Applications in different domains can be secured against cyberattacks by reducing security threats. During the development of an application, a number of phases like design, coding, testing, implementation, and maintenance are followed, and all these phases are prone to cyberattacks. Various threats to which different web applications are susceptible are denial-of-service attack, SQL injection, and cross-site scripting, whereas mobile applications are more prone to spyware, malware, and botnets.
- **Internet-of-Things (IoT) Security**: The IoT comprises sensors, actuators, processing devices, and a variety of other digital devices. Each device in

an IoT system has a unique identifier with the potential to transmit data to other things over the network. IoT security protects all mutually connected things and communication network constituents of a system. Threats in an IoT system comprise botnets and spyware.

Three very important aspects of cyber security are confidentiality, integrity, and availability. The security of a system against cyberattacks is parameterized on the basis of this triad. These three parameters are described below:

- **Confidentiality**: The fundamental idea behind confidentiality is to prevent sensitive information from unauthorized access. Identity theft, phishing, credit card fraud, wire tapping, etc. are attacks on confidentiality. These cyberattacks can be avoided using strong passwords, access control lists, and encryption.
- **Integrity**: It assures flexibility, veracity, and reliability of data. The fundamental objective is to avoid unauthorized access and modification of data. It assures the authenticity of data. A number of attacks like session hijacking, man-in-the-middle attack, etc., can violate the integrity of the data. Various mechanisms to assure integrity are encryption techniques, hashing, data access control, and checksums.
- **Availability**: It confirms the availability of the resources when needed. Consequently, the required data should be available for access to authorized users. Flood attacks and denial-of-service attacks are examples of cyberattacks which threat the availability of resources.

Cyber security basically focuses on people and the working facet of technology. It revolves around 3Ps, named as practice, people, and plan, depicted in Figure 3.2 and discussed below:

- **People**: The fundamental objective to focus on this aspect is to train the human resources to administer different kinds of security threats and to ensure the security of data and applications. Most of the organizations become sufferer of phishing. But suitable training and awareness programs

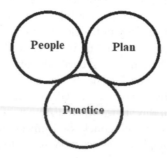

FIGURE 3.2   3Ps: important aspects of cyber security.

can make people aware of possible threats which can lead to a safer environment against security threats.

- **Plan**: There should be a suitable plan at all stages to ensure security against cyberthreats. To manage different security threats, there should be some technical way-outs. The availability of suitable mechanisms is also important to aid the process of data recovery and restoration. Necessary security protocols are also needed for the execution of the different security plans.

- **Practice**: To ensure the validity of security plans requires their practice/implementation. The process of implementation comprises training the people to work out the weakness of the planned mechanisms. Implementation also consists of exercising cyberthreat clues, execution of the plans, decision-making, and devising the procedure of response.

3.2   NEED FOR CYBER SECURITY

The fundamental idea behind cyber security is to protect cyberspace in which a system operates to safeguard the infrastructure from different types of cyberthreats. To avoid and manage various attacks, there is a need for suitable response, settlement, and resumption. There is also a requirement for a legal plan to facilitate a protected cyberspace. The need for different types of security mechanisms for the avoidance and preservation of security attacks is discussed below:

3.2.1   AVOID THREATS

To avoid different types of cyberattacks, it is very essential to study the potential threats and deploy suitable security protocols to facilitate secure communication of data over the communication networks. Symptoms of security threats need to be identified and reported using suitable mechanisms. Relevant security techniques need to be devised to avoid different types of security attacks.

3.2.2   RECOGNITION AND SYSTEM STRENGTHENING

One of the fundamental goals of cyber security is recognition of threats and strengthening the system to guard against those threats. The whole procedure comprises risk assessment and deployment of suitable security techniques. The main objective behind system strengthening is to minimize the security risks. Advanced system strengthening techniques are used to obtain the desired results.

3.2.3   MANAGE FUNCTIONAL, ARCHITECTURAL, AND TECHNOLOGICAL MODERNIZATION

The usage of appropriate vigorous techniques to administer the cyber risks safeguards the infrastructure against different cyberattacks.

3.2.4 Plan for Emergency

The concept of preparedness for emergency is the fundamental planning to deal with cyberattacks. It comprises suitable policies, mechanisms, techniques, strategies, and resumption plans.

3.2.5 Information Broadcasting

Adequate information needs to be broadcasted in the whole system. Different types of threats, attacks, susceptibilities, and events need to be broadcasted in the form of alerts.

3.2.6 Expert Training

The manpower must be trained to administer security threats including avoidance and management. Complete information should be available with all the stakeholders so that manpower can be prepared well to manage cyber incidents.

3.2.7 Harden System against Faults

The fault tolerance capability of any system is assessed by validating it against different vulnerabilities. Highly secure systems usually combat different types of cyberattacks.

3.2.8 Mitigate Vulnerabilities

There are a variety of techniques which aid to reduce different types of vulnerabilities against cyberattacks. Strong passwords and well-configured firewalls can help to avoid malicious attacks.

3.2.9 Enhance Usability

It describes the degree of ease for a system to be used. Along with the strength of the system to manage cyberattacks, this important characteristic also needs to be worked upon.

3.2.10 Authentication

It becomes very important in cyberspace to verify the authenticity of the users and the processes. Different devices may be verified using different authentication techniques.

3.2.11 Efficient Security Methods

Automated techniques help to deploy more efficient and better methods to assure cyber security. Automated methods ensure the avoidance of cyberattacks. Automated tools are also available to diagnose data leaks on communication networks.

3.2.12 INTEROPERATION OF DEVICES

It is the competence of any system to administer the diverse devices to work together. It leads towards an efficient spread of information in an organization which aids the functioning of a secure system against cyberattacks.

3.2.13 EMPHASIZING SUSCEPTIBLE EVENTS

All susceptible events which may cause a threat to the security of a system in cyberspace need to be highlighted. It will help to work out suitable security solutions. Listing these events will also strengthen the process of cyber security.

3.2.14 PROPOSE APPROPRIATE SECURITY MEASURES

Suitable security measures need to be proposed to avoid, detect, and handle cyber security attacks. Some of the methods to practice these security measures are firewalls, strong passwords, and advanced security protocols.

3.3 CYBER SECURITY FRAMEWORK

With the advancement in technology, cyberattacks are also turning into refined and sophisticated forms. So there is a requirement for advanced security techniques, mechanisms, and protocols. The NIST embodies some guidelines, policies, and practices to administer different challenges related to cyber security. The proposed framework comprises core, profile, and deployment tiers.

3.3.1 FRAMEWORK CORE

The core for the deployment of the framework consists of methods, classes, sub-classes, and descriptive references, presented in Figure 3.3. Under this framework, there are five fundamental functions, i.e., identify, recover, protect, respond, and detect to manage a system under different phases of the attack. Under each function, there are categories to determine various tasks and actions. For example, to recover a system from an attack, different mechanisms can be used. Categories with specified objectives are called subcategories. For example, to reconfigure and update software may constitute management and updating of the devices. Descriptive references comprise guidelines, standards, and various policies, e.g., if the user wants to update a windows system will follow some steps.

3.3.2 DEPLOYMENT TIERS

There are four different tiers for the deployment of the framework, i.e., Tier 1, Tier 2, Tier 3, and Tier 4, as shown in Figure 3.4. Tier 1 administers organizational risks caused by weaker security infrastructure. Tier 2 facilitates more advanced security than Tier 1 using suitable plans and infrastructure to protect a system against

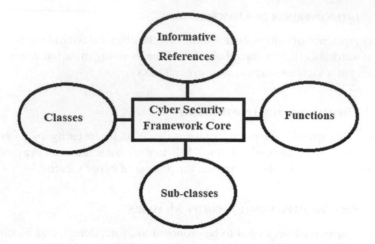

FIGURE 3.3 Cyber security: framework core.

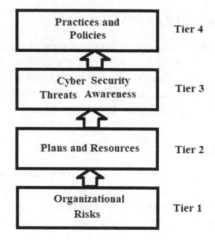

FIGURE 3.4 Cyber security deployment tiers.

cyberattacks. Tier 3 is also termed repeatable implementation. It mainly focuses on the awareness of the users related to various cyber security threats. Tier 4 is also referred to as adaptive implementation. Practices in this tier help in the prediction, detection, and handling of cyberattacks.

3.3.3 PROFILES

Usually, there are predefined objectives expected to be fulfilled in the deployed framework to ensure security against cyberattacks. The true scenario in an organization from the cyber security aspect is described by the profiles. Different profiles are used to identify weak links in the security framework of an organization. Profiles also facilitate the relationships among the functions and categories.

3.4 FUNCTIONS OF CYBER SECURITY

As previously discussed in Section 3.2, cyber security is spread over a broad domain. So, to ensure security against cyberattacks in an organization, checkpoints need to be marked at many stages for the security of the infrastructure from top to bottom. To ensure these security requirements, a variety of roles are undertaken by security experts. In this section, we will talk about various functions which are necessary to be performed to assure protection against cyberthreats (Newhouse 2017), as shown in Figure 3.5. Different cyber security functions which are performed to protect an organizational infrastructure in cyberspace are discussed below:

3.4.1 SECURE PROVISIONING

It comprises defended configuration, implementation, and administration of all the involved resources. Some of the crucial areas to ensure secure provisioning are risk management, secure software development, secure system architecture, development of advanced security mechanisms, secure system planning and development, system testing, and validation.

3.4.2 FUNCTIONING AND MAINTENANCE

Functions are responsible for facilitation, management, and maintenance for better performance and security of a system. The main tasks under this category are database administration, knowledge management, customer service and support, network services, system administration, and system analysis.

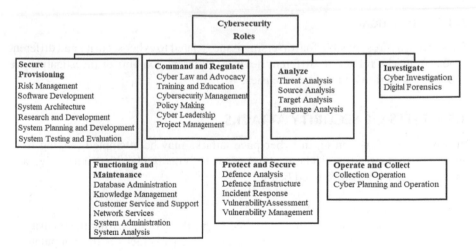

FIGURE 3.5 Functions of cybersecurity.

3.4.3 COMMAND AND REGULATE

The process of commanding and governing facilitates the tasks of mentorship, development, administration, and practicing of law and order for much-needed functioning of an organization. Some important tasks under this class of functions are cyberlaw assistance, training and education, cyber security administration, policy-making, cyber leadership, and project management to assure cyber security against different types of threats in an organization.

3.4.4 PROTECT AND SECURE

This sub-domain is responsible for the identification and study of cyber vulnerabilities in a system. Various tasks performed under this vertical are defense analysis, infrastructure management, incident response, vulnerability analysis, and administration.

3.4.5 ANALYZE

Analysis of a system comprises the study of the methods and solutions to ensure security against cyberthreats. Various techniques to analyze a system are threat analysis, source and target analysis, and language analysis.

3.4.6 OPERATE AND COLLECT

These tasks initiate dedicated operations to ensure cyber security which may help to develop intelligence. It provides protection of uncategorized data. Some important operations to realize these roles are collection operations, planning operations, and cyber operations.

3.4.7 INVESTIGATE

This process is responsible for traversing issues related to cyber security and different types of attacks related to different devices. Different domains of investigation are cyber investigation and digital forensics.

3.5 TYPES OF SECURITY ATTACKS

In any system functioning in cyberspace, attacks may be attempted ranging from networks to applications. These attacks can be broadly classified into active and passive categories as discussed below:

- **Active attacks**
  These types of attacks are attempted by breaking or bypassing the security system. The main aim of the attackers in active attacks is to manipulate the original data. This can be done through viruses, worms, introducing

malicious code, and stealing information. Some of the active attacks are masquerade, replay, and modification of message, and denial-of-service attack.

- **Passive attacks**

  In this type of attack, the attacker just observes and goes through all the activities. He does not make any alterations to the information or messages but actively monitors the communication. In a passive attack, taking out sensitive information and passwords is the main focus of the attacker. Some of the passive attacks are traffic analysis, the release of message contents, etc.

Some of the most frequently attempted attacks are discussed below:

3.5.1 REPUDIATION ATTACK

In a repudiation attack, the goal of the attacker is to perform either authorized or unauthorized actions. The attack may be performed by the sender or receiver. The basic motive of the attacker is to eliminate the evidence which may provide proof related to the identity of the attacker. In this type of attack, the sender or the receiver can deny the actions performed by them afterward. Figure 3.6 shows the repudiation attack, where User A requests for a transaction but denies later on taking the responsibility.

3.5.2 MODIFICATION OF MESSAGE

In modification attacks, intruders manipulate the true data over the network during communication (Pawar and Anuradha 2015). The data is removed, modified, and reinserted. As depicted in Figure 3.7, User A sends messages to User B, but the attacker attacks the network's traffic in between and hacks the system. He modifies the message over the network and the modified message is received by User B instead of receiving the original message sent by User A.

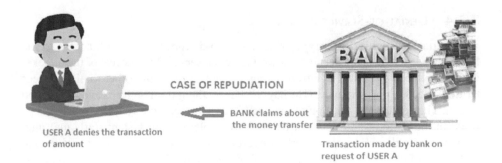

CASE OF REPUDIATION

BANK claims about
the money transfer

USER A denies the transaction
of amount

Transaction made by bank on
request of USER A

FIGURE 3.6   Repudiation attack.

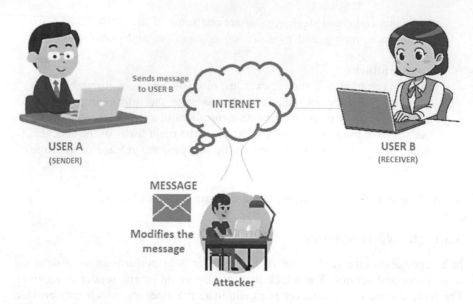

FIGURE 3.7 Modification of message attack.

3.5.3 Masquerade Attack

In this type of attack, one user assumes the identity of another. The attacker pretends himself to be the authorized user of the system for gaining the access to all the privileges of the authorized user. There are different possibilities for this type of attack. The attacker may get the user's account access by stealing authenticated user's password or by cracking the system's password using methods such as keylogger. Other reasons can be password misplaced by user or system left logged in, which gives a chance to the masquerader to misuse the system. As shown in Figure 3.8, User C is the attacker who sends messages to User B. He pretends to be authenticated User A by using his login credentials on the system. User B receives messages assuming that those messages are received from User A (Maiwald 2003).

3.5.4 Denial-of-Service Attack

The main idea behind this type of attack is to disrupt the network access to the legitimate user for basic services as well as to the server. The motive of the attacker is to stop the legitimate user from using system services and other vital resources to degrade the performance (Humayun, Niazi, Jhanjhi, Alshayeb, and Mahmood 2020). This leads to disruption of memory in disk space, inconvenience to access the files on the system, and network bandwidth problems. The system starts malfunctioning due to disabling of network or overload of messages, crashing of system, and restarting of the system repeatedly. As shown in Figure 3.9, User A trying to access services from the network server, which is disrupted by the attacker to prevent the access of User A to the internet services (Gunduz and Das 2020).

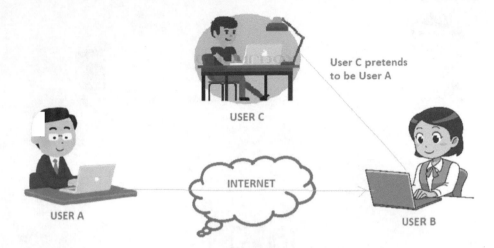

FIGURE 3.8   Masquerade attack.

FIGURE 3.9   Denial-of-service attack.

3.5.5 REPLAY ATTACK

In the replay attack, the attacker copies a block of messages communicated between the sender and the receiver and resends that same series of message to one or more users. When the hacker replays it again, he obtains the same access rights as the original user. Even if the system is enabled for the service of a password change or modification, the attacker can even replace that with his own. The example shown in Figure 3.10, where User A performs some action of online money transaction of $100, the attacker captures the network session packets of conversation and replays the action performed by User A and withdraws $100 by making a false transaction.

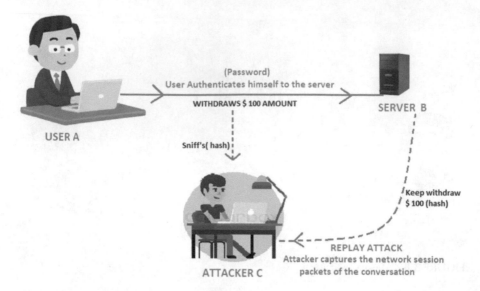

FIGURE 3.10   Replay attack.

3.5.6 Traffic Analysis

Traffic analysis is a kind of passive attack to observe, analyze, and examine the patterns of the information exchanged between the sender and the receiver. Normally, this type of attack is done by the attacker to conceive information even if the messages exchanged between users are encrypted. Normally such attacks are attempted on intelligence or military data. For example, Figure 3.11 shows the communication between User A and User B, where the attacker; i.e., User C observes the messages exchanged between them.

3.5.7 Cross-Site Scripting

It is a kind of security breach where the attacker inserts malicious scripts into the content on the original and reputed website. The victim user, who visits the website, ends up providing all the personal details and information to the hacker by accessing the vulnerable pages inserted by the hacker on the website. These attacks are very harmful to the victim users. As shown in Figure 3.12, the website visitor opens the website but the hacker has injected a malicious script on the website to steal the visitor's session cookies due to which the visitor's session cookies and desired information are automatically sent to the hacker.

3.5.8 Phishing

In phishing, the hacker creates a trap for the user. The hacker develops a clone of the original website for the target user to reach this page. The hacker then sends fake emails or messages to the victim users to trap them. The victim users reach that fake

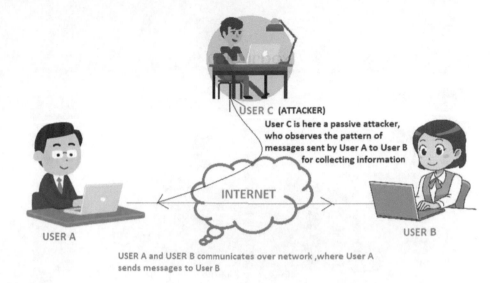

FIGURE 3.11 Traffic analysis attack.

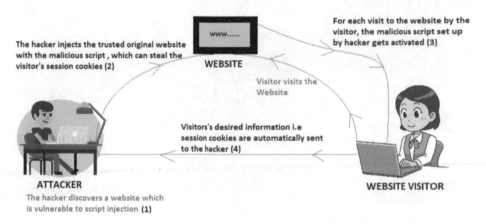

FIGURE 3.12 Cross-site scripting attack.

website by opening the link or malicious attachment shared by the hacker. When the user attempts to log in using their personal credentials and information, the hacker retrieves all the important information such as username and password. Figure 3.13 depicts where a hacker steals the information by creating a clone website referring to the original website.

3.5.9 RELEASE OF MESSAGE CONTENT

This is a kind of passive attack, where an attacker gets unauthorized access to confidential and sensitive information. It can be attempted using various modes such

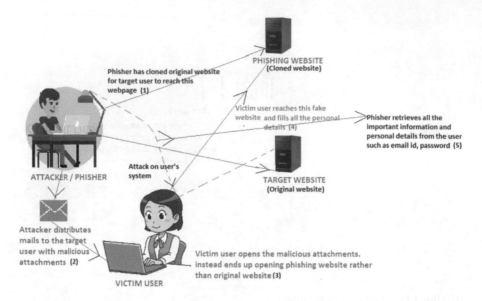

FIGURE 3.13 Phishing.

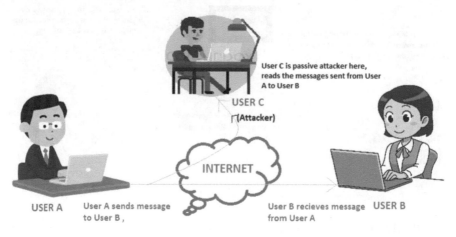

FIGURE 3.14 Release of message.

as email and file transfer whose access is only given to the authorized users. If the content of the message leaks, then it can be used by hackers and intruders for their benefit as shown in Figure 3.14.

3.5.10 HIJACKING

In hijacking, the hacker captures the session in between the conversation of two users. During this attack, the receiver is disconnected. The sender still believes that his conversation is going with the legitimate individual and might send some private information to the hacker who pretends to be that user, as depicted in Figure 3.15. This perception can be portrayed by the hacker to either of the users.

3.5.11 SPOOFING

In spoofing, a hacker modifies the source address of packets to portray that the messages are coming from a trusted user (Gaigole and Kalyankar 2015). This causes to bypass the firewall security. For spoofing, hackers use a variety of techniques. Figure 3.16 shows IP spoofing, where the victim assumes that the data packets are

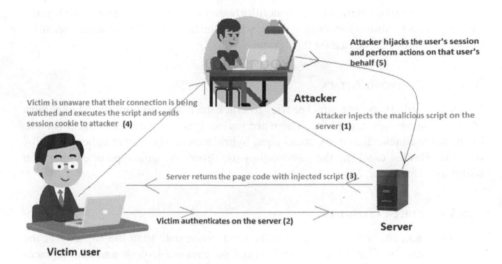

FIGURE 3.15   Hijacking.

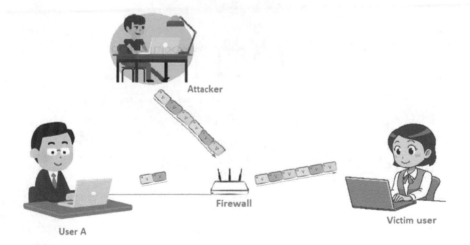

FIGURE 3.16   Spoofing.

sent by the legitimate User A, but actually those have been modified by the attacker and to the victim.

3.5.12 Sniffer Attack

In sniffer attacks, a sniffer application or device is used which reads, monitors, as well as captures network data packets. Unauthorized sniffers are very harmful to the systems as they can't be detected easily but can be inserted anywhere. A sniffer provides the full view of nonencrypted data packets. If the packets are not encrypted, they can be read without having any access key. Sensitive information such as passwords, email, and account information can be easily captured with sniffing. Figure 3.17 shows the sniffer attack where the hacker is able to access sensitive information using a device on the system.

3.5.13 Password Attack

In a password attack, the attacker tries to crack the password with illegal intentions from a password-protected file. There are various types of password attacks such as brute-force attack, dictionary attack, and hybrid attack. The hacker either uses a list of word files for cracking the password or tries every possible type of combination using all characters.

3.5.14 Buffer Overflow

In this attack, the attacker intentionally sends more data than the capacity of the buffer to store it. Due to this, it overwrites the executable code and also replaces

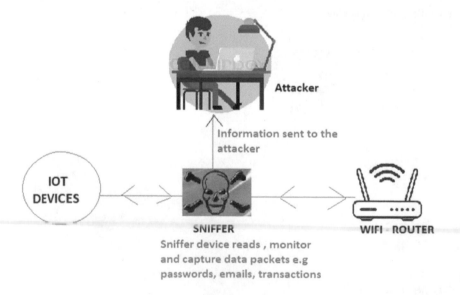

FIGURE 3.17   Sniffer attack.

the code with its own code. The hacker may also include extra code for gaining the access to the system by overwriting the existing code. By this type of attack, the hacker gains access to the system's command line.

3.5.15   EXPLOIT ATTACK

In this attack, the hacker takes the advantage of security problems of the communication network and operating system. Exploits try to control the system to steal the data transmitted over the network.

3.5.16   SNOOPING

Snooping is almost similar to eavesdropping, where the hackers' eye is always on the screen of the user. He observes emails and all other activities taking place on the user's system. The sophisticated type of snooping is done using typical software for monitoring and observing day-to-day activities of a computer system or a network device.

3.6   SECURITY MECHANISMS

To protect a system from different types of cyberattacks, a variety of tools and techniques are practiced which are termed security mechanisms. These mechanisms may function independently and even in collaboration with other techniques. These are designed to provide different types of security services in cyberspace. Different security mechanisms to administer cyberthreats are routing control, traffic padding, cryptography, digital signatures, notarization, access control, etc., and are discussed below:

3.6.1   ROUTING CONTROL

It is a dedicated network administration system designed to enhance internet services, better bandwidth, and overall network functioning in cyberspace. It is a conflux of hardware and software used to monitor all the traffic transferred over the communication network. It channelizes data through the most optimal routes to assure secure transactions. In addition, it allows changing the routing path for the data if there is any suspicion of security breach over the existing route.

3.6.2   TRAFFIC PADDING

This mechanism is used for the protection of data against traffic analysis attacks. Traffic padding actually produces continuous encrypted ciphertext even in the absence of plaintext. When there is an availability of plaintext, then the text is encrypted and transferred. But when the plain text is not available, then the random data is transmitted after encryption. This method helps to create a gap by insertion of bits into the data stream as shown in Figure 3.18, which makes it difficult for an attacker to differentiate between the actual data transferred and padding. It causes the traffic analysis attempts to become fatal.

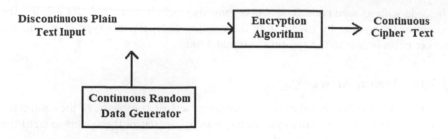

FIGURE 3.18 Traffic padding.

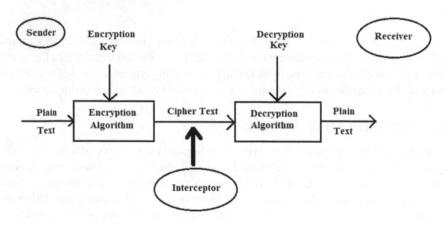

FIGURE 3.19 Encipherment.

3.6.3 ENCIPHERMENT

Encipherment is a technique used for translating plaintext into ciphertext. A mathematical function/algorithm transforms the data into an unreadable form, e.g., cryptography. Using this technique, the message is encrypted at the sender end and decrypted by the receiver using encryption and decryption algorithms, respectively, as shown in Figure 3.19.

3.6.4 DIGITAL SIGNATURE

A digital signature is authentication which gives an option to the sender to attach a code which acts as a signature for the validity of the digital message or document sent. This mechanism is based on the public key of the cryptosystem. Figure 3.20 shows the procedural steps to apply a digital signature to a document.

3.6.5 NOTARIZATION

Notarization is used for assuring some important properties of data exchange such as time, destination, location, integrity, etc., which is communicated between two

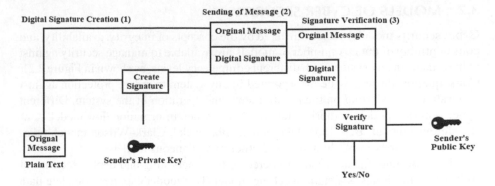

FIGURE 3.20   Digital signature.

or more than two parties (Song, Kim, Hwang, and Lee 2019). The assurance for the same is provided by the trusted third party using a specific process.

3.6.6   ACCESS CONTROL

An access control mechanism is used to depict the access rights for using different resources. Access rights specify the role of the authorities for important aspects of the data; i.e., all types of people cannot have access rights to important files and documents. The access control specifies the authority of people in terms of reading, writing, manipulation, and execution rights. It provides a security mechanism in which confidential files and documents aren't accessible to all but to only a limited number of users.

3.6.7   DATA INTEGRITY

This security mechanism is used for assuring the integrity of generated data. It is almost similar to the method of sending packets of information with the approval of sender and receiver where data is checked properly before and after data is sent or received, respectively, with which data integrity is maintained.

3.6.8   AUTHENTICATION EXCHANGE

This security mechanism ensures the identity of the person during the transfer of data. Data in communication can be secured using TCP/IP layer where a two-way verification process is used for ensuring about data, whether sent or not.

3.6.9   BIT STUFFING

In bit stuffing, extra bits are added to the data during its transmission. This supports the checking of data at the receiver's end by even/odd parity check.

3.7   MODELS OF CYBER SECURITY

Cyber security models are administered by the concepts of integrity, availability, and confidentiality of data. A number of models are available to manage security against cyberattacks in any system with different competency levels, as shown in Figure 3.21. Consequently, those may be incorporated in any system to assure protection against cyberattacks depending on the requirements and operation of the system. Different cyber security models comprise state machine model, information flow model, non-interference model, Bell–LaPadula model, Biba model, Clark–Wilson model, take-grant model, Brewer–Nash model, and other miscellaneous models.

The most fundamental model to perceive the functioning and deploy security of finite-state machines is a static machine model. This model captures complete data related to the states of a machine, actions, and transactions occurring. The basic idea is to protect the system to enter into an insecure state. An information flow model is an extension of the static machine model. Along with the basic features of the static machine model, it comprises entities, lattice states, and transitions among the states. This model facilitates to stop any unauthorized flow of information. A noninterference model manages the interference among the different levels. It controls the interference attacks among the objects and subjects belonging to the different levels. When an entity accesses unauthorized information for which it is not eligible, it is termed as an interference attack.

To incorporate security at multiple levels by using access control mechanisms, a Bell–LaPadula model encourages confidentiality. With this model, if a subject wants to access an object from a different level, it must be authorized to do so. In this model, certain security rules named simple security, star security, and strong star security are implemented to maintain confidentiality among different classification levels. A Biba model is used to ensure integrity. It is basically a lattice-based model. It ensures the integrity of the data flowing among different levels. The rules used by this model to ensure integrity are simple integrity, star integrity, and invocation property. This model does not consider the availability and confidentiality of the data.

Using Clark–Wilson model, it has been found that there is a well-defined classification of data and duties to practice integrity in commercial systems. But only authentic users can perform the tasks of duty definition and data classification.

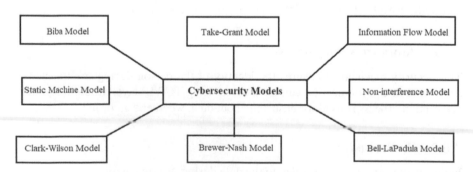

FIGURE 3.21   Models of cyber security.

TABLE 3.1

Domains of Implementation and Characteristics of Various Cyber Security Models

Model	Domain of Implementation/Features
Static machine model	• Used to protect finite-state machines • Stores states, actions, and transactions • Protects a system from entering an insecure state
Information flow model	• Used to protect finite-state machines • Stores states, actions, and transactions • Consists of entities, lattice states, and state transitions • Protects a system from entering an insecure state • Controls unauthorized flow of information
Noninterference model	• Manages security at different levels • Controls inference attacks among different levels
Bell–LaPadula model	• Deals with confidentiality • Manages cross-level authorized access • Implements simple security, star security, and strong star security
Biba model	• Lattice-based model • Ensures integrity of data accessed across different levels • Implements simple integrity and star integrity
Clark–Wilson model	• Manages integrity in commercial systems • Defined user rights for duty definition and data classification
Take-grant model	• Implements confidentiality • Fundamental functions include create, grant, take, and revoke
Brewer–Nash model	• Manages conflict of interest

A take-grant model implements confidentiality used for fundamental functions, i.e., create, grant, take, and revoke. Different subjects are allocated different functions to perform related tasks. The problem of conflict of interest is addressed by the Brewer–Nash model. It controls the flow of information to avoid any conflict of interest. Different domains managed using these models along with their characteristics are summarized in Table 3.1.

Along with all the models discussed above, Graham–Denning model, Harrison–Ruzzo–Ullman model, and lattice model are also among the important models to protect a system from cyberattacks.

3.8 CYBER SECURITY APPLICATIONS

Cyber security is playing a very vital role to protect different kinds of resources in a number of application areas. Prominent ones are corporate, government organizations, financial organizations, healthcare, and the military, where a huge volume of sensitive data is gathered, transmitted, processed, and stored over electronic devices (Patel, Srinivasan, Chang, Gupta, and Kataria 2020, Gupta 2017, Gupta and Rani

2013). In all these application areas, the role of cyber security can be divided into network security (Gupta, Rani, and Pant 2011), application security, information security, and operational security, as discussed below:

- **Network Security**: It helps to secure client data transmitted over different networks. It also facilitates secure access of data and safeguards against network threats (Kataria, Ghosh, Karar, Gupta, Srinivasan, and Hu 2020). Different methods to ensure network security are firewalls, network segmentation, authorized access control, remote access VPN, zero trust network access (ZTNA), intrusion prevention systems (IPS), hyperscale network security, cloud network security, etc.
- **Application Security**: The main aim to ensure application security is to protect data or code in an app against any theft. It aims to consider all the phases of the development starting from design, development, and finally deployment. It focuses on all the constituents of an application, e.g., software, hardware, and different methods of an application to reduce security threats. Application security revolves around authentication, authorization, encryption, logging, and testing of the final application.
- **Information Security**: It is an integration of mechanisms and policies designed to protect the information stored and transmitted in cyberspace against unauthorized access and manipulations. The main information security principles are confidentiality, integrity, and availability.
- **Operational Security**: It ensures the management of different types of cyberthreats which may expose sensitive data to cyberattacks. Operational security is practiced with different analytical operations like behavioral analysis and analysis of social media patterns. Some of the important operational security practices are to customize management processes, practice dual control, and use process automation.

3.9   CYBER SECURITY CHALLENGES

A number of security mechanisms and models are proposed by different researchers to administer that cyberthreats include a variety of domains like cyber-physical systems, smart homes, smart citifies, healthcare systems, smart grids, industry, business organizations, and e-commerce. But still, there are some challenges which need to be given special attention in the domain of cyber security. The very first long-term challenge to deploy cyber security is to plant it as a mandatory part of Information and Communication Technology (ICT), which is less considered due to economical constraints. It is also challenging to predict future security requirements with the fast evolution in communication technology. Traditional methods to ensure security are also not sufficient to protect the different resources in cyberspace. Cyberspace is among the fastest developing technologies. Consequently, the incorporation of new technologies such as the internet of things, artificial intelligence, machine learning, big data analytics, cloud computing, and mobile computing is making cyberspace a complicated platform to manage different types of cyberthreats (Kataria, Ghosh, and Karar 2020).

3.10 CONCLUSIONS AND FUTURE SCOPE

In this chapter, we have presented the notion of cyber security deeply. We have discussed the aims, platform, and architecture of cyber security. The need for cyber security is also presented in detail along with cyber security functions. Different types of security threats performed in cyberspace are discussed in detail. To manage these threats, different security mechanisms and security models are also presented in this chapter. At last, different security challenges that need to be addressed to secure different applications operating in domains like smart homes, smart cities, business organizations, and healthcare systems are discussed. From these research challenges, the following future research directions are derived:

- Requirement of standardized cyber security protocols to be designed for ICT
- Suitable security mechanisms need to be designed for all advanced technologies for their secure deployment in different application areas
- More versatile (in terms of security features) cyber security models need to be designed

REFERENCES

Gaigole, M. S., & Kalyankar, M. A. 2015. The study of network security with its penetrating attacks and possible security mechanisms. *International journal of computer science and mobile computing*, 4(5), 728–735.

Gunduz, M. Z., & Das, R. 2020. Cyber-security on smart grid: Threats and potential solutions. *Computer Networks*, 169, 107094.

Gupta, O. P. 2017. Study and analysis of various bioinformatics applications using protein BLAST: An overview. *Advances in Computational Sciences and Technology*, 10(8), 2587–601.

Gupta, O. P., & Rani, S. 2013. Accelerating Molecular Sequence Analysis using Distributed Computing Environment. *International Journal of Scientific & Engineering Research–IJSER.*, Vol. 4, 263–266.

Gupta, O., Rani, S., & Pant, D. C. 2011. Impact of parallel computing on bioinformatics algorithms. In Proceedings 5th IEEE International Conference on Advanced Computing and Communication Technologies (pp. 206–209).

Humayun, M., Niazi, M., Jhanjhi, N. Z., Alshayeb, M., & Mahmood, S. 2020. Cyber security threats and vulnerabilities: A systematic mapping study. *Arabian Journal for Science and Engineering*, 45(4), 3171–3189.

Kataria, A., Ghosh, S., & Karar, V. 2020. *Development of artificial intelligence based technique for minimization of errors and response time in head tracking for head worn systems* (Doctoral dissertation, EIED).

Kataria, A., Ghosh, S., Karar, V., Gupta, T., Srinivasan, K., & Hu, Y. C. 2020. Improved diver communication system by combining optical and electromagnetic trackers. *Sensors*, 20(18), 5084.

Kissel, R. (Ed.). 2011. *Glossary of key information security terms*. Diane Publishing.

Maiwald, E. 2003. *Network security a beginner's guide*. McGraw-Hill.

Newhouse, W., Keith, S., Scribner, B., & Witte, G. 2017. National initiative for cybersecurity education (NICE) cybersecurity workforce framework. *NIST Special Publication*, *800*, 181.

Patel, D., Srinivasan, K., Chang, C. Y., Gupta, T., & Kataria, A. 2020. Network anomaly detection inside consumer networks: A hybrid approach. *Electronics*, *9*(6), 923.

Pawar, M. V., & Anuradha, J. 2015. Network security and types of attacks in network. *Procedia Computer Science*, *48*, 503–506.

Priyadarshini, I. 2019. Introduction on cybersecurity. In *Cyber security in parallel and distributed computing: Concepts, techniques, applications and case studies*. Wiley.

Rani, S., Kataria, A., Sharma, V., Ghosh, S., Karar, V., Lee, K., & Choi, C. 2021. Threats and corrective measures for IoT security with observance of cybercrime: A survey. *Wireless Communications and Mobile Computing*. https://downloads.hindawi.com/journals/wcmc/2021/5579148.pdf

Song, G., Kim, S., Hwang, H., & Lee, K. 2019. Blockchain-based notarization for social media. In *2019 IEEE International Conference on Consumer Electronics (ICCE)* (pp. 1–2). IEEE.

Wang, E. K., Ye, Y., Xu, X., Yiu, S. M., Hui, L. C. K., & Chow, K. P. 2010. *Security issues and challenges for cyber physical system. In 2010 IEEE/ACM International Conference on Green Computing and Communications & Int'l Conference on Cyber, Physical and Social Computing (pp. 733–738)*. IEEE.

4 Secured Unmanned Aerial Vehicle-based Fog Computing Network
A Review

Akshita Gupta and Sachin Kumar Gupta

CONTENTS

4.1 INTRODUCTION

The growing interest of researchers in unmanned aerial vehicles (UAVs) helps in contributing to the smartness of the world. The massive benefits of UAVs in terms of coverage, capacity, prolonged connectivity, low cost, backhaul capacity, transmission range, etc., attract researchers to use UAVs in time-critical applications. Practically, in wireless communication technologies, UAVs have found promising applications not only to support existing telecommunications networks in circumstances of high demand and overload but also to provide remote connectivity in scenarios that lack facilities, such as battlefields or disaster zones, combat military zones, and pandemic situations [1]. UAV-assisted networks are very quick to deploy, self-configurable, and line of sight (LoS), and provide extensive coverage in geographical areas. UAVs can

DOI: 10.1201/9781003296034-4

67

be deployed as relay nodes of aerial control that act as the central point between the user equipment and base stations. UAVs aim to provide stable connections in areas vulnerable to high-link failures. It is simple to deploy a single UAV with regard to requirement, and it is very challenging and hard to deploy a range of UAVs in collaboration with each other due to the high probability of being disrupted by other UAV nodes [2]. The development of a controlled network by collaborating with another advanced network operating in a diverse mode is one of the significant UAV applications. The efficiency of UAV-assisted networks can be expanded by such a collaborative formation. The UAV-aided wireless network is a combination of flying relays, ground users, and base stations where ground users are linked to flying relays via communication links. While users are mobile, the optimum positioning of UAVs helps to minimize interference-related problems, ensuring high throughput and low delays [3].

An effective advanced technology can be used in collaboration with UAVs to offer benefits. Integrating UAVs with fog computing is a new platform. Fog computing has developed as a promising infrastructure to support scalable services nearer to the end of the network. It is a hierarchically distributed model of computing that bridges smart devices and cloud data centers. In order to provide a variety of software services to the end devices in a network, the fog system provides both architecture and platform. Fog computing expands the edge network to cloud-based facilities, reducing data transmission delay, and network traffic while improving the service quality. Fog nodes are usually heterogeneous in nature in terms of resource capability and software execution environment [4]. In a UAV-Fog system, the role of a UAV typically follows either of two types of communication: The first is UAV fog nodes act as relay nodes to provide connectivity to ground base stations; the second is UAV-Fog nodes maintain online connectivity with cloud servers for uploading data. A very popular research issue is the deployment of UAV as a fog node in collaboration to provide a real-time communication system as it is linked to energy consumption, latency, security, and performance of data transmission. To solve these problems, various algorithms are used to increase the performance of the system, such as CPU scheduling, neural and fuzzy approaches, data offloading, resource management, and load balancing [5, 6]. Apart from this, various optimization techniques and trajectory designs are designed to reduce the UAV fog node power consumption [7]. UAVs with processing and storage capacities function as fog nodes, enabling mobile users to offload applications by connecting with each other and other servers. It is, therefore, a promising solution to utilize fog computing and UAVs jointly, i.e., to use the UAVs as host fog nodes for ground users, thus called as UAV-based fog computing network [8].

4.1.1 Motivation and Contribution

In the modernized world, the advancement in technologies motivates researchers to use and deploy UAVs globally for wireless communication purposes, such as the delivery of goods, pandemic control, smart farming, e-healthcare, cordon operations, disaster management, emergencies, and many more. The motivation behind this contribution is that in diverse critical environments, if the UAVs and fog computing are deployed correctly, then it will successfully provide safe, on-demand, and low-cost services in wireless infrastructure for a variety of real-life situations [3]. Our contribution in this chapter is highlighted as follows:

1. The basic concept is to use UAVs and fog computing together as a node to provide various services at the network's edge, and UAVs facilitate to effectively optimize data bandwidth and minimize latency in real-time scenarios.
2. We provide a survey on UAV and fog computing networks (UAV-FCN) to understand the technical aspects of two advanced technologies. We also design the network model to depict the real scenario.
3. We discussed the quantum security in UAV-based fog computing network in which quantum cryptography and key distribution are used to provide secure communications.
4. Furthermore, we highlighted the challenges and opportunities of UAV-FCN for various applications.

4.1.2 CHAPTER STRUCTURE

The entire contents of this chapter are arranged as follows: Section 4.2 provides the overview of UAVs and fog computing. Section 4.3 discusses the quantum security in UAV-based fog computing networks. Section 4.4 describes the UAV-based fog computing network in which we discussed the collaboration of UAVs and fog computing and network design. Section 4.5 highlights the advantages and challenges of this network. Finally, Section 4.6 concluded with future scope.

4.2 OVERVIEW OF UAVS AND FOG COMPUTING

To understand the concept and technical implications of UAV-based fog computing networks, we include an overview of decentralized UAVs and fog computing in this section.

4.2.1 DECENTRALIZED UAVS

The UAVs are automatic self-configurable sensors in the sky for collecting data, maintaining connectivity, and providing services to ground users efficiently. UAVs can serve as a relay in the traditional cellular network, effectively distribute information between stations and nodes, and provide direct assistance for devices or things via the core network. The UAVs are categorized into two platforms: Low-altitude platform (LAP) and high-altitude platform (HAP). UAVs are optimally positioned at particular heights by entropy nets using the optimal placement algorithm, and then it serves as control nodes. The movement of ground users is controlled by these optimally positioned control nodes, which are random in nature, and each user's mobility is dynamic [9]. Another more challenging feasible architecture is decentralized multiple UAV networks where an operator communicates with an autonomous mission and payload manager, which manages a series of tasks for a number of highly autonomous vehicles. If we solve issues at the UAV stage, UAVs can communicate with each other in the pre-flight process to resolve their disputes in a decentralized manner. Decentralized UAV systems are very reliable particularly in terms of managing operator workload; also it is more flexible and more robust for single failure points [10]. With several benefits, one of the important UAV applications is the establishment of a controlled network via the collaboration of other heterogeneous networks. In addition, network degradation problems and latency issues can be effectively minimized by the optimum positioning of UAVs [11].

4.2.2   Fog Computing

The Cisco-originated term fog computing describes as an extended form of cloud computing. It is a decentralized computing system situated between the cloud and end devices, also called fog networking. This versatile system helps users position resources in logical places to improve performance, including applications and the data that devices generate [12]. Fog computing is a fully virtualized platform that combines end devices and traditional cloud-computing data centers to provide computing, storage, and networking services. A fog architecture with software-defined network (SDN) is to monitor networks programmatically. To allow fog nodes to be installed, the systems in the network should present a reliable, self-organized framework [13]. Traditional cloud computing presents scalability and reliability issues. When using a traditional client–server framework, the client identifies data and the server handles it. In a traditional client–server architecture, if the server gets overloaded due to data traffic, the other devices are considered inaccessible. So, fog computing aims to provide a flexible, decentralized solution to handle this problem [14]. Thus, fog computing offers additional benefits such as low latency, storage, and fast data processing to actually occur at the edge of the network, at the end computers, via fog nodes. Fog computing has the capability to provide intelligence and computing abilities for a variety of applications such as smart grids, traffic control, search and rescue operations, delivery of goods, disaster management, etc. [15]. Fog computing is considered to be a building block for the vast number of smart internet of things (IoT) devices in the near future to offer various solutions for more reliable, efficient, and manageable communication methods as compared to the cloud or edge computing. Mobile-edge computing (MEC), cloudlets, and mobile cloud computing (MCC) are quite similar to fog computing [16]. Fog nodes are one hop apart from edge devices and offer low-latency services in fog computing. Apart from this, fog computing provides location awareness and mobility support characteristics. As fog computing is an extended form of cloud computing, there are several security and privacy issues due to direct interaction with heterogeneous devices. This is a big challenge to take care of [17].

4.3   QUANTUM SECURITY IN UAV-FCN

In a UAV fog-computing network, security is a major issue. To implement a UAV fog environment, quantum security is one advanced way to provide strong security. Traditionally, various researchers build cryptography algorithms and intrusion detection mechanisms to provide security in UAV networks [18]. But for an attacker, breaking a traditional cryptographic encryption algorithm becomes very easy with quantum computing. To deal with this security breach, quantum cryptography provides a way to secure the network. In a UAV-assisted network, the UAVs act as a relay node and it is possible that there is the presence of an eavesdropper in the system. The active unauthorized party is supposed to obtain access to the device by breaching the UAV during user authentication. To identify the unauthorized network access, researchers from worldwide have contributed by proposing predictive models such as K-means clustering and one-class support vector machines (OC-SVM) [19]. Still, there is a possibility of low accuracy in the prediction of a security breach in a system. Quantum cryptography fills the gap by providing safe communication by offering encryption instead of using mathematical algorithms.

4.3.1   QUANTUM CRYPTOGRAPHY

Quantum cryptography is a very prominent area in which quantum mechanics principles are used to build a cryptosystem that is known to be the safest method. Quantum cryptography, also known as quantum encryption, uses the rules of quantum theory to symmetric encryption of messages so that no one except the receiver node can ever interpret them. Quantum cryptography is basically based on Heisenberg's uncertainty principle [20]. If in any case eavesdropper captures the keys during communication between UAV fog users and ground users, then quantum cryptography added the irregularities in the polarity of the photon and thus shows the violated communication. This helps to abort the ongoing communication and secure the infrastructure. The core of quantum cryptography arises from the fact that it incorporates the tiny individual particles, i.e., photons, which naturally occurs. These photon particles have great potential to reside concurrently in more than one state, and they alter their locations only when assessed [21]. Hua-Ying Liu and colleagues at Nanjing University in China developed the framework of quantum communications with UAVs. To establish a quantum communications channel between two ground stations nearby 1 km, a pair of UAVs were used. Multiple UAVs in pairs overcome the limitation of diffraction of photons [21, 22].

The benefits of quantum cryptography in UAVs are discussed as follows:

* The deployment of quantum UAVs is very easy and reliable.
* Quantum cryptography in UAVs provides secure communication, as it is unhackable, and if any case eavesdropper tries to intercept the messages, the receiver comes to know with the help of quantum key distribution and discard the intercepted messages.

- Industries and the government can possibly use the quantum-secure UAVs in future because it provides ultra-high security.
- Less manageable network than traditional cellular networks.

4.3.2 QUANTUM KEY DISTRIBUTION

Quantum key distribution is a technique that guarantees the distributed network's long-term security. The potential of the two interacting users to identify the existence of any third party attempting to obtain knowledge of the information flowing between ground users with the use of quantum key distribution. Quantum key distribution (QKD) uses the laws of quantum mechanics to enable parties, at least in some cases, to exchange cryptographic keys with complete security. A communication system may be developed that detects eavesdropping by using quantum superpositions or quantum entanglement and exchanging information in quantum states. The modification of a system can be possible by using a property called quantum entanglement [21, 23]. Quantum keys, i.e., a stream of photons, are distributed via a quantum channel, where encrypted information is transmitted via a public channel. The photons have a property of momentum and angular spin. There are two polarization modes: Rectilinear and diagonal, depending on the spin of photons. The users distributed the keys to other users by sending a stream of randomly polarized photons. If in any case someone attempts to capture the key, the recipient has the ability to read the malicious activity in the network. After that, the received key will be discarded and requests the sender to retransmit new arbitrarily polarized photon streams [24].

4.4   UAV-BASED FOG COMPUTING NETWORK

The UAVs and fog computing together help to provide the services at the edge of the network intelligently. In this section, we provide the collaboration of UAVs and fog computing and its network design for better understanding.

4.4.1 COLLABORATION OF UAVS AND FOG COMPUTING

We surveyed UAVs and fog computing to learn deployment strategies in order to provide real-time services with ultra-low latency. Several researchers focus on integrating UAVs and cloud, fog, or edge computing to provide storage capabilities, data processing, resource management, load balancing, energy efficiency, and low latency for different applications. Some of the important works by various researchers are discussed in this section.

To alleviate the burden on the base station and decrease the transmission delay during the peak time, the authors in [25], suggest a low-latency massive-connectivity vehicular fog computing system. User equipment's (UE) computing functions are offloaded to neighboring nodes with underutilized computation tools. It is observed that the vast amount of computing demands obtained at peak times will also exceed the small number of edge servers. As a consequence of the results, such tasks must be queued for a prolonged period of time, reducing delay and increasing communication machine reliability during processing. To deal with this problem, the authors use a two-dimensional pricing-based matching algorithm to manage task assignment and management issues between vehicular fog nodes and UE in order to minimize the overall network delay. The result shows an improvement in overall network performance. In [26], the authors have suggested a hybrid fog computing model (H-FVFC) that combines UAVs and vehicular fog computing (VFC) to perform highly challenging tasks with specific latency requirements. The authors have considered the computing capabilities in UAVs for post-disaster relief operations, and after that, the authors evaluate the task offloading using a hybrid fog model. The findings show that task offloading will substantially reduce the response latency in the UAV network.

The most popular approach is to offload tasks to external computers with higher processing and storage capacities that can be possibly supported in fog nodes or on edge by clustered servers using the paradigm of fog computing. To connect the network with a fog system in real time is a challenge. The authors in [27] suggested an idea to consider UAVs as a fog node and focus on the energy consumption of the computer component mounted onboard UAVs, which is important since it can impact the duration of the flight mission. To reduce energy consumption, computational power, and processing latency, reinforcement learning is used. In order to offer mobility and real-time support, fog computing will provide assistance to cope with a vast range of heterogeneous sensors and devices spread across large geographical locations. Also, a UAV-assisted network has been substantially developed and deployed for many real-time applications. In [28], the authors suggest UAV-Fog, a UAV-based fog computing framework for the internet of things (IoT) applications. In order to support any IoT applications successfully, the authors aim to use the strengths and capabilities of both technologies, fog computing and UAVs. To provide support in complex IoT environments, UAV-Fog nodes offer easy deployment of fog functionality at remote or difficult locations. The authors considered a service-oriented platform to implement for UAVs and fog computing. The deployment of UAVs in the environment of fog will face crucial challenges. GPS spoofing is an important security attack for UAVs since they rely heavily on GPS for flight control. In [29], the authors suggest a modern and reliable form of GPS spoofing identification that uses data fusion built on the inertial measurement unit (IMU) and monocular sensor. The authors use the Dji phantom 4 UAV for experimental purposes.

In a paper [30], the author has suggested self-aware communication architecture (SACA) for reliable and prolonged communication over IoT devices. The suggested scheme reflects the idea of mobile fog nodes and unmanned aerial vehicle (UAV) networks to act as a relay. The distributed node management (DNM) network is able to provide prolonged connectivity by increasing the stability and longevity of the network even in the event of failures. By creating a private near-user UAV fog infrastructure rather than the conventional static fog servers, the idea of fogging is pushed to another level. This serves to protect the logistics of fogging and provides versatility to cover a wide range of effective load balancing systems. The result shows that the network has less latency and less packet errors, the proposed solution is able to provide sustainable and stable connectivity. In a mobile edge computing (MEC) network, the author of this chapter [31] solved the sum power minimization problem by optimizing user association, power control, computing capacity distribution, and position planning all at the same time (UAVs). The incorporation of UAV-enabled connectivity with MEC will further boost computational efficiency due to the versatility of UAVs. The author decoupled the initial problem into several problems at limited sizes for computing power allocation problems. Since fog nodes have limited computing power relative to remote cloud servers, it becomes impossible to process all of the delegated data during activities at the primary fog node by the end-user-initiated deadlines. Therefore, the end-user offloads the mission data to its main fog node in this paper [32].

In the above survey, it is clear that very few works have been done in the area of collaborative UAV-based fog networks and their security. On analyzing the survey, we aim to deploy multiple UAV-based fog nodes to serve at the edge of the network with better quality of service (QoS). Table 4.1 demonstrates the comparison of existing work on a UAV-based fog network.

4.4.2 NETWORK DESIGN

UAVs have made great strides from the beginning, as in military surveillance, UAVs are the most common instrument for military units. UAV networks offer a major advantage over traditional wireless networking networks, can be quickly reconfigured and rearranged to accommodate differing traffic, can provide vital communication services in areas impacted by disasters like a landslide, forest fire, cyclone, and flood [33]. But as the demand and density of users increase in urban areas, this network poses a lot of challenges, such as coverage, capacity, latency, load balancing, connectivity, and security. The users were extremely requesting continuous data from UAVs, which causes a lot of traffic flow in the mobile network. The advantages of the UAVs attract researchers to use them widely. UAVs as a middleware helps to control the flow of the data from the ground station effectively. UAV also offers broad coverage to all recipient users with nearly congestion-free routes for data packets. Depending on the different criteria for applications, UAVs may be located at an optimum height ranging from 100 m to a few kilometers from the ground station. The UAVs should support mobility to communicate with ground users with full connectivity. These attractive benefits of UAVs inspired researchers to explore UAVs for commercial as well industrial purposes. Apart from the UAVs, the advanced technology called fog computing also attracts researchers because of its services, load balancing, storage capabilities, security, offloading, and data processing [34].

Figure 4.1 depicts the pictorial representation of the quantum secured UAV-FCN. The idea of merging UAVs with fog computing came into limelight because it completes the network by providing various benefits to users in terms of live video streaming, storage, low latency, fast processing, resource management, etc. UAVs become part of the fog computing infrastructure by linking the UAVs to the internet. Each UAV is considered as a fog server with a collection of resources and services to provide to users. In this infrastructure, most of the UAVs allow Wi-Fi connections

TABLE 4.1

Comparison of Existing Work on UAV-based Fog Network

Ref. No.	UAV	Fog	Problem	Technique Used	Key Focus	Future Scope
[25]	✗	✓	• Task assignment • Latency	Price-based matching scheme	Improvement in overall network performance by managing and assigning tasks using price-based matching scheme.	Combined machine learning approach with existing matching problems.
[26]	✓	✓	• Latency • Resource utilization • Energy consumption	Hybrid Vehicular Fog computing	Hybrid UAV-Fog model to offload tasks and reduce latency.	Energy-efficient hybrid vehicular fog computing with UAVs.
[27]	✓	✓	• Energy consumption • Latency	Reinforcement learning	Reduction in energy consumption of the onboard UAVs during take-off.	—
[28]	✓	✓	• Low latency • Resource management	Service-orientated UAVs and fog computing	Integration of two advanced technologies UAVs and fog computing to serve benefits in critical applications.	To develop an algorithm to reduce energy consumption in IoT applications.
[29]	✓	✓	• Security attacks in UAVs	GPS spoofing detection	Fusion of IMU and monocular sensor for detection of security attacks in UAV GPS system.	Design a decentralized and autonomous decision-making technique for collision avoidance without any central control.

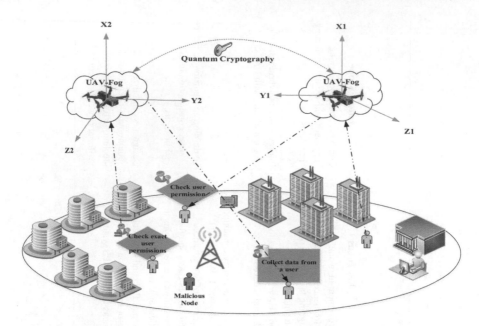

FIGURE 4.1   Quantum secured UAV-FCN.

and would have a special internet ID to connect with user equipment. The deployment of UAVs and their ability to deliver their services and resources via application
programming interfaces (APIs) are some of the requirements in incorporating UAVs
with the fog server. As a result, the UAV fog system consists of strong fog servers
for services and computing, as well as UAVs as relays offer services to communicate with the real environment [35]. Secure communication in a UAV-based network
becomes prior because in time-critical application security is a major issue. UAV-
Fog nodes connect with quantum internet to provide secure communications. Any
malicious activity in the network will be detected and discarded with this quantum
cryptography. In quantum cryptography, quantum key distribution plays a key role
as the stream of photons send to the receiver in a network.

4.5   ADVANTAGES AND CHALLENGES OF UAV-
BASED FOG COMPUTING NETWORK

In this section, we discussed the advantages and the challenges of UAV-based fog
network. Some of the important advantages include improved support for low cost,
reliable, long connectivity, low latency, mobility, save bandwidth, quick deployment,
low-cost solution, scalability, and robust interoperability with other systems, such as
fog or edge computing, AI, and blockchain [36, 37].

- **Low-Cost Solution**: The most effective and low-cost approach for improving computing capabilities and providing on-demand services by installing
  fog node properties into UAVs at the networks' edge.

- **Reliable**: This network is highly consistent and reliable, and it may be used in crowded areas where connectivity is difficult to build.
- **Quick Deployment**: UAVs are very quick to deploy and control in emergency situations. Thus, the UAV-based fog network is deployed very quickly wherever required.
- **Long-term Connectivity**: This network, in contrast to the existing traditional ground-based wireless network, provides long-term connectivity and consistency.
- **Quick Service Recovery**: Service failure is a major concern in mobile networks, but UAV-based fog network guarantees quick service recovery in any situation, whether partial or total loss of infrastructure due to hurricanes, landslides, flooding, natural disasters, and the data offloading of base stations in heavily crowded areas.
- **Security**: Quantum cryptography provides security in a UAV-based fog computing network. In case any effort by eavesdrop alter the status of the photons, then quantum security alerts the receiver to foul play. Thus, quantum security is much more reliable than traditional security.
- **Reduce Latency**: It is the primary advantage of this network because of the fog nodes the network deployed nearer to the ground station (at the edge of the network).
- **Save Bandwidth**: Although processing has chosen data locally, UAV-based fog computing will save network bandwidth instead of transferring it for analysis to the cloud. This will enhance the capacity of the network.
- **Storage Capacity**: UAV-assisted networks generally provide communication services to ground users, but with the integration of fog computing, the UAV-based fog network has the capacity to store data and offload to the ground users whenever required.
- **Computing Capabilities**: In a UAV-based fog computing network, the fog nodes have the ability to compute the data coming from ground users very efficiently.
- **Real-Time Services**: This network will provide real-time services in critical applications because of its best performance.

Apart from advantages, we highlighted some of the important challenges faced by the UAV fog network, which is highlighted as follows [2, 38]:

- **Energy Consumption**: The fog system's energy consumption is incredibly high due to the vast number of fog nodes involved, which necessarily involves a large amount of energy to function. This puts a challenge for researchers to reduce the usage of node energy during communication.
- **Authentication and Trust**: When the data facilities and services are provided on a wide scale, authentication and trust are some of the most troubling challenges of fog computing. Thus, it can make the whole network in trouble, and UAV fog functionality exacerbates the entire infrastructure. For example, in a military system, a malicious node acts as a fog node but it is not actually a fog node. This will cause a problem to the entire system to trust the data coming from the actual node.

- **Large Coverage**: The fog computing in UAV-based network puts a challenge of coverage in a network. As the fog nodes are placed at the networks' edge, they should not be able to cover large geographical areas.
- **Size, Weight, and Power (SWAP)**: SWAP limitations of UAVs, i.e., size, weight, and power, are one of the hardest problems in this network because they could restrict processing, connectivity, and persistence abilities.
- **Control and Coordination**: The involvement of UAVs in the network creates a challenge of control and coordination between multiple UAVs. Multiple UAVs cause interference with each other at adjacent cells. This challenge can be solved by optimization of task allocation and trajectory planning of UAV nodes.
- **Endurance**: The limited endurance of UAVs affects the practical deployment and longevity of UAV-aided communications. To deal with this challenge, the battery-powered system is being replaced by electric-powered UAVs to extend the endurance of UAVs in the entire network.

4.6 CONCLUSION AND FUTURE SCOPE

Traditional UAV networking is very limited to certain applications such as disasters, the military, and commercial use. With the advancement in technologies, researchers have grown their interest in the field of UAV communication and contributed to it. But with the increase in demands by active users for continuous data in UAV-assisted networks, the UAVs alone are unable to handle the data with efficiency. So the collaboration of UAVs and fog computing comes into broad light as both technologies share amazing benefits. Fog computing puts its properties in UAVs to serve intelligently in real-time applications. This chapter provides a survey on UAV-based fog computing and its network design. When the multiple UAVs communicate with ground users, there is a high chance of interception of data in a dense environment. To deal with security issues, we considered quantum security in a UAV-based fog computing network. We also highlighted the advantages and challenges of this network. The aim of this collaboration is to successfully deploy UAV-based fog computing to reduce latency, bandwidth saving, load balancing, on-demand services, high throughput, and overall high performance.

The future scope of the UAV-FCN is to deploy in disaster relief and search-and-rescue operations: Providing ultralow-latency relay network with the management of resources and data flowing in a loop. Apart from this, security is the main concern when the devices work at the networks' edge, and in further work, security policies and quantum security may be designed to implement UAV-FCN.

REFERENCES

1. Jiang, Fenyu, and Chris Phillips. "High Throughput Data Relay in UAV Wireless Networks." *Future Internet* 12, no. 11 (2020): 193.
2. Gupta, Akshita, Sachin Kumar Gupta, Mamoon Rashid, Amina Khan, and Manisha Manjul. "Unmanned aerial vehicles integrated HetNet for smart dense urban area." *Transactions on Emerging Telecommunications Technologies* (2020): 1–22.

3. Gupta, Akshita, Shriya Sundhan, Sachin Kumar Gupta, S. H. Alsamhi, and Mamoon Rashid. "Collaboration of UAV and HetNet for better QoS: a comparative study." *International Journal of Vehicle Information and Communication Systems* 5, no. 3 (2020): 309–333.

4. Mahmud, Redowan, Kotagiri Ramamohanarao, and Rajkumar Buyya. "Latency-aware application module management for fog computing environments." *ACM Transactions on Internet Technology (TOIT)* 19, no. 1 (2018): 1–21.

5. Bhushan, Shashi, Manoj Kumar, Pramod Kumar, Thompson Stephan, Achyut Shankar, and Peide Liu. "FAJIT: a fuzzy-based data aggregation technique for energy efficiency in wireless sensor network." *Complex & Intelligent Systems* 7, no. 2 (2021): 997–1007.

6. Aggarwal, Akarsh, Mohammed Alshehri, Manoj Kumar, Purushottam Sharma, Osama Alfarraj, and Vikas Deep. "Principal component analysis, hidden Markov model, and artificial neural network inspired techniques to recognize faces." *Concurrency and Computation: Practice and Experience* 33, no. 9 (2021): e6157.

7. Mozaffari, Mohammad, Walid Saad, Mehdi Bennis, and Merouane Debbah. "Drone small cells in the clouds: Design, deployment and performance analysis." In 2015 IEEE Global Communications Conference (GLOBECOM), pp. 1–6. IEEE, 2015.

8. Jeong, Seongah, Osvaldo Simeone, and Joonhyuk Kang. "Mobile edge computing via a UAV-mounted cloudlet: Optimization of bit allocation and path planning." *IEEE Transactions on Vehicular Technology* 67, no. 3 (2017): 2049–2063.

9. Hu, Jingzhi, Hongliang Zhang, and Lingyang Song. "Reinforcement learning for decentralized trajectory design in cellular UAV networks with sense-and-send protocol." *IEEE Internet of Things Journal* 6, no. 4 (2018): 6177–6189.

10. Ryan, Allison, John Tisdale, Mark Godwin, Daniel Coatta, David Nguyen, Stephen Spry, Raja Sengupta, and J. Karl Hedrick. "Decentralized control of unmanned aerial vehicle collaborative sensing missions." In 2007 American Control Conference, pp. 4672–4677. IEEE, 2007.

11. Merwaday, Arvind, and Ismail Guvenc. "UAV assisted heterogeneous networks for public safety communications." In 2015 IEEE Wireless Communications and Networking Conference Workshops (WCNCW), pp. 329–334. IEEE, 2015.

12. Yi, Shanhe, Cheng Li, and Qun Li. "A survey of fog computing: concepts, applications and issues." In Proceedings of the 2015 Workshop on Mobile Big Data, pp. 37–42. 2015.

13. Gedeon, Julien, Jens Heuschkel, Lin Wang, and Max Mühlhäuser. "Fog computing: Current research and future challenges." *GI/ITG KuVS Fachgespräche Fog Computing* 1 (2018): 1–4.

14. Khan, Saad, Simon Parkinson, and Yongrui Qin. "Fog computing security: a review of current applications and security solutions." *Journal of Cloud Computing* 6, no. 1 (2017): 1–22.

15. Mouradian, Carla, Diala Naboulsi, Sami Yangui, Roch H. Glitho, Monique J. Morrow, and Paul A. Polakos. "A comprehensive survey on fog computing: State-of-the-art and research challenges." *IEEE communications surveys & tutorials* 20, no. 1 (2017): 416–464.

16. Srivastava, Shashank, Sandeep Saxena, Rajkumar Buyya, Manoj Kumar, Achyut Shankar, and Bharat Bhushan. "CGP: Cluster-based gossip protocol for dynamic resource environment in cloud." *Simulation Modelling Practice and Theory* 108 (2021): 102275.

17. Yi, Shanhe, Zhengrui Qin, and Qun Li. "Security and privacy issues of fog computing: A survey." In International Conference on Wireless Algorithms, Systems, and Applications, pp. 685–695. Springer, 2015.

18. Sharma, Diwankshi, Sachin Kumar Gupta, Aabid Rashid, Sumeet Gupta, Mamoon Rashid, and Ashutosh Srivastava. "A novel approach for securing data against intrusion attacks in unmanned aerial vehicles integrated heterogeneous network using functional encryption technique." *Transactions on Emerging Telecommunications Technologies* 32, no. 7 (2021): e4114.

19. Hoang, Tiep M., Nghia M. Nguyen, and Trung Q. Duong. "Detection of eavesdropping attack in UAV-aided wireless systems: Unsupervised learning with one-class SVM and k-means clustering." *IEEE Wireless Communications Letters* 9, no. 2 (2019): 139–142.

20. Bhatt, Alekha Parimal, and Anand Sharma. "Quantum cryptography for internet of things security." *Journal of Electronic Science and Technology* 17, no. 3 (2019): 213–220.

21. Liu, Yeng, Hua, et al. "Quantum connection is made by flying drones." (2021). https://physicsworld.com/a/quantum-connection-is-made-by-flying-drones/.

22. Schirber, Michael. "Quantum drones take flight." *Physics* 14 (2021): 7. https://physics.aps.org/articles/v14/7.

23. Online Available: https://en.wikipedia.org/wiki/Quantum_key_distribution. Last accessed: 02 February 2021.

24. Online Available: https://www.rfwireless-world.com/Terminology/Advantages-and-Disadvantages-of-Quantum-Cryptography.html. Last accessed: 02 February 2021.

25. Xu, Chen, Yahui Wang, Zhenyu Zhou, Bo Gu, Valerio Frascolla, and Shahid Mumtaz. "A low-latency and massive-connectivity vehicular fog computing framework for 5G." In 2018 IEEE Globecom Workshops (GC Wkshps), pp. 1–6. IEEE, 2018.

26. Tang, Chaogang, Chunsheng Zhu, Xianglin Wei, Hao Peng, and Yi Wang. "Integration of UAV and fog-enabled vehicle: application in post-disaster relief." In 2019 IEEE 25th International Conference on Parallel and Distributed Systems (ICPADS), pp. 548–555. IEEE, 2019.

27. Faraci, Giuseppe, Christian Grasso, and Giovanni Schembra. "Fog in the clouds: UAVs to provide edge computing to IoT devices." *ACM Transactions on Internet Technology (TOIT)* 20, no. 3 (2020): 1–26.

28. Mohamed, Nader, Jameela Al-Jaroodi, Imad Jawhar, Hassan Noura, and Sara Mahmoud. "UAVFog: A UAV-based fog computing for Internet of Things." In 2017 IEEE SmartWorld, Ubiquitous Intelligence & Computing, Advanced & Trusted Computed, Scalable Computing & Communications, Cloud & Big Data Computing, Internet of People and Smart City Innovation (SmartWorld/SCALCOM/UIC/ATC/CBDCom/IOP/SCI), pp. 1–8. IEEE, 2017.

29. He, Daojing, Yinrong Qiao, Sammy Chan, and Nadra Guizani. "Flight security and safety of drones in airborne fog computing systems." *IEEE Communications Magazine* 56, no. 5 (2018): 66–71.

30. Sharma, Vishal, Jae Deok Lim, Jeong Nyeo Kim, and Ilsun You. "Saca: Self-aware communication architecture for IoT using mobile fog servers." *Mobile Information Systems* 2017, Article ID 3273917, (2017): 1–18.

31. Yang, Zhaohui, Cunhua Pan, Kezhi Wang, and Mohammad Shikh-Bahaei. "Energy efficient resource allocation in UAV-enabled mobile edge computing networks." *IEEE Transactions on Wireless Communications* 18, no. 9 (2019): 4576–4589.

32. Mukherjee, Mithun, Suman Kumar, Qi Zhang, Rakesh Matam, Constandinos X. Mavromoustakis, Yunrong Lv, and George Mastorakis. "Task data offloading and resource allocation in fog computing with multi-task delay guarantee." *IEEE Access* 7 (2019): 152911–152918.

33. Khan, Amina, Sumeet Gupta, and Sachin Kumar Gupta. "Multi-hazard disaster studies: Monitoring, detection, recovery, and management, based on emerging technologies and optimal techniques." *International Journal of Disaster Risk Reduction* 47 (2020): 101642.

34. Sharma, Vishal, Kathiravan Srinivasan, Han-Chieh Chao, Kai-Lung Hua, and Wen-Huang Cheng. "Intelligent deployment of UAVs in 5G heterogeneous communication environment for improved coverage." *Journal of Network and Computer Applications* 85 (2017): 94–105.
35. Mahmoud, Sara, Nader Mohamed, and Jameela Al-Jaroodi. "Integrating UAVS into the cloud using the concept of the web of things." *Journal of Robotics* 10 (2015): 10.
36. Curtis, Brian. "What are the issues with fog computing"? https://www.yourtechdiet.com/blogs/fog-computing-issues/. Last accessed: 02 February, 2021.
37. Syed, Farheen, Sachin Kumar Gupta, Saeed Hamood Alsamhi, Mamoon Rashid, and Xuan Liu. "A survey on recent optimal techniques for securing unmanned aerial vehicles applications." *Transactions on Emerging Telecommunications Technologies* 32, no. 7 (2021): e4133.
38. Gupta, Akshita, Shriya Sundhan, S. H. Alsamhi, and Sachin Kumar Gupta. "Review for capacity and coverage improvement in aerially controlled heterogeneous network." In *Optical and Wireless Technologies*, pp. 365–376. Springer, 2020.

5 Mars Surface Exploration via Unmanned Aerial Vehicles

Secured MarSE UAV Prototype

Manjula Sharma, Akshita Gupta, and Sachin Kumar Gupta

CONTENTS

DOI: 10.1201/9781003296034-5

5.1   INTRODUCTION

Space exploration is an exemplar of several types of integration, power, communication, and a host of others. It brings several technical fields together: Energy storage, biosciences, types of equipment, guidance, etc. The stars, Sun, planets (such as Mercury, Martian body, Earth, Venus, Saturn, Jupiter, etc.), various asteroids, comets, and meteoroids make up our solar system [1]. With the aid of space exploration, such parameters can be studied and explored. Space exploration and discovery, according to the superpowers of the 12th century, is a successful investment. It has contributed to different fields such as cancer treatment, global search systems, and rescue systems, among others. Landers, orbiters, rovers, flybys, telescopes, human crew, and other methods to space exploration have been used in the past for investigating several spatial bodies. However, there have been some limitations to these space exploration strategies, such as hindrance in surface exploration, the lesser amount of time spent closer to the planetary body, and insufficient quantity and consistency of the investigation [2]. Also, severe health complication develops in the body of the human crew [3] as a result of space exploration. Although these health conditions are generally just temporary, they may have a long-term impact as well [4]. These issues prompted us to consider a better choice, which led to the development of unmanned aerial vehicles (UAVs) for space exploration.

The use of UAVs would strike a balance between science, execution risk, and cost. UAVs must collect and process data in order to complete their missions. UAVs could be able to store a wide variety of data about a planet's atmosphere and strategic operations. Thus, it becomes evident that a methodical and accurate analysis of technical vulnerabilities is needed to secure communication through UAVs. It is because of cyberattacks, software and hardware flaws, and unintended defects introduced by the developer, space UAVs will tend to become more vulnerable and susceptible to faults and failures. As a result, UAVs must be built with keeping such dangers in mind; defensive capabilities and measures must also be included so that they can respond automatically and dynamically to both accidental and intentional faults and attacks

5.1.1   MOTIVATION AND CONTRIBUTION

Owing to the recent technical advances, UAVs are now considered a useful tool [5] for planetary exploration [6]. UAVs have made enormous progress in their application to space missions [7]. The latest planetary exploration methods are limited in mobility and resolution and provide little knowledge about Earth. To fix these concerns [8], we have been inspired to use UAVs for space exploration. The current study's main contributions are as follows:

- To securely deploy the UAVs for space exploration (for sensing and data collection, predict the environmental conditions in a spatial body).
- To provide the security aspects in space UAVs, including protocols, communication threats, crypto security, and quantum security.
- To learn about the challenges faced by UAVs' deployment and ensure the security in a UAV-based network in a spatial body.
- To simulate a prototype UAV for a successful flight on a Martian body.
- To observe the behavioral change in the UAV flight on the surface of Martian body and Earth.
- We provide a comparison of environmental parameters for Martian body and the Earth's surface.

The remaining sections of this chapter are as follows: Section 5.2 is about the earlier studies on space UAVs. Section 5.3 is with reference to the types of UAVs for space exploration. Section 5.4 provides the protocols and security threats in space UAVs. This section discusses various protocols for space exploration, communication threats and incidents, and the types of security algorithms such as crypto and quantum security. Section 5.5 discusses the deployment strategy for deploying a UAV on the surface of Martian body. Section 5.6 is about the environmental considerations on the surface of Martian body for a successful UAV flight. Section 5.7 is about the simulation results acquired while observing UAVs' behavioral change on the surface of Earth and Martian body. Section 5.8 discusses various possible research challenges related to the network security of space UAVs. Finally, Section 5.9 concludes.

5.2 PREVIOUS STUDIES ON SPACE UAVs

In this section, we have provided the previous studies on UAVs used for space exploration. As UAVs are used for space exploration, scientists from every corner of the world try to send UAV to Martian body for collecting information and making networks on the Martian surface.

The use of UAVs for space missions has increased significantly. A Mars helicopter landed recently on Jezero Crater on 18 February 2021 is one of the most popular examples of space UAVs. This mission is possible due to the advantages of low-speed forward flight, vertical take-off and landing (VTOL) aircraft, and hovering capabilities [9]. The key advantage of using UAVs for space exploration is wide area coverage and an enhanced quality of information [10]. Due to the differences in climatic conditions, the design, layout, flight, trajectory, and route planning differ for UAVs for a different planetary mission. The atmosphere of Martian body is very thin and dusty, consisting mostly of carbon dioxide, having traces of argon and nitrogen, as well as water and oxygen. The average surface pressure of Martian atmosphere is 0.4–0.87 kPa or around 1% of the pressure at sea level on Earth [11]. Due to its thin atmosphere and

TABLE 5.1

Various Space UAVs for Planetary Exploration

References	UAV Model	Solar Body	Mass (in kg)	Power Supply	Endurance (in min)
Koning *et al.* (2008) [16]	ExoFly-DelFly	Mars	0.02	Solar	12
Grumman (2014) [17]	Mars Helicopter	Mars	1.8	Solar	1.5
Zhu *et al.* (2015) [18]	VAMP AV	Venus	900	Solar and ASRG	–
NASA (2019) [19], (2015)	SESPA	Venus	–	Solar	–
Aggarwal *et al.* (2020) [20]	Dragonfly	Titan	–	Nuclear	–

greater distance from the Sun, the surface temperatures range from around 140°C in the winter to around 20°C in the summer. Despite the fact that Martian body has a lower density than Earth, due to the importance of Martian science, the concept of a drone that can fly on the planet has gotten a lot of attention. Venus is known as the "evil twin" of Earth because it is almost the same size as Earth but has a toxic carbon dioxide atmosphere and a scorching 470°C surface. Venus has an atmosphere that is similar to that of Earth; thus, the requisite power for flight is lower. As a result, research has been conducted on drones that can fly in Venus's climate.

Several UAV models have been proposed till now for exploring planets like Martian body, Titan, Venus, etc. Due to the possibility of life on Martian body, it is one of our solar system's most explored planetary bodies. The planetary body's climatic state is neither too cold nor too hot. Solar panels can be used while there is a lot of direct sunlight. Martian body has a gravity that is 38% that of Earth, making it one of the most suitable planets for drone exploration [11]. One of the most well-known examples of a Martian UAV is the Aerial Regional-scale Environmental Survey of Mars (ARES). It is a planned Mars Scout mission that will use an airplane to collect high-value science data on the planet's atmosphere, surface geology and mineralogy, and crustal magnetism [12]. It is also possible to fly a UAV on Venus (using solar power). It is possible to explore the regions of the atmosphere, including cloud tops, with a small aircraft carrying a suitable payload of scientific instruments. The aircraft under consideration are of a size that is appropriate for a low-cost Discovery-class mission [6]. Another solar body being considered for drone exploration is on Titan. Dragonfly is one of the well-known Titan drones in the near future. Dragonfly, NASA's next $1 billion planetary science mission, is set to launch in 2026. The aircraft, a quadcopter drone, with the size of a vehicle will arrive in 2034 and land across the frozen surface in search of chemistry that could support life [13]. Table 5.1 shows the comparison between the parameters of various space UAVs considered for different planetary exploration.

5.3 TYPES OF UAVs FOR SPACE EXPLORATION

It is not possible to fly on other solar bodies using conventional UAV geometry. The size and weight of the UAVs are typically limited due to the launch vehicle's

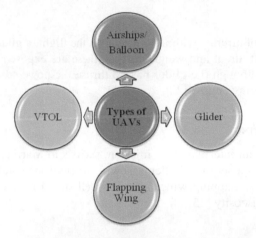

FIGURE 5.1   Types of UAVs for space exploration.

packaging constraints on the intended solar bodies [14]. In order to enhance the efficiency of UAVs, various aerodynamic, performance, legislative, and structural studies [15] are carried out during the design process. There are various configurations of UAVs for planetary exploration. Some of the examples are airships/balloons, gliders, cyclocopter, fixed wings, and VTOL. Figure 5.1 shows some of the types of UAVs for space exploration.

5.3.1 AIRSHIPS/BALLOONS

An airship or balloon is a type of aircraft carrier that navigates without the use of external power [15]. The balloon is a very simple technology that does not require any power to hold its height. Instruments and payloads are the only items that need electricity.

However, the changes in altitude and position are challenging for balloons. It is practically not possible for the balloons to last long in the heat. Balloons often have trouble holding their station, suggesting that balloons are inflexible in the field of atmospheric science. On the other hand, airships are difficult to position and deploy at low speeds [21]. The three kinds of balloons effective for space missions are superpressure balloons, standard helium balloons, and Montgolfiere balloons.

5.3.2 VERTICAL TAKE-OFF AND LANDING

The advantages of both multi-copter and fixed-wing aircraft are recombined to create VTOL for space exploration. Recent research has centered on the possibility of developing aerial VTOL vehicles to help in the exploration of various celestial bodies in our solar system. VTOL vehicles' efficacy is being examined in particular to support missions to Martian body, Titan, and Venus.

5.3.3 Glider

A glider is a type of aircraft without a motor. In the flight, a glider has three forces operating on it (lift, drag, and weight forces), these are exposed in each and every kind of aircraft. Although the glider has no thrust, the powered aircraft eventually has a thrust-generating engine [22].

5.3.4 Flying Wing

Flying a drone for an interplanetary mission, such as to Martian body, Venus [23], or Titan [24], poses a serious challenge, owing to environmental restrictions. New flying ideas, such as flapping wings, may be well suited for the atmosphere's low density and high viscosity [25].

5.4 PROTOCOLS AND THREATS IN SPACE UAVs

The interplanetary communication network is a put forward network that is often disrupted, with a wireless structure that is riddled with errors and delays varying from tens of minutes to hours [26]. During space exploration through UAVs, UAVs collect data from the planet. The data from the planet is collected through the near-field communication links. The orbiter then collects the data from UAVs. The data is then transmitted to the Earth ground station through direct links. Finally, the data is routed via Earth's internal communication network. Thus, one of the main concerns for space agencies is security in the area of space exploration. Guaranteed access to space and the right to freely use space for different purposes are two aspects of space security. The section comprises three parts: Protocols for space exploration, communication threats in space missions and incidents involving security issues, and security algorithms for preventing security threats during space missions using UAVs.

5.4.1 Protocols for Space Missions

A network of protocols has been developed for the transmission of data for interplanetary communication. These protocols are a set of rules that regulate how data is transmitted during an interplanetary mission. Traditionally, spacecraft telemetry was formatted using a time-division multiplexing (TDM) system, in which data objects were multiplexed into a continuous stream of fixed-length frames based on a predefined multiplexing law. Since there are no proven standards in this area, each project was forced to develop and implement a custom data system that was only used by that project, with the exception of the ground tracking network. In the early 1980s, the Consultative Committee for Space Data Systems (CCSDS) established an international standard for a Packet Telemetry protocol to transmit processed telemetry using a variable-length data unit known as the source packet. Shortly after Packet Telemetry, CCSDS established another international standard for transmitting commands to a spacecraft with a data unit known as the Tele Command (TC) Packet, based on a similar principle. CCSDS expanded the above requirements in the late

1980s to meet Advanced Orbiting Systems' (AOS) needs, such as the International Space Station (ISS) and developed AOS, a third standard. CCSDS later restructured these three specifications (Packet Telemetry, Tele Command, and AOS) in order to describe the protocols in a more standardized and unified manner. The modified standards were: Space Packet Protocol [26]; TM, TC, and AOS Space Data Link Protocols; TM and TC Synchronization, and Channel Coding [27].

5.4.2 COMMUNICATION THREATS AND INCIDENTS

For an interplanetary mission, radio frequency (RF) waves are used to communicate to and from the satellite. They are usually sent at frequencies in the GHz range. Telemetry, Tracking, and Control (TT&C) and data communications can be interrupted at any time during the satellite's lifespan, forcing the attacker to gather additional data and launch attacks on the ground segment. The most popular methods of data communication disruption are jamming, hijacking, eavesdropping, and spoofing.

5.4.2.1 Jamming

Jamming can effectively block communication on a wireless space channel, interrupt the predefined activity, trigger performance problems, and even harm the control device by simply emitting an interference signal. An intruder may deny legitimate communications by transmitting a continuous signal using an antenna, knowledge of the signal frequency, and the necessary power level. The AN/ALQ-218 UAV is one example of a jamming-resistant UAV. Emitters for cueing jammers are included in the AN/ALQ-218 UAV and electro-optical sensors, infrared radiation (IR) technology, and an on-board radar station.

5.4.2.2 Eavesdropping

Eavesdropping is the theft of data while it is being transmitted over a network. The RF signal is sent over the air for satellite and ground system communication. Here the communications are subject to interception. Data sent over RF signals is often unencrypted or uses low-grade encryption that can be broken to expose clear-text data. ELectronic INTelligence (ELINT) satellites are one of the devices that many countries use to eavesdrop on information transmitted across space.

5.4.2.3 Hijacking

In recent years, there have been several cases of satellite hijacking or the use of a satellite for a different purpose. This may entail manipulating or entirely altering valid signals. One of the well-known incidents of hijacking a space network was in 1999, J.J., a 15-year-old computer programmer who went by the moniker "c0mrade," confessed to hacking into NASA's computer network as well as a slew of other cybercrimes [28].

5.4.2.4 Spoofing

Spoofing is an electronic attack in which an attacker convinces a receiver that a false signal generated by the attacker is the real signal it is trying to obtain. Spoofing a satellite's downlink may be used to transmit incorrect or manipulated data to an adversary's communications device. An intruder who successfully spoofs a satellite's command and control uplink signal may take control of the satellite and use it for nefarious purposes [29]. Cryptography is one of the best suitable techniques to overcome spoofing.

5.4.3 SECURITY IN SPACE UAV NETWORK

For the purpose of space missions through UAVs, encryption algorithms should be selected carefully for various messages in order to protect sensitive information in the network.

5.4.3.1 Crypto Security in Space Network

As a consequence, the idea of cryptography is taken into consideration. The master key encrypts the sub-master key, which in turn encrypts the session and channel keys throughout the drone communication phases [30]. The sub-master, the session, and the channel keys are all delivered through key exchange messages. Since encryption and authentication are used to secure the communication system, the protection of the key exchange message is the most important aspect. Key exchange messages are transferred first in the channel during initialization, followed by the transmission of the sub-master key, channel key, and first session key to the drone [31].

5.4.3.2 Quantum Security in Space UAV Communication

Quantum security is another approach to the security challenges that space UAVs face. A new and improved protocol has been created for the purpose of safe communication [32]. An eavesdropper cannot keep a transcript of quantum signals that are sent in a quantum key distribution (QKD) operation due to the quantum noncloning theorem. In contrast to other communication methods, this latest quantum technique would use a low-orbit satellite to send encrypted messages over a much longer distance to ground-based stations. This improved framework has the potential to revolutionize how we exchange confidential data while still protecting people's data at a time when cyber security threats are on the rise. Quantum communication, also known as quantum key distribution, uses physics to provide protection when transmitting data. It enables two parties to exchange encrypted data that is sent via quantum bits or qubits [33]. Quantum communication is the most reliable method of data transfer, with a practical quantum network able to provide secure coverage in real time for any location and scale, from small to massive.

5.5 DESIGN MODEL OF UAV ON THE MARTIAN BODY

In our design model, we make a UAV prototype compatible enough to fly on the surface of Martian body. Lander at the surface of Martian body will deploy UAVs as a payload in the Martian surface. A communication link between the lander, UAV, and the Ground Control System (GCS) is done through satellite communication. Communication between UAV and GCS is through the part of the Ka band (uplink:

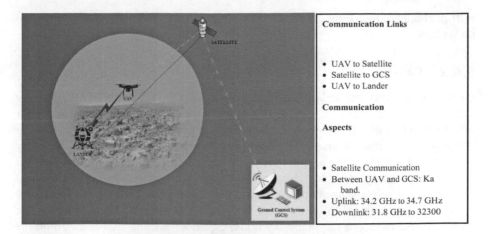

FIGURE 5.2 Deployment strategy of UAV on Martian body.

34.2 GHz to 34.7 GHz; downlink: 31.8 GHz to 32.3 GHz). Figure 5.2 shows the design model of UAV on the Martian surface.

5.6 ENVIRONMENTAL CONSIDERATIONS ON THE SURFACE OF MARTIAN BODY

To design an aerial vehicle for planet exploration, atmospheric conditions become a necessary part of being considered. Atmospheric pressure, air temperature, gravity, speed of sound, and air density are some of the mandatory parameters.

5.6.1 AIR PRESSURE

The air at any planetary body constitutes a weight, and it pushes against anything it comes in contact with. This pressure is known as atmospheric or air pressure. Air pressure is the force applied by the air on the planetary body (as gravity draws it toward the surface). The ability to fly vehicles to achieve lift is due to air pressure. Faster-moving airflow has a low temperature, whereas slower-moving air has a higher temperature, as per Bernoulli's principle. This indicates that the air pressure on the bottom would be higher, pushing the plane upward. The air pressure value at the surface of Martian body is approximately 610 Pa [34]. This means the air pressure on Martian body is less than 1% of that on the Earth's surface. The air on Martian body is much thinner than that on Earth. As a result, the key source of concern when developing a prototype UAV is whether there would be enough lift. UAV is possibly heavier than air. For a UAV to fly successfully in a planet's atmosphere, four forces are obligatory that are lift, drag, weight, and thrust. The engine of a flying vehicle generally provides thrust. Thrust must surpass the vehicle's drag for a successful flight. The lift of the vehicle is provided by the wings. UAV's lift should be equal to its weight for the flight to be flourishing. UAV's smooth shape will probably reduce drag, and the materials it is made up of will have an effect on its weight.

5.6.2 Gravity

Gravity is the force exerted on the object to pull it toward the center of the planetary body. Two major forces that are drift and weight are mainly required to get better off. The weight of a flying vehicle is the force of gravity acting to pull the UAV to the ground and resolve via lift. Lift and gravity are two opposite forces. It is very evident that for designing a prototype UAV, decreased weight and an increased lift are the two major goals to be achieved. On the basis of Newton's theory of Universal Gravitation, when talking about a spherical body like a planet, the gravitational force is directly proportional to the mass of the planet and inversely proportional to the square of the radius of the planetary body. Equations 5.1 and 5.2 are based on the Newton's theory of Universal Gravitation and show the formula for the gravitational force of Martian body [35]. Table 5.2 shows the notation and parametric values of Equation (5.1) [36].

$$g = Gm/r^2 \tag{5.1}$$

$$g = 3.711 \, \text{m/s}^2. \tag{5.2}$$

where g represents the gravity of Martian body,
$\quad$ G represents the gravitational constant,
$\quad$ m represents the mass of the Martian body,
$\quad$ r represents the radius of Martian body.

5.6.3 Air Density

Air density has a direct impact on UAV's performance, both aerodynamically and in terms of engine performance. Air density has an effect on nearly every aspect of a UAV's flight. In less dense air, standard measurements such as take-off distances, rate of climb, landing distance, and so on, would all be increased, thus reducing the performance. Atmospheric density, in general, is defined as the mass per unit volume of a planet's atmosphere.

TABLE 5.2
Notation and Parametric Values

Parameters	Values
Gravitational constant	$6.674 \times 10^{-11} \text{m}^3 \, \text{kg}^{-1} \, \text{s}^{-2}$
Mass of the Martian body	$6.42 \times 10^{23} \, \text{kg}$
Radius of the Martian body	3.38×10^6

5.6.4   AIR TEMPERATURE

Air temperature has a vital role toward the behavior of the flight of UAV. The lift generated by a UAV depends mainly on the air density. Air density depends on the air temperature and altitude. At higher temperatures, air density is reduced. UAV will travel faster to generate enough lift for take-off. The air temperature at Martian body is 210 K (approximately).

5.6.5   SPEED OF SOUND

Speed of sound is the distance traveled via sound waves per unit of time. This parameter plays a significant role in designing the UAV prototype: (1) useful in separating the flight regimes into two distinct areas with distinct flow conduct, (2) assisting in the conversion of compressible flow geometry to one that can be measured using simpler, incompressible methods, (3) for efficient air travel, and the maximum practical flight speed will be restricted, and (4) providing a hint to the designer about how to drive this boundary higher. The speed of sound at the Martian surface [37] is 240 m/s² and this is comparatively lower than that of Earth (343 m/s²).

5.7   PARAMETERS CONSIDERED IN SYSTEM MODEL AND SIMULATION RESULTS

In our proposed model, a UAV prototype has been simulated that can be made suitable enough to operate in the environmental conditions of Martian body. Comparative analysis of the behavior of the UAV prototype in the environmental conditions of Earth and that of Martian body has been studied. For the simulated model to operate on two different planets, various parameters are taken into consideration. Table 5.3 shows the reported environmental parameters of the planet Earth and Martian body is considered for the UAV prototype. A prototype of a UAV is observed in the atmosphere of Earth and Martian body. The environmental parameters are varied, and the behavior of the UAV is observed. Figure 5.3a graph of the UAV flight on the surface of Earth is observed; here, the UAV has a peak altitude of 1.58 m. UAV then acquires its stability after 3 s and hover at an altitude of 1.56 m. A similar UAV prototype graph for the flight on the Martian surface is observed. UAV has a peak altitude of 2200 m. For about 1 min and 40 s, the UAV will become stable and hover at an altitude of 380 m. We observed a major difference between the altitudes of the UAV flight on the surface of Earth to Martian body. Since Martian body's gravity is around one-third of Earth, which makes it simpler for the rotors to work, the rotors need not work hard on the Martian surface to combat its effort. However, on the surface of Earth since the gravity is higher, the rotors are not easy, thus having a lower altitude. The air density of the Martian surface is lesser than that of Earth. At lower air density, the altitude is increased, as seen in graph (b) of Figure 5.3.

The behavioral change in the acceleration of the UAV at the surface of Martian body and Earth is also studied. Figure 5.4 shows the rate of change of velocity of UAV at the surface of Martian body (a) and at the surface of Earth (b).

TABLE 5.3
Reported Environmental Parametric Values for Martian Body and Earth

Parameters	Martian Body (Reported Values)	Earth (Reported Values)
Volume (km³)	16.318	108.321
Mass (10^{24} kg)	0.64171	5.9724
Gravity (m/s²)	3.711	9.81
Air pressure (bars)	610.0e3	101.3e3
Air density	0.020	1.181
Speed of sound (m/s)	240	340
Atmospheric temperature	273 + 15	273 − 63
Latitude	40.695899600000000	42.299886000000000
Longitude	−80.01172539999999	−71.35044700000000
Flattening	0.00589	0.00335
Altitude	80.01172539999999	71.35044700000000
Equatorial radius (km)	33962	63781
Polar radius (km)	33762	6356.8

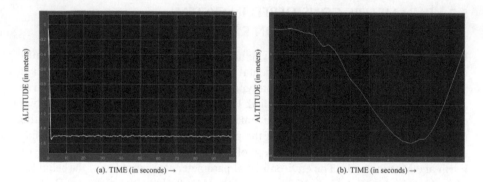

(a). TIME (in seconds) →   (b). TIME (in seconds) →

FIGURE 5.3 Comparison between the graph for the flight of UAV on Martian body (a) and Earth (b).

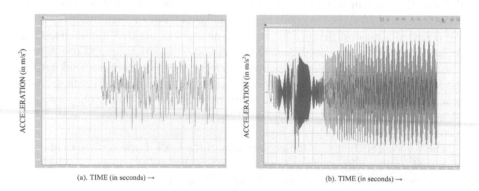

(a). TIME (in seconds) →   (b). TIME (in seconds) →

FIGURE 5.4 Acceleration of UAV on the surface of Martian body (a) and Earth (b).

From the results above, we have observed that it is possible to successfully deploy UAV on the Martian body surface. UAV will overcome the issues faced by other space-exploring techniques. In the near future, multiple UAVs can be used to get real-time information from the Martian surface with enhanced quality of service (QoS). Also, multiple UAVs can also be deployed at a certain height on the surface of Martian body to cover the wider area. In the future, if the multiple UAVs are success-fully deployed, then it is possible to collect the samples of the Martian surface and provide information to the GCS. As a result, the probability of life on Martian body, clues to the solar system's evolution, and a fascination with the chemistry, geology, and meteorology of the planet, etc., can be further be explored [38].

5.8 RESEARCH CHALLENGES

This segment addresses the potential research challenges related to network security in UAVs for space exploration.

5.8.1 ENDURANCE

Since the amount of energy available for an interplanetary mission is minimal, the UAV's endurance will be severely limited.

5.8.2 PRECONDITION

Fiber communication channels and satellite ground channels have so far proven to be the most effective quantum networks. However, none of them has met any of the prerequisites of space networks.

5.8.3 HIJACKING

There is no assurance that a fast factorization algorithm for classical computers will be discovered in the future or that existing algorithms will be implemented on a quantum computer, making traditional encryption "hacking" possible. Initial data replacement is another "hacking" technique. The possibility of encryption keys being stolen is a final weakness. As a result, a truly effective and easy encryption method is in high demand [32].

5.8.4 COVERAGE

The deployment of the UAVs should be nearer to the surface of the spatial body so that the maximum area is covered. When the UAV is placed nearer to the surface of the planetary body, then there are fewer chances of the network breakage. There is a strict Line of Sight (LOS) requirement between transmitter and receiver to get communication better off.

5.8.5 STABILITY

At the time of deployment of the UAVs in space, it is very necessary and important to ensure stability. Stability of multiple UAVs is affected by manipulative movements and environment contacts.

5.8.6 PATH PLANNING

An optimal path track for UAVs should be planned. The path planning should be from the start point to the destination point. The path planning should also satisfy the constraints of UAVs apparent performance and the environment of the planetary body.

5.9 CONCLUSION

The most recent planetary exploration methods are very limited in versatility and resolution, and they provide little information about Earth. To address these issues, our study discusses the use of UAVs for space exploration. Since the spatial missions' communication network is a store-and-forward device, there is a greater risk of it being disconnected. In a communication network, there are also risks such as jamming, spoofing, and hijacking. Technology algorithms such as cryptography and quantum security have been addressed in order to combat these threats, as well as several other concerns. Certain protocols for safe contact between the Earth station and space vehicles, as well as communication between space vehicles themselves, have been studied. This chapter discusses various space UAVs that have been considered for space missions to date, as well as the deployment technique for UAVs on the surface of a planetary body. The possibility of flying a UAV in the Martian body's atmosphere is explored. It has been found that there is a greater possibility of a successful UAV flight on the Martian body. The behavioral change in the UAV flight on both Earth and Martian body has been studied. It is found that the altitude of the UAV prototype is higher on the Martian surface than on Earth. Due to lesser gravity on the surface of Martian body, it becomes easier for the rotors to function with efficiency. The blades rotate and push the air downwards. As a result, the air pushes up the rotor, generating a lift. This gives UAV the optimal height on the surface of Martian body. It was also observed that on the surface of Earth UAV becomes stable to hover at a place in lesser time, whereas on the surface of Martian body stability is acquired after a certain amount of time. The stability, in this case, is directly linked with the number of rotations. The result is that the UAV acquires the optimal height of 1.56 m on Earth and 380 m on the Martian body. However, there are some research challenges for the practical purpose of communication security, which are addressed in the research challenges section.

REFERENCES

1. McFadden, L. A., Johnson, T., and Weissman, P. (Eds.). *Encyclopedia of the solar system.* Elsevier, 2006.
2. Rani, Anuj, Ajit Jain, and Manoj Kumar. "Identification of copy-move and splicing based forgeries using advanced SURF and revised template matching." *Multimedia Tools and Applications* (2021): 1–22.
3. Wikipedia. "Effect of spaceflight on human body." (n.d.). https://en.wikipedia.org/wiki/Effect_of_spaceflight_on_the_human_body (accessed October 26, 2020).

4. Syed, F., Gupta, S. K., Hamood Alsamhi, S., Rashid, M., and Liu, X. "A survey on recent optimal techniques for securing unmanned aerial vehicles applications." *Transactions on Emerging Telecommunications Technologies* (2020). https://doi.org/10.1002/ett.453 (accessed October 30, 2020).

5. Clarke, J.R., V. Abraham Kerem, and Richard Lewis. "A Mars Airplane... Oh really?." In 17th Aerospace Sciences Meeting, p. 67. 1979.

6. Hassanalian, Mostafa, and Abdessattar Abdelkefi. "Classifications, applications, and design challenges of drones: A review." *Progress in Aerospace Sciences* 91 (2017): 99–51.

7. Lone, Tufail A., Aabid Rashid, Sumeet Gupta, Sachin Kumar Gupta, Duggirala Srinivasa Rao, Mohd Najim, Ashutosh Srivastava, Abhishek Kumar, Lokendra Singh Umrao, and Achintya Singhal. "Securing communication by attribute-based authentication in HetNet used for medical applications." *Eurasip Journal on Wireless Communications and Networking* 2020, no. 1 (2020): 1–21.

8. Pergola, Pierpaolo, and Vittorio Cipolla. "Mission architecture for Mars exploration based on small satellites and planetary drones." *International Journal of Intelligent Unmanned Systems* (2016).

9. Gupta, Akshita, Shriya Sundhan, Sachin Kumar Gupta, S. H. Alsamhi, and Mamoon Rashid. "Collaboration of UAV and HetNet for better QoS: a comparative study." *International Journal of Vehicle Information and Communication Systems* 5, no. 3 (2020): 309–333.

10. Williams, Matt. "What is the atmosphere like on other planets." (2016). https://www.universetoday.com/35796/atmosphere-of-the-planets (accessed March 3, 2021).

11. MarsOne. "Why mars, and not other planets." (2020). https://www.mars-one.com/faq/mission-to-mars/why-mars-and-not-another-planet (accessed March 4, 2021).

12. Landis, Geoffrey A., Anthony Colozza, and Christopher M. LaMarre. "Atmospheric flight on Venus: a conceptual design." *Journal of Spacecraft and Rockets* 40, no. 5 (2003): 672–677.

13. Peeters, B., J. A. Mulder, S. Kraft, J. Leijtens, T. Zegers, D. Lentink, and N. Lan. "EXOFLY: a flapping winged Aerobot for R Autonomous flight in mars atmosphere." *Proceedings of the ASTRA* 2008 (2008): 2–6.

14. Guynn, Mark, Mark Croom, Stephen Smith, Robert Parks, and Paul Gelhausen. "Evolution of a Mars airplane concept for the ARES Mars scout mission." In 2nd AIAA "Unmanned Unlimited" Conference and Workshop & Exhibit, p. 6578. 2003.

15. Wikipedia. "Airship." (2020). https://en.wikipedia.org/wiki/Airship (accessed January, 21 2021).

16. Koning, Witold JF, Wayne Johnson, and Håvard F. Grip. "Improved Mars helicopter aerodynamic rotor model for comprehensive analyses." *AIAA Journal* 57, no. 9 (2019): 3969–3979.

17. Northrop Grumman. "Venus atmospheric maneuverable platform (VAMP)." (2019). https://www.northropgrumman.com/vamp/ (accessed December 5, 2020).

18. Xiongfeng, Zhu, Guo Zheng, and Hou Zhongxi. "Sun-seeking eternal flight solar-powered airplane for Venus exploration." *Journal of Aerospace Engineering* 28, no. 5 (2015): 04014127.

19. NASA. "NASA's dragonfly will fly around titan looking for origins, signs of life." (2019). https://www.nasa.gov/press-release/nasas-dragonfly-will-fly-around-titan-looking-for-origins-signs-of-life (accessed November, 25 2020).

20. Aggarwal, Akarsh, Mohammed Alshehri, Manoj Kumar, Purushottam Sharma, Osama Alfarraj, and Vikas Deep. "Principal component analysis, hidden Markov model, and artificial neural network inspired techniques to recognize faces." *Concurrency and Computation: Practice and Experience* 33, no. 9 (2021): e6157.

21. NASA. "Space shutter as a glider." (2020). https://www.grc.nasa.gov/www/k-12/airplane/glidshuttle.html (accessed January 23, 2021).

22. Michelson, Robert C., and Messam A. Naqvi. "Beyond biologically inspired insect flight." *von Karman Institute for Fluid Dynamics RTO/AVT Lecture Series on Low Reynolds Number Aerodynamics on Aircraft Including Applications in Emergening UAV Technology* (2003): 1–19.

23. Landis, Geoffrey A. "Robotic exploration of the surface and atmosphere of Venus." *Acta Astronautica* 59, no. 7 (2006): 570–579.

24. Voosan, Paul. "NASA to fly dron on titan." (2019). https://science.sciencemag.org/content/365/6448/15.1.summary (accessed March 4, 2021).

25. Book, B. "Space packet protocol." (2003). https://public.ccsds.org/Pubs/53x0b2e1.pdf (accessed November 8, 2020).

26. Dimov, Daniel. "Interplanetary hacking: How the space industry mitigates cyber threats." (2015). https://resources.infosecinstitute.com/topic/interplanetary-hacking-how-the-space-industry-mitigates-cyber-threats/ (accessed March 3, 2021).

27. Harrison, Todd, Kaitlyn Johnson, and Thomas G. Roberts. *Space threat assessment 2019.* Center for Strategic & International Studies, 2019.

28. Sharma, D., Gupta, S. K., Rashid, A., Gupta, S., Rashid, M., and Srivastava, A. (2020). A novel approach for securing data against intrusion attacks in unmanned aerial vehicles integrated heterogeneous network using functional encryption technique. *Transactions on Emerging Telecommunications Technologies*: 4–5. https://doi.org/10.1002/ett.4114

29. Han, Maojie. "*Authentication and encryption of aerial robotics communication.*" PhD diss., San Jose State University, 2018.

30. Liu, Hua-Ying, Xiao-Hui Tian, Changsheng Gu, Pengfei Fan, Xin Ni, Ran Yang, Ji-Ning Zhang et al. "Drone-based entanglement distribution towards mobile quantum networks." *National Science Review* 7, no. 5 (2020): 921–928.

31. Rabie, Passant. "Quantum communication takes a major leap with satellite experiment." (2020). https://www.space.com/quantum-communication-major-leap-satellite-experiment.html (accessed March 6, 2021).

32. Raheja, Supriya, Mohammad S. Obaidat, Balqies Sadoun, Sahil Malik, Anuj Rani, Manoj Kumar, and Thompson Stephan. "Modeling and simulation of urban air quality with a 2-phase assessment technique." *Simulation Modelling Practice and Theory* 109 (2021): 102281.

33. Wikipedia. "Atmosphere of Mars." (2020). https://en.wikipedia.org/wiki/Atmosphere_of_Mars#:~:text=It%20also%20contains%20trace%20levels,1%25%20of%20the%20Earth's%20value (accessed April 7, 2021).

34. Byjus. "Value of g." (2020). https://byjus.com/physics/value-of-g/ (accessed April 7, 2021).

35. NASA. "Sounds of Mars." (2020). https://mars.nasa.gov/mars2020/participate/sounds/#:~:text=With%20an%20average%20surface%20temperature,meters%20per%20second)%20on%20Earth (accessed April 8, 2021).

36. Wikipedia. "Phoenix mars mission." (2020). http://phoenix.lpl.arizona.edu/mars111.php#:~:text=Mars%20is%20only%20about%20one,Mars%20has%20no%20liquid%20water (accessed April 6, 2021).

37. NASA. "Planetary factsheet." (2020). https://nssdc.gsfc.nasa.gov/planetary/factsheet/marsfact.html (accessed April 6, 2021).

38. Gupta, A., Gupta, S. K., Rashid, M., Khan, A., & Manjul, M. (2020). Unmanned aerial vehicles integrated HetNet for smart dense urban area. *Transactions on Emerging Telecommunications Technologies*. https://doi.org/10.1002/ett.4123.

6 Quantum-Safe Asymmetric Cryptosystems

Current Solutions and Future Directions against Quantum Attacks

Sagarika Ghosh, Marzia Zaman, and Srinivas Sampalli

CONTENTS

DOI: 10.1201/9781003296034-6

6.1   INTRODUCTION

Cryptography is a crucial part of securing all cyber-physical systems to attain confidentiality and integrity as security goals. The security level of cryptographic algorithms, including Rivest–Shamir–Adleman (RSA) and elliptic curve cryptography (ECC), relies on the intractability of certain problems using traditional computers. However, the boom of quantum computing has placed current cryptographic algorithms at stake.

Quantum computers exploit the principles of quantum physics, mainly superposition and entanglement principles, to process information.

The standard quantum algorithms, mainly Shor's [20] and Grover's [16] algorithms, are a threat to RSA and ECC cryptosystems, respectively. Researchers and organizations have been developing various quantum attack-resistant algorithms, using either complex mathematical problems or exploiting quantum physics [23, 24]. The algorithms that exploit quantum physics principles are quantum cryptography, and the algorithms based on hard mathematical problems are post-quantum cryptography. While quantum cryptography relies on quantum hardware, post-quantum cryptography can be deployed on the same hardware infrastructure of the current networks [8]. In this chapter, we review post-quantum cryptography that is resistant to quantum attacks.

6.1.1   SECURITY THREAT FACED BY QUANTUM COMPUTING

The progress in developing quantum computers on a large scale has threatened the most commonly used symmetric and asymmetric key cryptosystems. A modern computer encodes information in bits with a value of either 0 or 1. However, a quantum computer or hardware encodes information in qubits that follows the rules of quantum physics. The qubit can be in s state 0 or 1 or both at the same time, as per the superposition principle. The two qubits are in an entangled state when their states are allied with each other. The superposition and entanglement principles make quantum computers much faster than any modern computers [14, 34].

6.2   SHOR'S ALGORITHM

In 1994, Peter Shor [30] developed an algorithm to derive the prime factorization of any positive integer. We denote it as N. Shor's algorithm has two phases: classical and quantum. The first section uses the Euclidean algorithm to derive an order-finding problem reduced from the factoring problem. Moreover, the quantum phases find the approximate superposition of periods of the function by applying Quantum Fourier Transform (QFT) [6, 14].

The widely adopted RSA generates its public key using a product of p and q such that $N = p*q$, where both p and q are private prime numbers. Thus, RSA's security depends on the complexity of obtaining the factors p and q [22]. Thus, Shor's algorithm, when applied to quantum hardware, can crack the RSA cryptosystem. Moreover, Gidney et al. [15] proved that Shor's algorithm efficiently cracks RSA-2048 within 8 h with 20 million qubits [14].

6.3 GROVER'S ALGORITHM

In 1996, Lov Grover [16] developed an algorithm that searches databases faster than a classical algorithm. Grover's approach is based on amplitude amplification and the property of quantum physics to provide a quantum search algorithm that can find a particular element, given an array of x number of elements. A classical search algorithm takes $O(N)$ while a quantum search algorithm by Grover has $O(\sqrt{N})$, a quadratic speedup.

Grover's algorithm can be used for the problem of obtaining a key or for the study of block ciphers. Thus, Grover's algorithm weakens the commonly used cryptosystem, namely AES-256/128 [2, 6, 14].

6.4 EXISTING POST-QUANTUM SECURITY SCHEMES ADDRESSING CONFIDENTIALITY

The emergence of quantum computing in recent years has brought both benefits and risks to stable cyber-physical systems [34]. The most threatened cryptosystems are widely used public-key algorithms, key management schemes, and digital signatures dependent on factorization, elliptic curve cryptography, and discrete logarithms [1]. This has motivated researchers to focus on the study and development of post-quantum cryptography. They are resistant against quantum as well as classical attacks and can be deployed in the existing network infrastructure [1]. Currently, there are five categories of primary post-quantum cryptography, namely [6, 8]:

- Code-based cryptography [6, 8]
- Lattice-based cryptography [6, 8]
- Supersingular elliptic curve isogeny [6, 8]
- Multivariate-based cryptography [6, 8]
- Hash-based cryptography [6, 8]

We divide post-quantum cryptography into two security goals: confidentiality and integrity. The following sections provide post-quantum cryptography based on the type of algorithms used.

6.5 CODE-BASED CRYPTOGRAPHY

Code-based cryptography is cryptosystem, including symmetric and asymmetric, based on the difficulty of error-correcting codes [8]. It can be categorized into the following:

- Public-key encryption
- Digital signature
- Zero-knowledge protocols
- Pseudo-random number generator and stream cipher
- Hash functions

In this survey chapter, we review the code-based public-key cryptosystem as discussed in the following subsection. The most commonly known algorithm is the McEllice cryptosystem [1].

6.5.1 McEllice Cryptosystem

In 1978, a public-key encryption scheme that was based on hidden Goppa code [33] was proposed by Robert McEllice. Goppa codes are the relation between algebraic geometry and codes and are used as error-correcting codes. They rely on the NP-hard problem of decoding linear codes. The basic concept of the Goppa code depends on modular arithmetics. When a number series approaches a higher number, and once it reaches a specific number, the series starts from 0 again [1, 8]. A classic McEllice cryptosystem includes the following phases (assuming Alice and Bob are the two legitimate participants) [28, 33].

Key Generation: Bob selects a Goppa polynomial $g(z)$ of degree t, computes its corresponding generator matrix G, selects a random invertible matrix denoted as S and a random permutation matrix denoted as P. Bob uses all the parameters to compute $G' = SGP$ and announces his public key that includes (G', t). Bob's private key includes (S, G, P).

Encryption: Alice encrypts her message, represented in binary strings, by selecting and combining a random error vector, e, that has weight $\leq t$, to mG'. Thus, Alice sends the following cipher, y in Equation 6.1.

$$y = m \times G' + e \tag{6.1}$$

Decryption: Bob uses his matrix, P, to derive y' as shown in Equation 6.2. Then, Bob applies the decoding algorithm, computing e', to y' to correct the errors and derive the codeword, m'. The m' is mS. Thus, Bob can easily derive m by $m' * S^{-1}$.

$$y' = y \times P^{-1} \tag{6.2}$$

According to the National Institute of Standards and Technology (NIST) Post-Quantum Cryptography (PQC) Standardization report [1], the McEllice cryptosystem is suitable for replacing traditional cryptosystems. It is quantum safe and provides security against Chosen Ciphertext Attack (CCA) and One-Wayness against Chosen Plaintext Attack (OW-CPA). Moreover, the McEllice cryptosystem is faster than most cryptosystems. However, it also comes with its drawbacks. It generates large public keys that can cause an implementation problem, especially in resource-constrained devices. Moreover, the ciphertexts are smaller than other post-quantum Key Encapsulation Mechanisms (KEMS), but the ciphertexts are larger than the plaintexts. The McEllice cryptosystem is not applicable to generating authentication scheme or digital signature scheme [1].

6.6 LATTICE-BASED CRYPTOGRAPHY

Lattice-based cryptography has been proven to be strongly resistant to subexponential as well as quantum threats. They are based on the concept of lattices, sets of points within an n-size periodic structured space as shown in Figure 6.1 [13]. In simple terms, lattice can be considered as any regularly spaced grid of points. The security of the lattice-based cryptography depends on the complexity of lattice problems, mainly the shortest vector problem (SVP), the closest vector problem (CVP), or the shortest independent vector problem (SIVP) [7, 13]. The SVP is deriving the minimum nonzero vector in the current lattice and is an NP-hard problem, unsolvable by the present quantum algorithm [7].

6.6.1 NTH-DEGREE TRUNCATED POLYNOMIAL RING UNITS

In 1996, Hoffstein *et al.* [17] published an encryption scheme called the Nth-Degree Truncated Polynomial Ring Units (NTRU). It is public-key cryptography focused on SVP within a lattice [17]. It does not rely on factorization or disjunctive logarithms as the traditional public-key cryptosystem does. The basic NTRU operation is performed in the truncated polynomial rings as shown in Equation 6.3, such that N is a prime number and Z_q is the ring of integers modulo q [17].

$$R_q = \frac{Z_q[X]}{X^N - 1} \tag{6.3}$$

A polynomial, f, in R_q can be written in Equation 6.4.

$$f = [f_0, f_1, \ldots, f_{N-1}] = \sum_{k=0}^{N-1} f_k X^K \tag{6.4}$$

Moreover, we denote the multiplication as *. Thus, $f * g$, where f and g are two polynomials, is given as a cyclic convolution product as shown in Equation 6.5.

$$f * g = h = [h_0, h_1, \ldots, h_{N-1}] \tag{6.5a}$$

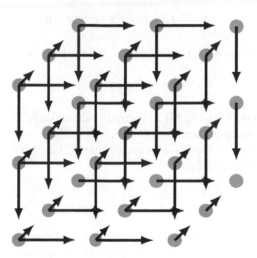

FIGURE 6.1   A lattice space in 3D.

$$h_k = \sum_{i+j=k \bmod N} f_i g_j \qquad (6.5b)$$

The NTRU uses the above parameters to derive key pairs, encrypt the message, and then decrypt the cipher. Thus, we list the public parameters of the NTRU algorithm as follows [17, 28].

- N denotes a large prime number.
- p and q are positive numbers. $Gcd(p, q) = 1$, and, $p \ll q$.
- d_p, d_g, and d_r are integers to generate polynomials. The polynomials from which the private keys are uniformly chosen belong to the set $B(d_f)$, $B(d_g)$, and $B(d_r)$. The binding values in $B(d_r)$ are used during encryption.

Key Generation: Two random small polynomials, f and g, are selected, such that $f \epsilon B(d_f)$ and $g \epsilon B(d_g)$, $f_p = f^{-1}(\bmod p)$ and $f_q = f^{-1}(\bmod q)$. Then h is computed. Thus, the obtained public key is (N, h) and the private key is (f, f_q) [17, 28].

Encryption: To encrypt a message, m, a polynomial r is chosen randomly such that $r \epsilon B(d_r)$. Then, the message is encrypted to generate a cipher e as shown in Equation 6.6 [17, 28].

$$e = p * r * h + m \,(\bmod)\, q \qquad (6.6)$$

Decryption: The first step of decryption is to compute $f * e \,(\bmod\, q)$, and transform the obtained value, a, to polynomial whose coefficients are in the range $[-q/2, q/2]$. The following equations are used during decryption. The value of m can be derived from $f_p * a \,(\bmod\, p)$ [17, 28].

$$a = f * e \,(\bmod q) \qquad (6.7)$$

$$\Rightarrow a = f * (p * r * h + m)(\bmod q) \qquad (6.8)$$

$$\Rightarrow a = f * p * r * g * f_q + f * m (\bmod q) \qquad (6.9)$$

$$\Rightarrow a = p * r * g + f * m (\bmod q) \qquad (6.10)$$

As per the NIST report [1], the NTRU remains unbreakable against current attacks as well as attacks using present quantum hardware. Moreover, it generates shorter key pairs as compared to McEllice's cryptosystem. Thus, NTRU is declared a suitable alternative to RSA and ECC.

6.6.2 Ring-LWE

Ring learning with errors (Ring-LWE) [21] is a post-quantum cryptosystem that relies on the learning with errors (LWE) problem assigned to polynomial rings over finite fields. In Ring-LWE, the coefficients of polynomials can be added and multiplied within a finite field, $F*q$, such that the coefficients are less than q [21, 28]. The Ring-LWE can be deduced to an SVP within a lattice.

A classic Ring-LWE problem follows the following steps, assuming Alice and Bob are the two participants [21].

6.6.2.1   Alice and Bob accord on a shared complexity value of n, such that n is the highest coefficient power.

6.6.2.2   They both derive q such that $q = 2^n - 1$.

6.6.2.3   The polynomial operations are computed with a modulus of q.

6.6.2.4   Alice creates a set of polynomial values, A, as in Equation 6.11.

$$A = a_{n-1}x^{n-1} + ... + a_1x^2 + a_1x + a_0 \qquad (6.11)$$

6.6.2.5   Alice divides A by $\varphi(x) = x^n + 1$.

6.6.2.6   Alice computes two polynomials: Error polynomial (e) and secret polynomial (s).

$$e\_A = e_{n-1}x^{n-1} + ...e_1x + e_0 \qquad (6.12)$$

$$s\_A = s_{n-1}x^{n-1} + ... s_1x + s_0 \qquad (6.13)$$

6.6.2.7   Alice, then, computes v_A using A, e_A and, s_A as shown in Equation 6.14.

$$v_A = A * s_A + e_A \qquad (6.14)$$

6.6.2.8   Alice sends A and v_A to Bob, and Bob follows the same algorithm to generate his own error polynomial e_B and secret polynomial s_B.

6.6.2.9   Bob also creates v_B and sends it to Alice.

6.6.2.10 Alice multiplies the v_B with her own secret polynomial, and further computes it as shown in Equation 6.1

6.6.2.11 In the meantime, Bob uses the same algorithm to generate its own shared secret key as in Equation 6.16.

Then, both Alice and Bob extract the noise from the shared secret key to obtain the same shared secret value [21]. This algorithm can be implemented in the key-exchange scheme, digital signature, and homomorphic encryption, and the public and private key sizes are larger than that of a traditional public-key cryptosystem [21]. One of the post-quantum algorithms that focuses on Ring-LWE is called New Hope [1].

6.7   SUPERSINGULAR ELLIPTIC CURVE ISOGENY-BASED CRYPTOGRAPHY

Supersingular elliptic curve isogeny cryptography is quantum-safe cryptography that depends on the hardness to find isogenies among the supersingular elliptic curves. Feo *et al.* [10] developed a post-quantum cryptography algorithm, Supersingular

Isogeny Diffie–Hellman (SIDH) key exchange, analogous to Diffie–Hellman, and is based on supersingular isogeny problem defined as following [9, 29].

Definition 6.1. [9, 29] Given two supersingular elliptic curves, E_1, E_2, in a finite field

k, where $|E_1| = |E_2|$, solve an isogeny function f: $E_1 \longrightarrow E_2$.

Public Parameters: The public parameters are, first, agreed upon by both participants (Alice, Bob) during the SIDH protocol. Alice and Bob establish a large prime p based on a supersingular elliptic curve, denoted as E, over a field, F_p2 such that F refers to the set of integers modulo, p, and E can be represented as the following [9, 29].

$$E : y^2 = x^3 + ax + b \tag{6.17}$$

$$p = 2^a + 3^b - 1, \tag{6.18}$$

where a and $b \in N$. Moreover, they also agree on the basis P_A, Q_A of $E[2^A]$ and P_B, Q_B of $E[2^B]$.

Key Generation: Alice selects a number, r_A, randomly extracted from the set $0 \le r_A < 2^b$-1. She uses her basis and the selected random number to compute the kernel to generate her isogeny function φ_A. Alice, using her isogeny function with ker φ_A (Equation 6.19), generates the public key denoted as $E_A = \varphi_A(E), \varphi_A(P_B), \varphi_A(P_B)$. Her private key is r_A [9, 29].

$$\ker\varphi_A = \langle P_A + r_A Q_A \rangle \tag{6.19}$$

Parallely, Bob follows the same algorithm to generate his own key pairs. His private key is r_B randomly extracted from the set $0 \le r_A < 3^b - 1$. His public key is her public key denoted as $E_B = \varphi_B(E), \varphi_B(P_A), \varphi_B(P_A)$.

Shared Secret Key Generation: The public keys, E_A, E_B, are exchanged by Alice and Bob. Alice generates another isogeny function, ψ_A, with kernel function based on the basis parameters, P_A, Q_B, as described in Equation 6.20 [9, 29].

$$\ker\left(\psi_A\right) = \langle \varphi_B\left(P_A\right) + \left[r_A\right] \cdot \varphi_B\left(Q_A\right) \rangle \tag{6.20}$$

Alice then generates j-invariant of the curve $E_{AB} = \psi_A(E_B)$. Similarly, Bob calculates ψ_B and then proceeds to derive the j-invariant of curve $E_{BA} = \psi_B(E_A)$. The j-invariant derived by both Alice and Bob are the shared secret key as described in Equation 6.21 and is simply described in Figure 6.2 [9, 29].

$$j(\varphi_B\left(E_A\right)) = j\left(E_{BA}\right) = j(E_{AB} = j(\varphi_A\left(E_B\right)). \tag{6.21}$$

The post-quantum scheme that relies on the complexity of supersingular isogeny curve problem provides enough resistance against attack using a quantum algorithm. A key encapsulation mechanism based on SIDH, named supersingular isogeny-based key (SIKE), provides the smallest public key sizes as that of other

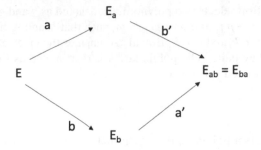

FIGURE 6.2 Isogeny computation by Alice and Bob to obtain the common shared secret key.

post-quantum schemes, as well as small ciphertexts. However, the performance of the supersingular isogeny-based cryptosystems is lower than that of other post-quantum cryptosystems. Thus, it requires efficient optimization algorithms to increase the performance [1].

6.8 EXISTING POST-QUANTUM SECURITY SCHEMES ADDRESSING INTEGRITY

In this section, we provide an overview of the types of post-quantum cryptography addressing integrity as a security goal. Currently, three types of post-quantum cryptography implement a signature scheme, mainly, lattice-based, multivariate-based, and hash-based cryptography.

6.8.1 LATTICE BASED

The widely used and known lattice-based cryptographies are NTRU sign and BLISS. Lattice-based signatures mainly depend on the NP-hardness of the short vectors in lattice spaces [28]. The following subsections describe the NTRU signature and BLISS.

6.8.1.1 NTRU Signature

NTRU signature [18] is a signature scheme that follows after the NTRU encryption algorithm to provide authentication to the encrypted message. Like NTRU encryption, its security relies on the difficulty of solving the SVP. The basic operation of NTRU Signature occurs in the ring of polynomials, R, of degree less than $N-1$ represented as in Equation 6.3. The NTRU signature has three phases, mainly, Key Generation, Signature, and Verification [18]. The parameters used in the NTRU sign are as the following [18].

- Integer parameters: $(N, p, q, D_{min}, D_{max})$. p and q are relatively prime, and N denotes a large prime number. D_{min}, D_{max} are the deviations caused by the reduction modulo function.
- Set of polynomials: F_f, F_g, F_w, F_m.

Key Generation: Bob selects two polynomials, denoted as, f and g. They are further represented as $f = f_0 + p \cdot f_1$ and $g = g_0 + p \cdot g_1$, such that f_0 and g_0 are fixed universal polynomials, and, $f_1 \in F_f$ and $g_1 \in F_g$. Bob also computes the inverse of f modulo q and thus deriving the key pairs. The public key h is represented as Equation 6.22. The pair (f, g) is the obtained private key.

$$h \equiv f^{-1} * g \bmod q \tag{6.22}$$

Signing: Bob selects a polynomial w, such that $w \in F_w$. And w can be represented as in Equation 6.23.

$$w = m + w_1 + p \cdot w_2 \tag{6.23}$$

In Equation 6.23, w_1 and w_2 are small polynomials. The w was further used to compute the signature, s, in Equation 6.24. The final signature includes the set (m, s).

$$s \equiv f * w \,(mod\, q) \tag{6.24}$$

Verification: Alice now verifies Bob's signature, (m, s). At first, Alice verifies the signature is null or not. Alice then tests whether the deviation satisfies, and then proceeds to use Bob's public key denoted as h. The h and the polynomial, t, is further computed as described in Equation 6.25. She then further verifies the deviation of t as well.

$$t \equiv h * s \,(mod\, q) \tag{6.25}$$

The performance of NTRU Sign is similar to NTRU Encrypt, as it provides almost similar public and private key sizes as compared to RSA and ECC and provides higher performance and a higher security level against traditional and quantum attacks. Thus, it is suitable for the current network infrastructure [1].

6.8.1.2 BLISS

BLISS [26] is a signature-generating algorithm whose operation relies on the ring R_q with a power of 2 where q is the prime number as represented in Equation 6.26 [28, 31].

The $x^n + 1$ has a root in Z_q. Moreover, $q = 1 \bmod 2n$. It also has three phases such as key generation, signing, and verifying as the following [26, 31].

$$R_q = \frac{Z_q[X]}{X^n - 1} \tag{6.26}$$

Key Generation: We denote two polynomials as f and g with d_1 coefficients in $\{\pm 1\}$ and d_2 coefficients in $\{\pm 2\}$, where $d_1 = \delta_1 n$ and $d_2 = \delta_2 n$. The private key $S \in R_{2q}^2$ and the public key $A \in R_{2q}^2$ are generated by computing the following equations.

$$S = (s_1, s_2) = (f, 2g + 1) \tag{6.27}$$

$$a_q = (s_2 / s_1) \bmod q \tag{6.28}$$

$$A = (2a_q, q - 2) \tag{6.29}$$

Signing: The message to be signed is denoted as μ from the message space, M. At first, two polynomials y_1 and y_2 are selected from a disjunctive Gaussian distribution D_σ, where σ is the width parameter of the distribution. And, y is a set of (y_1, y_2). Then, using a Hash function, H, a challenging variable is generated as described in the following.

$$c = H(A \cdot y, \mu) \tag{6.30}$$

$$H : R \times M - \to R \tag{6.31}$$

The signing involves Greedy approximation algorithm that produces a variable v, where $v = Sc'$ for $c' = c \bmod 2$. Then, we select a bit value, b, such that $b \in \{0,1\}$ to further compute the signature $sign = y + bv$.

Verification: The receiver receives the sign and c is verified if it is smaller than the discrete Gaussian parameter that has a width variable σ. If the sign satisfies the condition, the receiver further verifies Equation 6.32.

$$H(az + qc \bmod 2q, \mu) \overset{?}{=} c \tag{6.32}$$

BLISS is a lattice-focused signature algorithm [28, 31]. It generates key and signature size similar to the RSA algorithm, and is resistant against quantum attack [28, 31].

6.8.2 MULTIVARIATE CRYPTOGRAPHY

A multivariate public-key cryptosystem is dependent on the NP-hardness of deciphering the multivariate polynomials over the finite fields [12, 13]. The NIST report claims that various multivariate public cryptosystems have been proposed. However, some of them are broken [1]. The class of trapdoor one-way functions is an integral property of PKC. For example, NTRU depends on the lattice structure, and ECC depends on the elliptic curve group. Multivariate cryptography depends on the one-way function as a multivariate quadratic polynomial public map over a finite field [1, 12, 13]. We denote the set of quadratic polynomials as $P = (p_1(w_1, \ldots w_n), \ldots, p_m(w_1, \ldots w_n))$, where each p_i is a quadratic polynomial in $w = (w_1, \ldots w_n)$ [1, 12, 13]. One of the multivariate cryptography is Rainbow that has been selected as Round 3 finalists by NIST [1].

6.8.2.1 Rainbow

In 2004, Ding et $al.$ [11] developed a multivariate post-quantum signature focused on the Oil-Vinegar signature scheme. Its security relies on the NP-hardness of solving a set of random multivariate quadratic schemes. Like any other signature scheme, it has three phases, including key generation, signature, and verification as the following [11, 12].

Key Generation: Two keys are generated in this phase. The private key includes two invertible affine maps, L_1 and L_2. It also includes the map, denoted as, F. Moreover, the public key consists of the field referred to as K as well as the composed map, $P(x)$ [11, 12].

Signing: In the signature generation phase, given a document $d \epsilon \{0,1\}_*$, the sender uses a hash function, $h = h(d)$. Then, it computes it further, as shown in the following equations, to generate the signature, z.

$$x = L_1^{-1}(h) \tag{6.33}$$

$$y = F^{-1}(x) \tag{6.34}$$

$$z = L_2^{-1}(y) \tag{6.35}$$

Verification: The receiver computes the hash of the composite map on z, where $h' = P(z)$, and then further computes the hash of the document. If the generated hash matches with the received hash, the signature is validated and accepted.

Rainbow offers shorter signatures, only 258 bits for the NIST level 1 security compared to other post-quantum signature schemes. Moreover, the algorithm used in signing the document and verifying the signature is highly efficient and faster than other post-quantum schemes. One drawback of the Rainbow algorithm is that the key generation process is slow and needs to be more efficient [1].

6.8.3 Hash-based Signature Scheme

HSS schemes are signature-generating algorithms that rely on cryptographic hash functions addressing at least one of the following security properties: preimage, second pre-image, and collision resistance [6, 25]. The hash-based signature scheme can be further classified into two, mainly, stateless and stateful schemes. A stateful hash-based signature scheme relies on Merkle's tree using OTS parameters, whereas a stateless hash-based signature scheme includes a hyper-tree with both a One-Time Signature (OTS) scheme and a few-time signature (FTS) schemes [32].

6.8.3.1 Stateful Signature Scheme

Lamport Signature: In 1970, Leslie Lamport [19] proposed a one-time signature algorithm which is resistant against traditional as well as quantum attacks. The primary advantage of the Lamport signature is that it exploits a secure cryptographic hash function to derive a public key, which is further processed to sign a message [19]. Thus, the security of Lamport primarily depends on the secrecy of the hash function [19]. Moreover, the Lamport signature generates large key sizes as well as signature sizes. Thus, it is unsuitable for almost any network infrastructure. The

public key and private key (of size 256 bit) of the Lamport signature can be represented as the following [4].

$$\text{Private Key} = \left(x_0, y_0, x_1, y_1 ..., x_{255}, y_{255} \right) \tag{6.36}$$

$$\text{Public Key} = \left[h(x_0) h(y_0) \| h(x_1) \| h(y_1) .... \| h(x_{255}) \| h(y_{255}) \right] \tag{6.37}$$

Winternitz One-time Signature Scheme (WOTSS): To address the large key sizes
of the Lamport signature scheme (LSS), WOTSS is proposed. The primary idea of
WOTSS is to implement a certain count of the chain of functions that start from
feeding on random inputs [4]. In WOTSS, the random data are the secret key, and the
public key includes the output derived from the chains [4]. A message is signed by
mapping it to one of the intermediate values of each chain. WOTSS is an optimized
version of LSS that uses a parameter, w. The Winternitz parameter, w, is inversely
proportional to the signature size. A larger w generates a smaller signature. Thus,
WOTSS is suitable for memory-constrained devices. However, the time complexity
increases exponentially as w increases [4].

  Merkle's Signature Scheme: To address the drawbacks of one-time signature
(OTS), Ralph Merkle proposed an algorithm named Merkle Signature Scheme
(MSS). It merges various OTS key pairs and obtains multiple concatenated key pairs
into a single binary hash tree [4]. During the tree construction, the signature keeps
concatenating the string of intermediate nodes with respect to the tree root to generate the authentication path. The authentication path verifies the signature and generates the path of the tree [4]. A simple Merkle's tree is a binary tree with each node is
a hash of its following child node. Thus, the root of the tree is considered to be the
final public key, and the Merkle tree leaves are the hashes of the OTS public key.
Figure 6.3 illustrates a simple Merkle tree [4].

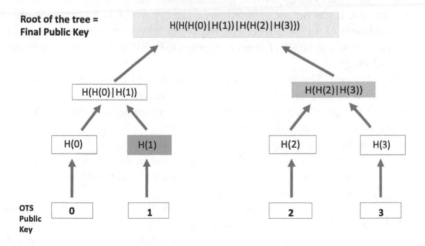

FIGURE 6.3 A simple illustration of Merkle tree. The gray-shaded nodes are authentication
path, and the root of the tree is the public key.

The OTS signatures generate large public keys, and it needs to generate a novel public key every time a message needs to be sent. Thus, it increases the computation cost [4]. The MSS obtains a public key for signing multiple messages, such that the frequency of messages must be a power of 2 [4]. Given $M = 2^n$, it generates the public key, X_i, and private key, Y_i, such that Y_i is within the interval $1 \leq i \leq 2n$, where $i = n$, being the root level of the tree [4].

HORS: Reyzin *et al.* [27] proposed a few-time signature (FTS) scheme, using hash functions, that generates a secret key that contains n random numbers generated from a pseudo-random number function. The public key is derived from computing the n hashes of the random elements in the secret key. The signature generated contains k secret key values [27].

$$m = k \log n = k\tau \tag{6.38}$$

The relationship between the message (m), public key, and secret key values are shown in Equation 6.38, where $k \in \mathbb{N}$ and $n = 2^\tau$ for $\tau \in \mathbb{N}$ [27].

6.8.3.2 Stateless Signature Scheme

SPHINCS: It is a stateless signature scheme that is quantum resistant, and its general construction involves hyper-tree with height h-layer and d-layer. Each intermediate tree is a Merkle tree with height h/d. The security parameters of a SPHINCS tree are, mainly, n refers to the HORS tree (HORST) and WOTS hash bit sizes, m refers to the bit-length of the message, h refers to the height of the hyper-tree, d refers to the layers of the hyper-tree, w is the WOTS parameter, t is the frequency of HORST secret key elements, and k is the count of published HORST secret key elements [3, 5].

The general construction of a SPHINCS tree has the four following trees and has been shown in Figure 6.4[3, 5].

- The hyper-tree: The hyper-tree is the main tree that generates the root as the public key. It has height denoted as h. The hyper-tree is further segmented into d-layers of a *type-2* tree. The hyper-tree leaves are the instances of the *type-4 trees,* the HORST tree. For example in SPHINCS-256, h is 60 and d is 12 [3, 5].
- The sub-trees: The sub-trees are the intermediate trees that are based on Merkle trees and have a height of h/d. The leaves of the sub-trees are the root of the *type-3* trees; that is, the roots are compressed WOTS public keys that feed as the leaves to the next layer's tree.
- WOTS public-key compression tree: They are known as L-trees of height $\log_2 l$, where l is the count of leaves. The leaves in the sub-trees are derived from the WOTS public keys by computing an unbalanced binary tree that has l leaf nodes, known as L-trees [3, 5].
- HORS public-key compression tree: In 2015, Bernstein *et al.* [5] proposed HORS tree (HORST) for implementing at the lowest level of the SPHINCS tree as the FTS. The bottom layer of the hyper-tree also contains the Merkle tree of height $\tau = \log_2 t$, such that t is the count if HORST public-key

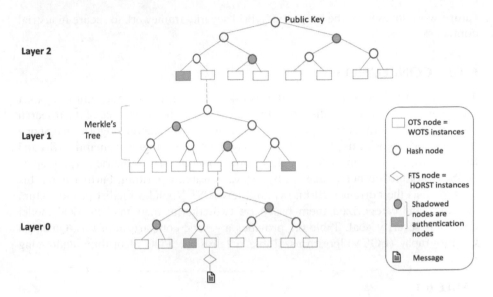

FIGURE 6.4 General SPHINCS tree construction with $h = 9$ and $d = 3$.

instances. Unlike stateful hash-based schemes, the stateless signature scheme does not keep a history of used key pairs. Thus, SPHINCS uses multiple HORST key pairs to correctly use key pairs more than once [3, 5].

SPHINCS' proof of security solely depends on the underlying hash function. As per NIST [1], SPHINCS provides robust security against traditional and quantum algorithms. Thus, NIST declared SPHINCS to be the Round 3 finalist. Moreover, the public keys of SPHINCS are small enough. However, the signatures are large, and the signature generator process is slow. Thus, SPHINCS requires optimization techniques to increase the speed such that it is well suitable for memory-constrained devices [1].

6.9 A GENERIC HYBRID CRYPTOSYSTEM AGAINST CLASSICAL AND QUANTUM ATTACK

Currently, various cyber-physical fields and their frameworks including industrial control systems used in nuclear power plants, oil and gas industry, traffic management, and space stations rely on classical cryptography protocols. The emergence of quantum computing threatens the security framework of the current cyber-physical systems. Thus, we propose an abstract concept of a generic hybrid cryptosystem to enhance the security of current cyber-physical systems against both classical and quantum attacks. The hybrid cryptosystem comprises a post-quantum key encapsulation mechanism, such as a code-based algorithm followed by the classical encryption scheme, such as a widely used advanced encryption standard (AES) algorithm along with a post-quantum digital signature or a classical quantum-resistant signature. Our future work focuses on the proposed hybrid security framework to secure industrial control systems.

6.10 CONCLUSION

This chapter provides a study of the well-known post-quantum signatures against the quantum attack. It first discusses the motivation of the emergence of the research area on post-quantum cryptography by focusing on two quantum algorithms, Shor's and Grover's algorithms. The traditional asymmetric cryptography, mainly RSA and ECC, is already broken by Shor's algorithm. However, the symmetric cryptography, AES, is not broken but weakened by Grover's search algorithm. Furthermore, this chapter lists the current well-known and few NIST Round 3 finalist post-quantum schemes and categorized them based on two criteria: their mathematical model and their security goal. Table 6.1 provides a generic comparison of Post-Quantum Cryptography (PQC) algorithms. Table 6.2 lists the PQC algorithms addressing

TABLE 6.1
Comparison of Post-Quantum Cryptography (PQC) Algorithms

Category	PQC Algorithms		Advantages	Disadvantages	Examples
Addressing confidentiality	Code-based encryption		Strong proof of security. Fast encryption. Ciphertext size is small.	Public keys are large	McEllice cryptosystem
	Lattice-based encryption		Ciphertext size is short. Public and private keys are small. Fast encryption process.	Need more understanding of the security. Further security analysis is required.	NTRU Encrypt Ring-LWE
	Supersingular elliptic curve isogeny		Generates the smallest public key sizes of all PQC schemes. Generates small ciphertexts.	Computation cost is high Optimization techniques are needed.	SIDH SIKE
Addressing integrity	Lattice-based signature		Generates short public and private keys. Fast signature generation.	Need more understanding of the security. Further security analysis is required.	NTRU Sign BLISS
	Multivariate-based signature		Generate short signatures.	Need more understanding of the security. Further security analysis is required.	Rainbow
	Hash-based signature	Stateful	Smaller signature size. Faster signature generation.	Need maintenance in usage of non-repeated key pairs	Lamport signature WOTS MSS HORS
		Stateless	Do not need to monitor non-repeated key pairs usage.	Larger signature size. Signature generation process is slower.	SPHINCS

TABLE 6.2

Comparison of Post-Quantum Cryptography (PQC) Algorithms That Addresses Confidentiality

PQC Encryption Algorithm	Overview	Advantage	Disadvantage	NIST Round 3 Finalist	Research Gap
McEllice cryptosystem	It is based on hidden Goppa code	Faster than most cryptosystems CCA-resistant and one-wayness CPA resistant. Smaller ciphertexts than that of other PQCs.	Large public keys. Not suitable for resource-constrained devices.	Yes	Compression technique needed.
NTRU encrypt	It is based on the hardness of SVP within a lattice.	Quantum resistant. Smaller public and private keys than McEllice. Suitable alternative to RSA and ECC.	Need more understanding of the security.	Yes	Further security analysis is required.
Ring-LWE	It relies on the learning with errors problem referred to rings of polynomials over finite fields.	Versatile algorithm. Can be implemented as key management, digital signatures and encryption scheme.	Public and private keys are larger than that of traditional cryptography.	No	Compression algorithm is required.
SIDH based SIKE	It focuses on hardness to find isogenies among supersingular elliptic curves.	Strong security against quantum and classical attacks. Smallest public keys of all PQCs. Generates small ciphertexts as well. Suitable for resource-constrained devices.	Performance is low.	Yes	Optimization is required to increase the efficiency.

TABLE 6.3
Comparison of Post-Quantum Cryptography (PQC) Algorithms That Addresses Integrity

PQC Signature Scheme	Overview	Advantage	Disadvantage	NIST Round 3 Finalist	Research Gap
NTRU sign	It relies on the hardness of SVP in a lattice.	Smaller public and private keys compared to RSA and ECC. Provides high performance.	Is complementary with NTRU encrypt.	Yes	Further security analysis is required.
BLISS	It relies on a ring with a power of 2 in a lattice space.	Key and signature size similar to RSA	Need more understanding of the security. Further security analysis is required.	No	Further security analysis is required.
Rainbow	Based on Oil-Vinegar Signature scheme.	Generates shorter signature, for NIST security level 1, as compared to other PQCs. Signature and verification are efficient and fast.	Key generation process is slow.	Yes	Optimization technique is needed.
Lamport signature (LOTSS)	It relies on a secure cryptographic hash algorithm to sign a message.	Versatile.	Security solely lies in the secrecy of the hash function. Generates large key size.	No	Key sizes need to be compressed.
WOTS	Optimized version of Lamport signature	Smaller signature size	Time cost increases exponentially as signature size increases.	No	Optimization algorithm is required.
HORS and HORST	It is a few-time signature scheme	Both of them are quantum resistant. HORST has smaller public key and signature size than that of HORS.	Signature size is larger than WOTS. Time cost of HORST is greater than that of HORS.	No	Optimization and compression technique is required.
MSS	Stateful hash-based scheme that uses a single binary hash tree to generate public keys and signature.	Uses one public to sign more than one messages.	Signature size and key sizes are still large in MSS. They were improved in the extension of MSS.	No	Need maintenance of the usage of non-repeated key pairs
SPHINCS	It is a stateless hash signature scheme based on hyper-tree including Merkle tree, OTS and FTS scheme.	Do not need maintaining the non-repeated key pairs usage.	Larger signature size. Signature generation process is slower.	Yes	Optimization and compression techniques are required.

confidentiality. Table 6.3 provides the comparison of PQC algorithms that focuses on integrity. Post-Quantum Cryptography can be divided into the following five categories based on the types of mathematical models: code-based, lattice-based, supersingular elliptic curve isogeny-based, multivariate-based, and hash-based scheme. The hash-based scheme can further be categorized into two: stateless signature and stateful signature. Based on their security goal, the algorithms can be further categorized into two: algorithms addressing confidentiality and algorithms addressing integrity. Furthermore, this chapter also provides the research gap in the algorithms and provides a foundation for future research and improvements.

REFERENCES

1. Alagic, G., Alperin-Sheriff, J., Apon, D., Cooper, D., Dang, Q., Kelsey, J., Liu, Y.-K., Miller, C., Moody, D., Peralta, R., et al. (2020). *Status report on the second round of the NIST post-quantum cryptography standardization process*. US Department of Commerce, NIST.
2. Amy, M., Di Matteo, O., Gheorghiu, V., Mosca, M., Parent, A., and Schanck, J. (2016). Estimating the cost of generic quantum pre-image attacks on sha-2 and sha-3. In International Conference on Selected Areas in Cryptography, pages 317–337. Springer.
3. Aumasson, J.-P. and Endignoux, G. (2018). Improving stateless hash-based signatures. In Cryptographers' Track at the RSA Conference, pages 219–242. Springer.
4. Becker, G. (2008). *Merkle signature schemes, merkle trees and their cryptanalysis*. Ruhr-University Bochum, Tech. Rep.
5. Bernstein, D. J., Hopwood, D., Hu¨lsing, A., Lange, T., Niederhagen, R., Papachristodoulou, L., Schneider, M., Schwabe, P., and Wilcox-O'Hearn, Z. (2015). Sphincs: Practical stateless hash-based signatures. In Annual International Conference on the Theory and Applications of Cryptographic Techniques, pages 368–397. Springer.
6. Bernstein, D. J. and Lange, T. (2017). Post-quantum cryptography. *Nature*, 549(7671):188–194.
7. Bl¨omer, J. and Naewe, S. (2009). Sampling methods for shortest vectors, closest vectors and successive minima. *Theoretical Computer Science*, 410(18):1648–1665.
8. Chen, L., Chen, L., Jordan, S., Liu, Y.-K., Moody, D., Peralta, R., Perlner, R., and Smith Tone, D. (2016). *Report on post-quantum cryptography*, volume 12. US Department of Commerce, National Institute of Standards and Technology.
9. Costello, C. (2019). Supersingular isogeny key exchange for beginners. In International Conference on Selected Areas in Cryptography, pages 21–50. Springer.
10. De Feo, L., Jao, D., and Pluˆt, J. (2014). Towards quantum-resistant cryptosystems from supersingular elliptic curve isogenies. *Journal of Mathematical Cryptology*, 8(3):209–247.
11. Ding, J. and Schmidt, D. (2005). Rainbow, a new multivariable polynomial signature scheme. In International Conference on Applied Cryptography and Network Security, pages 164–175. Springer.
12. Ding, J. and Yang, B.-Y. (2009). Multivariate public key cryptography. In *Post-quantum cryptography*, pages 193–241. Springer.
13. Fern´andez-Caram´es, T. M. (2019). From pre-quantum to post-quantum iot security: A survey on quantum-resistant cryptosystems for the internet of things. *IEEE Internet of Things Journal*, 7(7):6457–6480.
14. Ghosh, S. and Sampalli, S. (2019). A survey of security in scada networks: Current issues and future challenges. *IEEE Access*, 7: 135812–135831.

15. Gidney, C. and Eker°a, M. (2019). How to factor 2048 bit rsa integers in 8 hours using 20 million noisy qubits. *arXiv preprint arXiv:1905.09749.*
16. Grover, L. K. (1996). A fast quantum mechanical algorithm for database search. In Proceedings of the Twenty-Eighth Annual ACM Symposium on Theory of Computing, pages 212–219.
17. Hoffstein, J., Pipher, J., and Silverman, J. H. (1998). Ntru: A ring-based public key cryptosystem. In International Algorithmic Number Theory Symposium, pages 267–288. Springer.
18. Hoffstein, J., Pipher, J., and Silverman, J. H. (2001). Nss: An ntru lattice-based signature scheme. In International Conference on the Theory and Applications of Cryptographic Techniques, pages 211–228. Springer.
19. Lamport, L. (1979). Constructing digital signatures from a one-way function. pp. 1–7. SRI International.
20. Lomonaco, S. (2002). Shor's quantum factoring algorithm. *Proceedings of Symposia in Applied Mathematics*, volume 58, pages 161–180.
21. Lyubashevsky, V., Peikert, C., and Regev, O. (2010). On ideal lattices and learning with errors over rings. In Annual International Conference on the Theory and Applications of Cryptographic Techniques, pages 1–23. Springer.
22. Minni, R., Sultania, K., Mishra, S., and Vincent, D. R. (2013). An algorithm to enhance security in rsa. In 2013 4th International Conference on Computing, Communications and Networking Technologies (ICCCNT), pages 1–4. IEEE.
23. Nurhadi, A. I. and Syambas, N. R. (2018). Quantum key distribution (qkd) protocols: a survey. In 2018 4th International Conference on Wireless and Telematics (ICWT), pages 1–5. IEEE.
24. Padamvathi, V., Vardhan, B. V., and Krishna, A. (2016). Quantum cryptography and quantum key distribution protocols: A survey. In 2016 IEEE 6th International Conference on Advanced Computing (IACC), pages 556–562. IEEE.
25. Perlner, R. A. and Cooper, D. A. (2009). Quantum resistant public key cryptography: a survey. In Proceedings of the 8th Symposium on Identity and Trust on the Internet, pages 85–93.
26. Pessl, P., Bruinderink, L. G., and Yarom, Y. (2017). To bliss-b or not to be: Attacking strongswan's implementation of post-quantum signatures. In Proceedings of the 2017 ACM SIGSAC Conference on Computer and Communications Security, pages 1843–1855.
27. Reyzin, L. and Reyzin, N. (2002). Better than biba: Short one-time signatures with fast signing and verifying. In Australasian Conference on Information Security and Privacy, pages 144–153. Springer.
28. Roy, K. S. and Kalita, H. K. (2019). A survey on post-quantum cryptography for constrained devices. *International Journal of Applied Engineering Research*, 14(11):2608–2615.
29. Seo, H., Anastasova, M., Jalali, A., and Azarderakhsh, R. (2020). Supersingular isogeny key encapsulation (sike) round 2 on arm cortex-m4. *IEEE Transactions on Computers*, 70.10(2020): 1705–1718.
30. Shor, P. W. (1999). Polynomial-time algorithms for prime factorization and discrete logarithms on a quantum computer. *SIAM Review*, 41(2):303–332.
31. Staffas, R. (2016). Post-quantum lattice-based cryptography, pp. 1–67. KTH SCI.
32. Suhail, S., Hussain, R., Khan, A., and Hong, C. S. (2020). On the role of hash-based signatures in quantum-safe internet of things: Current solutions and future directions. *IEEE Internet of Things Journal.* Jul 30; 8(1): 1–7.

33. Valentijn, A. (2015). Goppa codes and their use in the mceliece cryptosystems. Syracuse University Honors Program Capstone Projects. 845. pages 1-40. Available: https://www.semanticscholar.org/paper/Goppa-Codes-and-Their-Use-in-the-McEliece-Valentijn/6cd1b5657d1c228c30d7705f41dcb2e3a6fe2d74
34. Zhang, X., Dong, Z. Y., Wang, Z., Xiao, C., and Luo, F. (2015). Quantum cryptography based cyber-physical security technology for smart grids. 10th International Conference on Advances in Power System Control, Operation & Management (APSCOM 2015): 5-61.

7 Cyber Security Technique for Internet of Things Using Machine Learning

Swati Goel and Monika Agrawal

CONTENTS

7.1 INTRODUCTION: BACKGROUND

Since the 1960s, the internet has served as a vital link between individuals, businesses, and organizations. People's geographical barriers have been broken down by the internet, which has provided them with a reliable, productive, and low-cost means of communication.

Nowadays, it appears that things are going to be different in the internet space as an outcome of the introduction of smart things that can generate and communicate data over the web in a manner like human beings. The internet of things (IoT) is a new stream to be explored, and it is a system that has the ability to transform our lives. IoT can be thought of as a two-component technology.

DOI: 10.1201/9781003296034-7

Any object which can collect data about its surroundings or for itself is referred to as a "Thing." Depending on the object's type, intelligence, and capabilities, it can analyze and interact intelligently with connected devices through the internet.

In the internet of things, communication does not take place only among IoT things. It further extends focusing on humans in such a manner which makes life simpler, healthier, and more enjoyable. There has been a lot of research into how IoT can help to improvise human health by remotely assessing their health and removing the requirement for frequent hospital visits. The Internet of Things (IoT) is widespread and is used in almost every aspect of our lives. Governments all over the world are implementing IoT in order to gather raw data through various sectors and improve facilities in areas such as health, transportation, security, and development [1].

Attacks on IoT are becoming more common as it becomes more widespread. Statistics show that the number of devices attached to the IoT framework has increased drastically in recent times. The overall global market for IoT is expected to reach around $1.6 trillion by 2025 as per a forecasting report.

Medical, geopolitical, environmental, governmental, or a similar type of dataset with varying significance may be included. Hence, it's critical to protect these types of information and devices [2].

Physical and logical controls can be used to keep an information system secure. Hardware devices are prevented from attackers using various physical controls.

Intrusion detection and prevention mechanisms [3] are tools for detecting familiar attacks or abnormalities in computer networks. When an intrusion prevention system detects or matches an attack signature or anomaly, it takes predetermined and systemic steps to stop the attack. Detection of anomalies can be done based on signature or on anomalies. In case of signature-based techniques, known attacks are detected by observing patterns in data stored in a system's memory or in network traffic. Unknown attacks are detected using anomaly-based detection, which performs a comparative analysis of the objects, entire system, or traffic. Attackers are now capable of creating malware which can change its structure while in execution in order to avoid detection. Artificial intelligence (AI) and machine learning (ML) are used in anomaly-based IDS [4, 5] and IPS to detect anomalies. The main objective of the latest hot technology AI and ML is the ability to develop such a model which can design an algorithm based on previously existing data and make predictions about normal and abnormal behaviors when some input is given to the model. Supervised, unsupervised, and reinforcement learning is a broad-level categorization of machine learning algorithms as claimed by various researchers.

A machine must be taught to be able to predict, regardless of the method used to teach it. Several machine learning methods have been in practice to detect intrusions. K-means has been the most globally used algorithm for data grouping.

To serve the purpose of classifying abnormal and normal data using machine learning, a decision tree classifier is well known. Anomaly-based intrusion detection systems, according to the author [6], suffer from false positives, which occur when IPS or IDS mistakenly considers normal activity in place of abnormal activity.

7.1.1 Purposes of Research

Using a hybrid approach based on partitioning around medoid (PAM) and decision tree (DT) algorithms, this study aims to develop an intrusion detection system by observing anomalies that lie in data coming in and out of the network. The objective of the research can be briefed as follows:

1. To gain a thorough understanding of the internet of things and how it functions
2. To gain a thorough understanding of the PAM and DT anomaly detection methods
3. To create a model to detect anomalies based on PAM clustering and decision tree classifier and to apply it to the internet of things
4. To assess the model
5. Make suggestions for how to improve the model

7.1.2 Methodology of Research

The purpose of this study is to develop a novel system for IoT by combining two algorithms: PAM and decision tree classification. Data collection is required, just as it is for any other type of study, in order to construct the system and then test the system.

For detection of anomalies in IoT networks, a few of the freely available datasets are KDD 99, network intrusion detection dataset, Intel lab dataset, etc. However, these datasets contain general information about the IoT network. In order to satisfy our current study's requirement, we have used a modified version of the Intel lab dataset. Various researchers have already thrown light onto difficulties found in collecting datasets specific for anomaly detection.

The model will use an altered copy of the Intel Lab IoT dataset fed as the input. First, the dataset will be clustered into two groups to divide the data in the dataset into two groups based on data record similarities. The groups are classified as "normal" and "abnormal" once clustering is finished. The input data has been segregated into two sections: Training data (70%) and testing data (30%). The classification system is created based on training data.

7.2 OVERVIEW OF INTRUSION DETECTION TECHNIQUES

This section presents a brief review of intrusion detection techniques developed previously, especially in the terms of internet of things. We examined various methods of intrusion detection in IoT networks.

IDS is generally built using a hybrid approach of clustering and classification. Similar work has been discussed by Golman (2014) [6]. Goldman proposed a combined IDS which was based on support vector machine (SVM) and classifier C5.0. The author emphasizes that by combining these algorithms, the accuracy of IDS can be improved significantly.

Hajare [7] mentioned that attacks are continuously increasing against IoT connected network IDS are not much efficient in detecting such attacks because these are "unknown" attacks.

Hajare proposed a new intrusion detection model based on MapReduce. It arranges large unstructured and structured data into key-value pairs. MapReduce uses a combination of clustering and classification techniques. It uses Fuzzy C-Means (FCM) as a clustering technique and SVM as a classification technique. FCM clusters data into separate groups by using features.

Tanpure *et al.* [8] proposed a hybrid intrusion detection system by combining two data mining techniques which are K-means for clustering the data and naïve Bayes for classifying data. The model proposed by him has been designed to identify denial of service (DoS), U2R (user to root), R2L (remote to local), and probe.

After observing IDS proposed by various authors including Golman (2014), Tanpure *et al.* (2016), and Hajare (2016), it can be inferred that to detect network-based attacks, data mining techniques are broadly used to cluster and classify data.

Sherasiya and Upadhyay [9] proposed a novel intrusion detection system which targets the detection of nodes within an IoT framework having multiple identities. The model proposed by them is limited to be used only within wireless networks as it depends on the strength of the signal in order to detect genuine nodes as well as adverse nodes.

Fu *et al.* [2] proposed a new IDS for anomaly detection in IoT. They pointed out various challenges in the IoT environment. The method proposed by the author is designed to cater to these problems by using an anomaly mining algorithm and distributed intrusion scheme.

To evaluate their model, the author used the Intel Lab Project dataset. This dataset contains sensors that capture various attributes like temperature, light, humidity, and voltage in every 30 s and then report these readings to a centralized point.

Quinlan [16] stated that the primary responsibility of the intrusion detection system is to analyze network traffic data. To cope with this issue, the authors have proposed a well-defined classification technique. They have applied support vector machine (SVM) and naïve Bayes methods of machine learning for classification purposes. In order to evaluate the intrusion detection system, the authors have applied a classification approach to the NSL-KDD dataset. The output reveals that SVM performs comparatively better than naïve Bayes. Finally, they concluded the results by misclassification rate and accuracy matrices.

Ning [17] discussed on the concepts, application, and performance measurement of anomaly-based strategies for intrusion detection based on unsupervised algorithms.

7.3 METHODOLOGY

This chapter focuses on the detection of anomalies in an IoT-based network which combines two algorithms: Partitioning around medoid (PAM) clustering and decision tree classifier method. It includes a depiction of the process of applying clustering and then classification techniques to the sensitive dataset in order to gain insight into the inconsistencies. To achieve this goal, data collected from communication among IoTs devices is fed as input to the clustering algorithm which results in dividing the dataset into two groups: Normal and abnormal. The proposed anomaly detection method using decision tree (ADMDT) comprises three phases:

Input data pre-processing: In this step, data collected from IoT devices is taken and pre-processed to filter certain relevant attributes out of it.

Handling: In this step, pre-processed data is fed as input to the PAM clustering algorithm, and it is followed by the classification technique. The pre-processed data is separated into two categories: One category is utilized for preparing and constructing a decision tree, and the second category is utilized to test the precision of the decision tree in order to recognize typical and unusual data. The decision tree is received as output after this stage.

Prediction: This step is concerned with utilizing the currently built DT for further prediction (Figure 7.1).

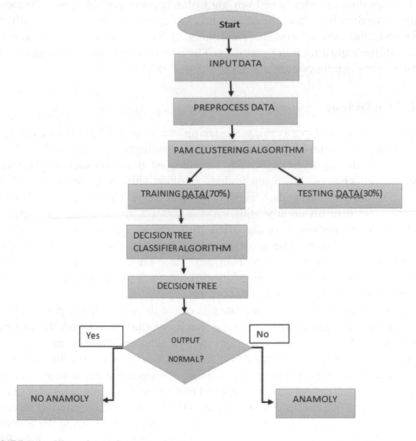

FIGURE 7.1   Flow chart of proposed system.

7.3.1 Pre-process Data

When a dataset is chosen for intrusion detection in an IoT-based network, then the biggest challenge has been experienced in getting labeled data. Kurniawan *et al.* [12] drew attention toward this which has been faced by other researchers of the same time. Besides this, various datasets are also available free for researchers such as the KDD Cup 1999 dataset. This dataset comprises a large number of records gathered from a military network. To cope with these problems, unlabeled data has been acquired from. To overcome these challenges, the unlabeled IoT dataset from Intel Lab was taken. This data set consists of nearly 2.3 million records which is the data collected from 54 sensors. The processing complete dataset may be computationally too expensive; therefore, random records have been placed in a separate excel sheet named input_data.csv. Also, as all the columns of the dataset are not relevant for our proposed methodology of detecting anomalies, those columns have been removed by copying the dataset into the input_data.csv file. The columns which were deleted are sensor ID, date and timestamp when readings were taken, voltage, and light parameter. Besides this, in order to test our algorithm in every possible case, 500 records having anomalies have been added to the existing dataset intuitively. Familiar [1] has followed the same approach of manipulating the input dataset in order to get the insights of the algorithm more precisely. The modified input dataset consists of two attributes namely temperature and humidity and 7500 records.

7.3.2 Clustering

The main objection of performing clustering over to any dataset is to identify the objects that possess some natural attribute of belongingness.

The clustering algorithm [10] may be classified based on various parameters. Various approaches of clustering include partition clustering, density-based clustering (DBSCAN), hierarchal clustering, grid-based clustering, etc. Different algorithms perform differently with varying datasets and working environmental conditions. Many authors have classified clustering methodology based on density, centroid, or distribution. The most generally used algorithm for intrusion detection includes approaches based on centroid. These are considered more suitable to the anomaly's detection-based application [11] as each group of data is represented through a separate vector named as centroid.

K-means algorithm has been accepted as one of the most popular clustering algorithms by various researchers. As per the number of clusters required, this algorithm can reproduce data by segregating them into "K" clusters. Partition around medoid (PAM) is the clustering algorithm that also divides the dataset into a fixed number of partitions, and it attempts to decrease the distance between different data points in each cluster and between data points and centroid of the cluster. K-means also tries to minimize the distance in a similar manner, but PAM has been tested as a stronger algorithm by various researchers. The K-means algorithm works on minimizing the Euclidean distance, whereas the total sum value of dissimilarity is reduced in the case of the PAM.

7.3.2.1   PAM Algorithm

It operates in two stages [13], which include the build and then swap stage. The first stage, "build," stepwise chooses centrally found n elements, whereas the swap stage calculates the final cost for every pair of data points that are taken from chosen or non-chosen elements.

Input:

```
D={d1, d2, ..., dn} // Data points set
Ad_mat // Adjacency matrix showing distance among data points
noc // Count of desirable clusters
```

```
Output
```

```
C // Set of clusters.
```

Algorithm
1. Randomly select c Medoids from D, provided c is given.
2. Assign each instance to the nearest Medoid x.
3. Compute objective function TCmn where TCmn is the total cost for each pair of selected and non-selected elements. It is the sum of dissimilarities of all instances to their nearest Medoids.
4. Arbitrarily select an instance y.
5. Swap x and y is swapping results in decreasing value computed by the objective function.
6. Repeat steps 2 to 5 until no change.

7.3.3   CLASSIFICATION

Algorithm C4.5(D)[14] is described as given below.

```
Input: an attribute values dataset D
1.    Tree={}
2.    If D is "pure" OR other stopping criteria met then
3.    Terminate
4.    end if
5.    for all attribute ε D do
6.    Compute information-theoretic criteria if we split on a
7.    end for
8.    abest=Best attribute according to above computed criteria
9.    Tree=Create a decision node that tests abest in the root
10.   Dv=Induced sub datasets from D based on abest
11.   for all Dv do
12.     Treev=C4.5(Dv)
13.     Attach Treev to the corresponding branch of Tree
14.   end for
15.   return Tree
```

7.3.4 EVALUATION METHOD

The confusion matrix is a method for describing and characterizing the efficiency of a classification model [11].

The matrix is easy to understand, but it has some doubtful items: True negative values (TNV), false negative values (FNV), true positive values (TPV), and false positive values (FPV). It is a matrix of 2×2 dimensions, and it shows the association between real and predicted values as shown in Figure 7.2.

If a classifier makes a prediction about a hidden abnormality in the underlying dataset and the actual data is not normal, then it is said as a true positive attempt. Based on this count of TPV, TNV, FPV, and FNV, the TP rate of a suggested model is estimated (Figure 7.2).

If the proposed model indicates that the data being tested has no anomalies and in actual, it is true, then this attempt is considered to be true negative (TN).

If a classifier makes a prediction that there may be an inconsistency or anomaly in statistics even as the statistics are really ordinary and no longer include an anomaly, then it is considered as a false positive (FP).

Similarly, if a classifier forecasts that no anomaly in data but in real data has an anomaly, in that case it is considered as a false negative (FN) attempt. Based on the number of false-negative values found during testing in the dataset, the FN rate of our system is estimated. This term is an indication of the extent of failure that occurred in the model.

Using the above four computed values (TPV, FPV, TNV, FNV), the overall accuracy of the system may be computed as given by Equation 7.1:

$$\text{Overall Accuracy} = \frac{\text{TPV} + \text{TNV}}{n} \qquad (7.1) \dots$$

where n is the overall count of records fed as the input in a classification model, and these records have been separated into another file named input.csv.

The misclassification rate signifies how many times a classifier gave wrong results.

$$\text{Misclassification rate} = \frac{\text{FPV} + \text{FNV}}{n} \qquad (7.2) \dots$$

Equation 7.3 can be used in order to compute the true positive rate (TPR) of the suggested system:

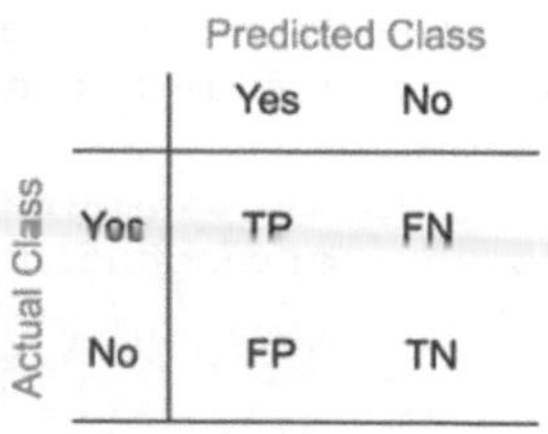

		Predicted Class	
		Yes	No
Actual Class	Yes	TP	FN
	No	FP	TN

FIGURE 7.2   Estimation.

$$TPR = \frac{TPV}{Count\ of\ actual\ abnormal\ records\ in\ given\ input} \qquad (7.3)\ ...$$

The false-positive rate (FPR) of the system can be estimated as given in Equation 7.4:

$$FPR = \frac{FPV}{Count\ of\ actual\ normal\ records\ in\ given\ input} \qquad (7.4)\ ...$$

The true negative rate (TNR) of the model can be calculated as given in Equation 7.5:

$$TNR = \frac{TNV}{Count\ of\ actual\ normal\ records\ in\ input\ data} \qquad ...(7.5)\ ...$$

In order to get insight into how accurately our proposed system is working, the precision of the prescribed model is computed as given below:

$$Precision = \frac{TPR}{Count\ of\ predicted\ abnormal\ records\ in\ given\ input\ data} \qquad (7.6)\ ...$$

The performance of the proposed method is going to be inferred using metrics discussed in Equations 7.1–7.6.

7.4 RESEARCH OVERVIEW

The area of IoT has grown extensively in the past few years. Technically, in this field, numerous smart devices named as "Things" are connected to the internet using various kinds of sensors, these devices continually gather various kinds of information about the surrounding environment. This data is then shared with authorized third parties which monitor and control these devices through the internet. The concept of IoT first came into the picture in 1999 at the Massachusetts Institute of Technology (MIT) where researchers had a vision of creating a network that would be entirely based on the internet and would include all smart devices in the world. But as most IoT things are generally made up of semiconductors which were not cost effective and simultaneously it was heavily based on IPv4, the technology could not grow at a large scale. But, as IPv6 technology was introduced, it allowed vastly larger address space that allowed billions of billions of devices to connect to the internet as compared with the IPv4, and semiconductor prices, IoT has resurfaced. Although the widespread use of IoT objects makes it simpler, it also increases the chances of attacks. Various smart devices connected to the IoT network contain data of varying criticality. Based on the criticality of data, the loss incurred due to exposure of data can result in loss ranging from minimal to severe.

7.4.1 PROBLEM DEFINITION

The need for studying cyberattack in an IoT network [15] has grown steadily. As an IoT system comprises various components, these components are vulnerable to miscellaneous kinds of attacks. A few of these include physical attacks, whereas a few capture data when it is being exchanged among devices over the network. Any attack can target these objects' default routing configurations, causing them to transmit their data to unauthorized parties. According to the existing data, several current studies are based on defending IoT networks from various attacks at network levels. An intrusion detection approach is used to mitigate the risk of any device getting compromised over the network.

7.4.2 EXPERIMENTATION AND RESULTS

Anomaly detection is being done by various machine learning techniques approached extensively. The current research work proposes a novel and unique method for detecting anomalies in an IoT network on the basis of a hybrid approach that combines two machine learning techniques: Partition around clustering (PAM) and decision tree algorithm. PAM is a famous clustering algorithm that has been considered a better method than K-means algorithm by various researchers. It can be used to create different clusters of data points based on the similarity found between them. C4.5 is a broadly utilized decision tree method, which may be used to construct a decision tree in order to classify data. In order to implement a proposed system, a dataset for the IoT network has been taken from Intel Lab. After pre-processing, irrelevant columns are filtered out and the dataset contains only two attributes: Humidity and temperature. The input dataset was fed as input to the clustering algorithm, and it generated the output that was segregated into two clusters. Further, the dataset was divided into two subsets: Training and testing dataset. The testing dataset contained 70% of records and testing data contained 30% of records.

The proposed system has been implemented using MATLAB. It is very easy to use a language with extensive processing capabilities. The fundamental unit of representation in MATLAB is the matrix.

The used Intel Lab IoT dataset consists of 2.3 million readings of various sensors. Four types of information are retrieved by these sensors, i.e., temperature, humidity, light, and voltage. After downloading the dataset, the dataset is opened using Microsoft Excel. The starting four columns of the downloaded dataset signify the date and timestamp of data collection, reading, and node ID, respectively. The unwanted attributes will be removed, and only desired attributes will be kept in for further processing steps (Table 7.1).

After the removal of unwanted attributes, the resultant dataset would appear as shown in Table 7.2 It will contain a dataset having two attributes that signify temperature and humidity. Out of nearly 2.2 million records, 7000 records were selected arbitrarily in order to construct the input dataset. Then 500 entries having anomalies had been inserted in the input data. So a total of 7500 readings will be there in the input dataset (Table 7.2).

After pre-processing, data is given to the PAM clustering algorithm. This algorithm has been implemented as a function in MATLAB, which takes the following two inputs:

1. Pre-processed data in the form of a matrix
2. Desired numbers of clusters

TABLE 7.1

A Sample of Input Dataset before Pre-processing

2005-04-30	04:28:16.575351	3	1	121.163	−.3.879	14.06	2.04567
2005-03-29	01:55:34.02845	2	1	18.7754	35.0833	44.09	2.56742
2005-03-23	02:02:26.35393	15	1	18.3024	37.7629	45.06	2.62354
2005-03-23	02:06:46.772088	11	1	18.1652	39.9039	45.06	2.67451
2005-03-23	02:08:45.962524	28	1	19.567	36.2379	45.06	2.60348

TABLE 7.2

Pre-processed Sample Input Data

121.163	−3.879
18.7754	35.0833
18.3024	37.7629
18.1652	39.9039
19.567	36.2379

TABLE 7.3

Clustered Data in the Form of Matrix

38.45	55.017	2
39.353	56.319	2
40.253	56.619	2
38.453	38.145	1
40.253	38.025	1

TABLE 7.4

Result of Proposed Model

D = 2600	Predicted Anomalies	Predicted Normality
Actual anomalies (216)	True positive = 208	False negative = 8
Actual normality (2384)	False positive = 87	True negative = 2297

After execution, the function returns the clustered data in the form of a matrix (Table 7.3).

The output of the clustering algorithm is fed as the input to classification. C4.5 is used as a classifier. Before constructing the decision tree, data has been classified into two groups. The training group is formed using 4900 records and the other group is formed using 2600 records for testing purposes.

After execution of the classifier on the test data, the output is generated as a confusion matrix. Table 7.4 reflects the result of the proposed anomaly detection model.

It is prominent from the results that the proposed system was able to predict anomalies in the existing dataset with an accuracy rate of 96.32%. The false-positive rate (FPR) has been observed as 3.68%.

7.4.3 Contribution and Impact

The efficient and reliable hybrid approach of PAM and C4.5 in identifying irregularities in IoT data is the main contribution of research work. The scope of current research is limited to those networks where IoT sensors share information about humidity and temperature attributes only. If sensors share information about more parameters than the proposed method, it cannot be applied to detect anomalies in that case.

7.5 CONCLUSION

In this chapter, we used multiple machine learning approaches to try to improve the protection of IoT-connected devices by performing experimentation for the purpose of anomaly detections on the modified version of the Intel Lab dataset. After implementation, we could achieve better accuracies while maintaining high efficiencies as compared with other existing similar algorithms. Using various machine learning algorithms, the findings were consistent.

7.6 FUTURE SCOPE OF WORK

This study focuses on a hybrid approach to detecting anomalies among IoT devices. But this approach is based on numerical input data. Textual data cannot be handled using this approach. Furthermore, the model's intrusion detection capabilities are limited to detecting an intrusion.

REFERENCES

1. Familiar, B. (2015). *Microservices, IoT and Azure: Leveraging DevOps and Microservice Architecture to deliver SaaS Solutions*. Apress.
2. Fu, R., Zheng, K., Zhang, D., & Yang, Y. (2011). An Intrusion Detection Scheme Based on Anomaly Mining in Internet of Things. In: IEEE International Conference on Wireless, Mobile & Multimedia Networks (ICWMMN 2011), Beijing, 27–30 Nov. 2011, pp. 315–320. DOI: 10.1049/cp.2011.1014.
3. Cyber Security Intrusion Detection. (2016). *IEEE Communications Surveys and Tutorials*, vol. 18, no. 2, pp. 1153–1176. Second quarter 2016. DOI: 10.1109/COMST.2015.2494502
4. Pajouh, H. H., Javidan, R., Khayami, R., & Ali, D. (2016). A Two-layer Dimension Reduction and Two-tier Classification Model for Anomaly-Based Intrusion Detection in IoT Backbone Networks. *IEEE Transactions on Emerging Topics in Computing*, vol. PP, no. 99, pp. 1–11. DOI: 10.1109/TETC.2016.2633228.
5. Haq, N., Onik, A., Hridoy, A., Rafni, M., Shah, F., & Farid, D. (2015) Application of Machine Learning Approaches in Intrusion Detection System: A Survey. *International Journal of Advanced Research in Artificial Intelligence*, vol. 4, no. 3, pp. 9–18.

6. Golman, V. (2014). An Efficient Hybrid Intrusion Detection System based on C5.0 and SVM. *International Journal of Database Theory and Application*, vol. 7, no. 2, pp. 59–70.

7. Hajare, S. A. (2016) Detection of Network Attacks Using Big Data Analysis. *International Journal on Recent and Innovation Trends in Computing and Communication*, vol. 4, no. 5, pp. 86–88.

8. Tanpure S. S. et al. (2016) Intrusion Detection System in Data Mining using Hybrid Approach. *International Journal of Computer Applications*,vol. 5, pp. 0975–8887.

9. Sherasiya, T., & Upadhyay, H. (2016) Intrusion Detection System for Internet of Things. *IJARIIE-ISSN(O)*, vol. 2, no. 3, pp. 2395–4396.

10. Aggarwal, C. C., & Reddy, C. K. (2013) *Data Clustering: Algorithms and Applications*. Chapman and Hall/CRC.

11. Bhushan, S., Kumar, P., Kumar, A., & Sharma, V. (2016). Scantime Antivirus Evasion and Malware Deployment Using Silent-SFX. In 2016 International Conference on Advances in Computing, Communication, & Automation (ICACCA) (Spring), 2016, pp. 1–4. DOI: 10.1109/ICACCA.2016.7578894.

12. Kurniawan, H., Rosmansyah, Y., & Dabarsyah, B. (2015). Android Anomaly Detection System Using Machine Learning Classification. In International Conference on Electrical Engineering and Informatics (ICEEI). DOI: 10.1109/ICEEI.2015.7352512.

13. Jung, E., Cho, I., & Kang, S. M. (2014). An Agent Modeling for Overcoming the Heterogeneity in the IoT with Design Patterns. In: Park, J., Adeli, H., Park, N. and Woungang, I. (eds) *Mobile, Ubiquitous, and Intelligent Computing*, Vol. 274, pp. 69–74

14. Diwakar M., Singh P., Kumar P., Tiwari K., Bhushan S., & Kaushik M. (2022) Secure Authentication in WLAN Using Modified Four-way Handshake Protocol. In: Tomar A., Malik H., Kumar P., Iqbal A. (eds) *Machine Learning, Advances in Computing, Renewable Energy and Communication. Lecture Notes in Electrical Engineering*, vol 768. Springer.

15. van der Laan, M. J., Pollard, K. S., & Bryan, J. (2002) *A New Partitioning Around Medoids Algorithm*. Hosted by The Berkeley Electronic Press.

16. Quinlan, J. R. (2014). *C4.5: Programs for Machine Learning*. Morgan Kaufmann Publishers. Zhao, K. & Ge, L. (2016). A Survey on the Internet of Things Security. In 9th International Conference on Computational Intelligence and Security (CIS). DOI: 10.1109/CIS.2013.145.

17. Ning, H. (2013). *Unit and Ubiquitous Internet of Things*. CRC Press Inc., 68.

8 Image Encryption and Decryption through Quantum Cryptography

Renjith V. Ravi, Manoj Kumar,
Pramod Kumar, and Shashi Bhushan

CONTENTS

8.1 INTRODUCTION

Today, we are in a technologically advanced age of mass information transmission through a reliable communication network (Friggeri *et al.* 2011). To have complete details, databases nowadays are put and maintained by the government, banks, commercial, and private institutions. Knowledge sharing on social networking sites poses a severe threat to any organization. Our current world is facing enormous difficulties

DOI: 10.1201/9781003296034-8

because of digital development in emerging technology. The secrecy of knowledge is one of the necessary items. This is the era of relentless digital image processing that plays a significant role in our lives because of these digital materials. Remote digital images have a degree of redundant information, making it difficult for outdated encryption schemes like RSA (Andalib and Azad 2014), DES (Biryukov and De Cannière 2011), IDEA (Hoffman 2007), and AES (Heron 2009) to process. Different approaches were taken in technology to protect digital images. Chaos theoretic methods include an innovative mixture of chaos and diffusion. Many researchers made significant approaches for developing nonlinear components of block ciphers. The concept of quantum computers is gaining recognition as it is an important topic that needs to be discussed. The fundamental idea behind quantum computers is to encode the matching pertaining output by converting input states that can be represented by a linear combination of various related input states. The quantum scheme consists of quantum gates that act on qubits. In this chapter, the discussion will be on quantum cryptography and how quantum cryptography helps to provide a secure image encryption and decryption scheme (Khan and Waseem 2018).

Quantum computing is a modern compression model used in parallel computation to obtain quantum overlay, enclosure, and other qualities (Akl and Nagy 2009). It could solve several computer problems that cannot be calculated in classic computers efficiently. For instance, many traditional encryption algorithms, including RSA algorithms, are based on NP problems (non-deterministic time polynomial) (Liu *et al.* 2015). These encryption algorithms are easily broken and not stable with the advent of quantum computing. Thus, quantum cryptography in recent years has become a hot subject. Quantum image encryption is a cross-research area used to secure quantum and quantum image encryption.

Le *et al.* (2011) proposed a versatile flexible representation for quantum images (FRQI), which represents gray and the photo's location as a standardized quantum superstructure. Since then, Zhang *et al.* (2013) and others have suggested a novel enhanced quantum representation (NEQR) approach, making it simpler to extend some classical picture processing algorithms to quantum pictures to achieve their purpose. A new generalized quantum image representation (GQIR) approach was suggested in 2017 (Zhou *et al.* 2017). The NEQR representation method is an improvement based on the GQIR. It can display any H to W quantum pictures in which H and W are arbitrarily positive integers. In addition to gray images, the GQIR representation can indicate color imagery. At the same time, an extensive range of transformations were suggested for the quantum picture, including Arnold and Fibonacci image scrabbling (Jiang *et al.* 2014a), scratching the Hilbert image of the quantum (Jiang *et al.*, Quantum Hilbert image scrambling 2014b), compression in the quantum image (Horng 2012). Many algorithms for quantum image encryption based on various methods are proposed. These encryption algorithms can be divided into two groups. One is based on the image transformations, including transforming Fourier (Tyo and Alenin 2015), encoding random phase, changing the quantum wavelet (Yin *et al.* 2010), decomposition of the image correlation (Wang *et al.* 2017), the transformation of Arnold (Loebbecke and Picot 2015), and so forth.

Quantity imaging research is very closely associated with the processing of quantum image. Quantum image representation performs quantic state storage of images (Yao *et al.* 2017). Venegas-Andraca *et al.* (2010) proposed a method of imagery in 2003 that was used to map electromagnetic waves into the quantum states and named the memory cell a quantum grid. On the basis of the quantum grid concept, Yuan *et al.* (Lim *et al.* 2005) introduced simple quantum representation (SQR), a quantum imaging tool called infrarouge photos. The most widely interwoven state of the picture was used in Venegas-Andrea *et al.* (Splendiani *et al.* 2010) in 2010, and a method of representation of quantum images based on interweaving. It can solve the problem of image processing more quickly and efficiently with the intricate state. However, only the binary picture of simple forms, limiting the scale of applications, can be stored and processed by the quantified image representation system.

Using quantum wave transformation and diffusion, Wang *et al.* (Liu and Wang 2010) proposed a new quantum pictorial algorithm. Yan *et al.* (2015) proposed a quantum encryption algorithm based on various transforms in 2015. This encryption method typically uses various transformations to scramble information about where the picture is stored and colored. No secret encryption strategy can be classified. The cipher is a different kind of quantum picture encoding method which encrypts the picture using the chip. Gong *et al.* (2016) proposed the XOR-based quantum image encryption algorithm. This article uses a quantum key image which is more straightforward for introducing a new quantity encryption algorithm than other quantum imaging algorithms. The quantum key image is produced by means of a key stream formed with a classical encryption algorithm (Aljawarneh *et al.* 2017). Let's look at Figure 8.1 which displays the encryption of the images using the SHA-512 algorithm in which the color image is encrypted to the cipher image.

In Figure 8.1, the steps that are used to perform the encryption of the images are as follows:

a. First, we have input the color images.
b. Second, they are converted into three different images of different colors such as red, green, and blue.
c. Splitting these colored images into small blocks of matrices.
d. Then the mod operation will be performed on the blocks using SHA-512 algorithms (Velmurugan and Karthiga 2020).
e. All the blocks will be joined to get the image after performing the mod operation.
f. Finally, the Game trick will be applied to get the cipher image and it is in the form of the gray color [30].

Current quantum image encryption algorithms focus mainly on gray color, or dual-quantity image encryption although with only limited investigation. A dual quantic picture encryption algorithm is suggested based on the quantum Arnold transform (QAT) (Zhou *et al.* 2015) and qubit random rotation, and it is proposed to use a double quantic picture encryption algorithm. In the first instance, the encrypted two images employ a flexible representation of quantum images (FRQI) (Le *et al.* 2011).

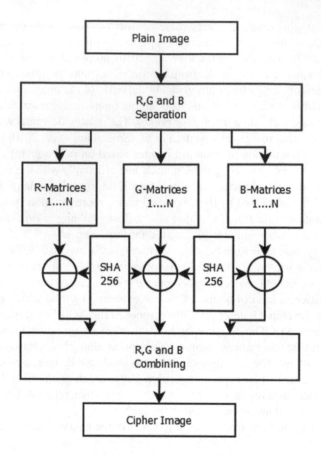

FIGURE 8.1   Flow of encryption of the image (Butt *et al.* 2020).

The two quantum states are then scratched by different QAT parameters, one of which is encoded in amplitude and the other in phase. The independent random-qubit rotation then works in the quantum transformation Fourier (QFT) in the spatial and frequency domains to achieve pixel unsafety and spread once. The reverse QFT (Shao 2017) is finally the noise-like chip photo. Without cross-talk, the original images can be precisely restored. Parallel quantum computations accelerate the encryption and decryption of double images. The numerical impacts of simulation and theoretical analysis indicate the efficiency and sophistication of algorithms. The chapter's contribution is as follows:

i. Section 8.2 covers the background work done in cryptography through quantum computing
ii. Section 8.3 explains the methodology used for the encryption and decryption performed by quantum computing
iii. Sections 8.4–8.7 cover the result analysis with future works followed by conclusion and references

8.2 LITERATURE SURVEY

Lee and Tsai have transformed HSV target images and the reversible image hiding process that worked out a stable picture-transmission technique for mosaic pictures (Lee and Tsai 2013). When a secret vision is transformed into a mosaic, the image can be transferred and hidden in color, which can be further divided into frames. The proposed work demonstrated that messages sent using this method were nearly loss-free. This demonstrates that this method is unsuitable for transmitting medical images. Kapur and Baregar (2013) used stitching and image steganography to secure an image sent over the network in which the photos are partially separated. The second part is the process of embedding the chip text in any secret image section to be submitted. In the output picture of the embedding phase, the third component is the hiding process and steganography.

The article written by van der Walt (2016) shows that it is possible to use a collection of values that generate a specific system since the hardness of a large number depends on most of these cryptographic algorithms. But a stringent test of complexity is needed for the latest collection of quantum cryptographic algorithms. This was the motive for this proposed work to use quantum cryptography. Quantum computing is the field in which computer power and other properties based on quantum-mechanical concepts are studied. An essential goal is to find quantum algorithms that considerably solve the same problem as a classical algorithm. The assumption for quantum-safe cryptographic research is that mathematical problems are more difficult to break with a quantum computer. In the presence of a quantum computer, RSA and ECC cannot be used.

Khan *et al.* (2009) developed an alternative key distribution protocol that allowed Alice and Bob to have a second set of bases on which they used "0" and "1" when an expeditious manner could be required. The system's safety becomes an expansion-based minimum transmission exponent (Exponent IT) that causes photon states with a higher dimension to produce a minimum index error. This provides more room for more noise in the transmission to travel between Alice and Bob, who are closer to one another.

KMB09 is another protocol based on the quantum key distribution (QKD), and it is safer as it doesn't need the least bit error rate (LIBER) (Chen *et al.* 2008). The encryption/decryption protocol uses the principles of the public and private keys. The process of keeping public–private and private keys separate is called "public-private key cryptography." Cryptography based on public and private keys S13 protocol (Singh *et al.* 2014) is more stable, but implementation is more difficult due to the multiple exchanges of qubits. It's also a modern protocol; it resembles the BB84 protocol, but it differs from that by using RC and asymmetric cryptography (Epping *et al.* 2017). It's also a modern protocol. The Heisenberg uncertainty principle can be applied to any current device as long as those system-level functions are kept the same.

Bedington *et al.* (2017) stated that quantum key distribution (QKD) is a series of protocols used to create a private coding key between both sides. All ground-based QRD approaches are advancing at a distance due to air losses or in-fiber attenuation despite a lot of development. These limitations make a global delivery network of purely ground-based structures impractical. However, satellites equipped with high-quality optical connections will broaden the range of communication. This chapter provides a summary of research and development that QKD starts with satellites. It includes protocols and infrastructures and a high-level overview of the ongoing QKD satellite projects around the world. They also address technological issues involved in implementing such systems.

Pirandola *et al.* (1906) provided theoretical and experimental overviews of recent developments in the field and a state-of-the-art summary. They begin by examining quantum key distribution protocols based on discerning variable systems. Next, platform independence, satellite problems, and high-quality protocols based on variable plans were taken into account. The authors addressed the absolute limits of private communications point to point and how quantum repeaters and networks can resolve these constraints. Finally, several aspects of quantum cryptography, including quantum data locks and quantum digital signatures (Lv *et al.* 2019), have been discussed outside normal quantum key distributions.

Pradhan *et al.* (2019) offered a significantly higher degree of security, and the average number of cryptography problems on lattice appears to be the biggest problem. Furthermore, lattices will convince any quantic machine. Quantum computational security is used to prevent the attack during cryptanalysis. This chapter will explore the cryptosystem based on lattices, its dimensions of security, an overview of how this works the potential of the future, applications, and areas of interest. Mavroeidis *et al.* (2018) aim to clarify the consequences of quantum computing in the current cryptographing and introduce the reader to simple algorithms after quantity. The readers can study in particular: current (symmetric and asymmetric), discrepancies in quantum and classical computation, quantum-computing problems and quantum algorithms, public-key encoding schemes, symmetric schemes affected, the effect on hash functions, and the after-quantum encryption. The reader can explore the following topics. In particular, the author deals with a wide range of quantum and mathematical solutions such as BB84 protocol, cryptography based on grids, multivariate cryptography, Hash-based signatures, and code-based encryption.

8.3   INTRODUCTION TO QUANTUM COMPUTING IN CRYPTOGRAPHY

In this section, we will describe the role of quantum computing in different phases of cryptography.

8.3.1   KEY DISTRIBUTION

This scheme allows dispersing the sequence of random bits, which the laws and the philosophy of quantum mechanics guarantee their restraint and privacy. These sequences can be used as hidden keys and also as a safeguard for the transmission of information. For transmission, QKD requires an optical environment, such as optical fibers (Moll *et al.* 2019). Quantum key distribution has functional limitations. The QKD range is about 60 or 100 km long, with research reaching up to 250 km

(Makarov 2007). One important aspect is that QKD is used to distinguish third parties during user processing. Quantum keys are not used for messages and data only to generate and distribute keys. In quantum cryptography, several symbols are used to polarize the photon (Kour *et al.* 2017).

A quantum key distribution is a non-commuting operator property that reveals the Heisenberg phenomenon's property (Parkinson and Farnell 2010). Where Eve discovers the angle at foundation one before Bob, Mea must differ from that of base 1 to base 2, when Eve finds the angle at base 1 before Eve at base 2.

8.3.1.1 Main Parameters for Quantum Key Distribution

The study of quantum computing, namely size, error bit rate, data rate, etc., has several parameters (Li *et al.* 2011). Many theoretical and practical experiments have been carried out on long-term transmission via an optical fiber cable, but quantum computing distance is a great challenge. Effective distribution of links over 200 km can be achieved. Quantum error bit rate with the distance QBER/1/distance can be analyzed (Table 8.1) (Upadhyay 2018). Four protocols on quantum distribution BB84 were suggested by Bennett and Brassard in 1984 (Rusca *et al.* 2018). A pair of states is used in this protocol, and these pairs are mutually orthogonal. Alice selects a random bit like 0 or 1 and then sets with the base. The basis is of two forms. Some basic symbols are indicated.

Figure 8.2 shows the rectilinear and diagonal foundations. In that state, Alice sends one photon to Bob before no bits are sent. Bob also goes with the base randomly. If the bit has the same base at both ends, then the key was shared successfully. Take an example, like Alice, to produce a random bit 0 or 1 and choose a random bit to submit Bob. There is also an opportunity to create excitement. Bob also selects a

TABLE 8.1

Quantum Computing Parameters

	20 km	100 km
Fiber distance	20 km	100 km
Secure key rate	1.02 Mbit/s	10.1 Kbit/s
Security	More	Experimentally less
Quantum bit error rate	Less	More

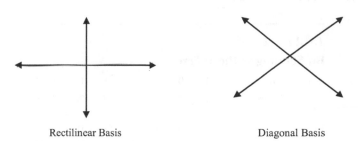

Rectilinear Basis   Diagonal Basis

FIGURE 8.2   Encoding of bits.

basis randomly if Alice sends a bit as horizontal as the basics, but Bob doesn't prefer that way.

Table 8.1 displays the quantum parameters in the computation range of 20 km fiber with safe key speeds of 1.02 Mbit/s and 10.1 Kbit/s (Sidhu and Kok 2020). The error rate of quantum bit with experimentally less protection gives more cryptography of quantity: A survey will take place with the probability that both will fit 1 (horizontally), but the probability of D/A is 45°, and D/A is −0.5 (for 135°). Still, if Eves isn't present, the likelihood of accepting bits between is 0.75. As mentioned below, the BB84 protocol has some fundamental phenomena.

1. Alice selects bits (4*n+$), is encoding, and is sending Bob randomly.
2. Bob tests even random foundations.
3. At least 2*n cases dependent on the probability likelihood would be decided.
4. Bob throws away all the bits that do not fit the foundation.
5. In the event of a minor mistake, the other n bits will be used as a one-time pad for safe communication (Figure 8.3).

In the following tables, this can be understood by two instances, such as:

First, Table 8.2 indicates that there is just Alice and Bob between them and no Eve. Alice needs a message to Bob, first Alice selects random bases and sends bits

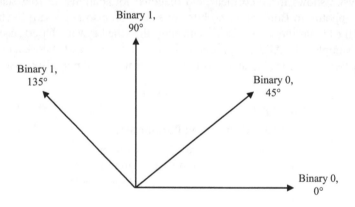

FIGURE 8.3   Polarization of photon.

TABLE 8.2
Bit Sending without Error

Alice	Bit	1	0	0	1	1	0	0	0
	Bases	⊕	⊗	⊗	⊕	⊗	⊕	⊕	⊗
Bob	Bit	1	0	0	0	1	0	0	0
	Bases	⊕	⊕	⊗	⊗	⊕	⊗	⊕	⊗
	Second Key	1	–	0	–	–	–	0	0

and Bob, and if Bob has a matched base, Bob will also receive the same bits as he has picked. Alice will send messages to Bob.

Second, Table 8.3 shows that three of them are Alice, Bob, and Eve. Alice wants to submit Bob's letter, and, based on specific criteria, Alice then selects random bits and sends them on the channel between Alice and Bob. Eve is present, and she selects the random base and steals the foundation and its bits. Now all three bases are paired with the final protected key. E91 protocol is also called Eckert and is based on interlocking photonic pairing. The EPR pair is used to identify Eve's presence in the scheme.

In that way, someone like Alice, Bob, and even Eve could produce these photons. There are two situations: One is the same product in both Alice and Bob steps with a 100% probability of either a horizontal or vertical polarization (Table 8.2). Bit sending error-free 1 0 0 1 1 0 0 Alice Bit Basic Foundation 1 0 0 0 1 0 0 BB Bit Key 1 – 0 —- 0 0 Secured Key (Table 8.3). Bit error sending 1 0 0 1 1 0 0 Alice Bit 1 1 0 0 0 1 0 1 1 0 1 1 0 0 0 1 0 0. A B92 scheme has only two states of four which are identical to the BB84 protocol [54]. Alice encodes its foundation in this protocol in a default way—the computer encoding of 0, but bit 1 in some way is not orthogonal.

When Alice wants to encode the bits, in that case, the traditional bits are converted into two non-orthogonal states. No measurement can separate two non-orthogonal states so that the problem is created, which does not allow the bits to be identified with certainty. This code allows the recipient party to learn whenever the bits are dispatched with Alice without discussion. To decide the basis for measurement, Bob uses a coin toss. Suppose Bob picks bit 1, Alice can't pick a bit, and if Bob picks bit 1, Alice can't pick bit 1. When Bob chooses bit 0, there is no measurement.

8.4 QUANTUM-BASED DIGITAL ENCRYPTION AND DECRYPTION SCHEME

Let the size of the image $g\ (i, j)$ is $M*N$ where $g\ (i, j)$ is a pixel value at ith row and jth column. The system suggested applies to misunderstanding and distribution. Figure 8.4 shows the procedure for encrypting an image. Below are the

---

TABLE 8.3
Bit Sending with Error

Alice	Bit	1	0	0	1	1	0	0	0
	Bases	⊕	⊗	⊗	⊕	⊗	⊕	⊕	⊗
Eve	Bit	1	1	0	0	0	1	0	1
	Bases	⊕	⊕	⊗	⊗	⊗	⊕	⊗	⊕
Bob	Bit	1	0	0	0	1	0	0	0
	Bases	⊕	⊕	⊗	⊗	⊕	⊗	⊕	⊗
	Second Key	1	–	0	–	–	–	0	0

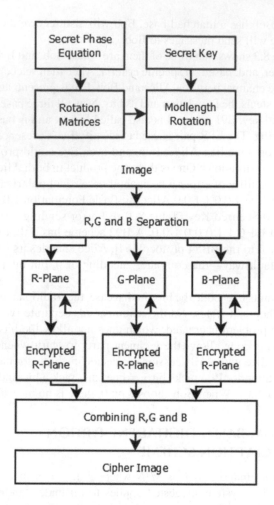

FIGURE 8.4   Encryption algorithm (Butt *et al*. 2020).

two-dimensional mathematical expressions of rotating operators which will help to improve the algorithmic image encryption [6].

8.4.1   ENCRYPTION OF IMAGES

1. Read a picture and convert each image layer (RGB) into four separate commands
2. Choose the sender and recipient-known encoding process
3. Put the phase to obtain the M_i matrices
4. Choose a key of any length in mod 24 and take the matrix of each matrix of the set **M**
5. Encrypt each digital picture layer with the rotary arrays picked
6. Shift encrypted layers dimensions to original dimensions

7. Mix all encrypted layers into an encoded RGB image
8. The conditions for encrypting the key can also be decided: Suppose $n \in [a, b,$ $c, d, ...]$ and if you dig the key out of the odd $[a\ b\ c]$, compute the matrix of b here and convert b to binary, and check if b is the last, select the matrix for encrypting the other key in the c-screen. If a number of keys even $[a\ b\ c\ d\ d$ $e\ f]$ are calculated, calculate $n/2$, equivalent to c, convert c to be binary and check if the final c is 0, select the matrices with respect to $[a\ b]$ to encrypt the key, select $[d\ e\ f]$ to encrypt the key

8.4.2 IMAGE DECODING

1. Study and convert RGB encrypted image into $4 \times n$ order
2. Extract the encrypted image from the RGB layers
3. The phase determined by equation and the set M
4. Now remove the source keys from the encrypted keys and take M matrices and reverse them
5. Decrypt the inverse matrix and matrices for each layer
6. Transform the layer dimensions as encoded
7. Merge the layers to form the original image

8.5 IMPLEMENTATION OF THE ALGORITHM

Assume that we want to encrypt the image of "Lena," "Fruit," and "Parrot" dimension of 512×512 and then analyze it differently with key [1 3 7 14 29 59]. We select the image of "Lena," "Fruits," and "Parrot," then extract and analyze their RGB layers. Then decide to choose the secret equation of the phase:

$$y = 330 \times (2^M - 1) \bmod 720, \text{where } M \in [1, 24] \text{and } \theta = \text{mean}(y) \tag{2}$$

While using this equation, we have (tangent angle) tangent angle: $\theta = 382.5$. By the mentioned algorithm, one must be in control of the key. When one increases, the other increases as well, we can determine parameters that apply to each level of protection, which will ensure a constant level of privacy. Thus, the third term of the n key is 7, and the last binary digit of the key is 1. Let's pick our moduli from set M: 14 mod 24 = A, 29 mod 24 = B, and 59 mod M = A11. Now apply the zero map to A14, A5, A11 with respect to dimension and apply the measured process to each A. Let's use the provided key to encrypt the picture.

8.5.1 PERFORMANCE PARAMETERS

We also completed several steps on different normal and implemented encryption using digital photos. These employ a process known as data-based testing, for examining and dissecting the encrypted files, as well as an irregularity test for application. These processes are extensively defined in the subsections.

8.5.1.1   Cipher Randomity Evaluation

For a long-term, uniform distribution, high complexity, and efficiency, security of the cryptosystem needs to take some shape. NIST SP 800-22 is used to measure the haphazardness of digital photography with a clear end objective to achieve these locations (Bastos *et al.* 2020). Some of these tests have different subsets. The scratched 24-bit Lena optical picture is used for all NIST studies. The great deals of the first keys are helpful in order to measure the figure's haphazardness. Our projected digital image encryption scheme effectively passes the NIST tests by breaking down those results. In view of the results achieved, random ciphers can therefore be asserted that are very irregular in their production in our encryption algorithms.

8.5.2   Pixel Consistency

Among others, the histogram's uniformity of encompassed contents is a significant highlight in estimates of the safety of the digital information encryption framework (Wang 2012). Three 256 optical dark-level images of 512 to 512 were taken with different compounds and histograms. The histograms of plain images have large sharp ascents, and the histogram of all enciphered images is truly uniform, and in essence not entirely the same as that of the original picture, which makes measurable attacks difficult. It then provides little insight into the use of the digital encrypted images in an observable analysis (Khan and Waseem 2018)

8.5.3   Check for Correlation Pixels

It is remarkable that adjacent pixels are either in horizontal, vertical, or corner directions very closely related. This connection to increase obstacles to the observable investigation should therefore be evacuated by the secured encrypted plan. The accompanying method has been completed to test connections between nearby pixels in a single and encrypted image. Original, 10,000 sets of two close-up pixels were selected arbitrarily from a clear and encrypted image (Venegas-Andraca and Bose 2003).

8.5.3.1   Association of Original Images with Encryption

The relationship between different pairs of original/encoded images is measured by the 2D coefficients of the relationship between original and encrypted images (Planat and Solé 2008). The following equation is used to calculate the correlation coefficients.

$$r = \frac{\sum_{i=1}^{M}\sum_{j=1}^{N}\left(X_{ij} - \bar{X}\right)\left(Y_{ij} - \bar{Y}\right)}{\sqrt{\left(\sum_{i=1}^{M}\sum_{j=1}^{N}\left(X_{ij} - X\right)^{2}\right)\left(\sum_{i=1}^{M}\sum_{j=1}^{N}\left(Y_{ij} - \bar{Y}\right)^{2}\right)}} \tag{3}$$

where X and Y represent the plain and cipher images, $\bar{X}$ and $\bar{Y}$ represent the mean of X and Y, M represents the height, and N represents the width of the initial/encrypted picture. The correlation coefficients between different pairs of flat and cipher images are very small or virtually nil, resulting in a wide range of flat and cipher images. Findings have indicated that lower correlation values allow for an effective image-encoding technique in real-time applications (Anirudh *et al.* 2020).

8.5.4 THREE-DIMENSIONAL, SINGLE, AND ENCRYPTED PICTURE COLOR STRENGTH

The color intensity (RGB) controls the presence of the pixel [60]. The amount of information in a pixel determines the depth of colors. The color depth governs the colors of the pixels and the bit depth can also be named and the number of pixels matching the degree of intensity over images. The 3D histograms for simple images are made up of sharp pictures in the distribution of the pixels, whereas the 3D color intensities for encrypted images are very standardized to produce the flat plan in RGB coordinates (Wan Ishak and Rahman 2010). These three-dimensional representations demonstrate that our anticipated image encryption scheme is highly robust, preventing an eavesdropper from accessing or evaluating any information contained in the uniform distribution of the encrypted image pixels.

8.5.5 ENTROPY RESEARCH

Randomness is the most significant function of entropy (Knill *et al.* 2008). The source of independent random events has been defined from a set of possible discrete events $\{y_1 y_2, \ldots y_i\}$ with the related probableness

$$H = -\sum_{i=0}^{2^N-1} p(y_i) \log_2 p(y_i) \tag{4}$$

The UACI (unified average intensity) value improves the encryption protection. In order to determine the sensitivity of a plain image, the single pixel is encrypted first, and a plain image is randomly selected and modified. The NPCR estimates are consistent with the ideal estimate of 1, and the UACI estimate is over 34%. The results show that the intended scheme has a great deal to make a small change in the original image, irrespective of whether there is a 1-bit difference between these two scrambling single pictures, the two images that are scraped/enciphered would be very different. Consequently, in examination with alternative systems, the design has a superior capability to avoid various entire attacks. In any word, the magnificence and versatility of outlined algorithms alter cipher images quickly, and only single matrices and phase ÚTE cannot unscreen the encrypted image. To decipher the encrypted, the two matrices and the step uterus should be known. Since TER has huge focuses, a smidgen shift like 0.01 in the stage will change the enciphered picture. We have also compared our NPCR and UACI findings with well-known results (Yang and Liao 2018). The implemented system is very resistant to differential and linear attacks and has agreed with its performance.

8.6 FUTURE RESEARCH IN QUANTUM CRYPTOGRAPHY

Cyberspace security should be safeguarded on the internet since it is the gathering for human existence of all information systems and information environments (Pang and Li 2020). Quantum cryptography is the first concern for the rising safety issue in cyberspace (Majenz 2018.).

8.6.1 UNQUALIFIED SAFETY

Today's internet connectivity is primarily made up of cable and light. Alice and Bob are authorized device users, whereas Eve serves as a scout. They encrypt messages before sending them over the public channel to ensure their security. The classical cryptosystem is loosely classified into two types: symmetric and asymmetric cryptosystems (Meher and Midhunchakkaravarthy 2020). Their security is primarily dependent on the complexity of the machine for these two cryptosystems. The swift development of hardware and modern sophisticated algorithms has, however, brought the safety of the classical cryptosystems with unparalleled challenges. In addition, several difficulties in classic mathematics have arisen in the area of quantum physics as a result of the fast development of quantum computing. For instance, in 1994, the DLP and the problem of integer factorization were solved. In this way, it will be important for the future of the internet to explore quantum cryptographic protocols. In the 1950s, Shannon, the founder of the theory of knowledge, conducted a pioneering study on unreserved safety.

In this analysis, the "one-time pad" was given unconditional security conditions (Rahim *et al.* 2018). Instead of a pseudo-random number, the encryption/decryption key is truly random, and this key is used only once. Additionally, the key is the same length as the plaintext and is executed bit by bit alongside its operation. The problem of one-time pad key distribution was never solved. It should be remembered that the theory of quantum mechanics will solve this problem of key distribution. Figure 8.4 depicts a model of the well-known QKD protocol (Horng 2012). In this model, the sender wishes to share a standard conference key with her counterpart to encrypt/decrypt communicated messages. The actual randomness of the key is guaranteed in this QKD protocol by the fundamentals of the quantum: the theory of ambiguity (Wang *et al.* 2019). In addition, if it occurs, an intruder is definitely found.

8.6.2 DETECTION OF SNIFFING

Information is shared on public networks by Alice and Bob. For confidentiality, their information is encrypted; however, an intruder cannot be blocked by a channel. In addition, it is impossible to detect the eavesdropper in cable communications or optical fiber communication on the basis of the characteristics of the system itself. A millimeters or oscilloscope may be used for cable communications to track (O'Malley 2019). In optical fiber communications, the eavesdropper will obtain information from a portion of the light signal. Take note that environmental factors such as temperature and pressure affect fiber loss, but this does not make eavesdropping losses perceptible. The eavesdropper will undoubtedly be observed due to quantum communication's no-clone principle. To be more precise, an eavesdropper monitors the quantum channel and uses the same measuring base as the sender to obtain a small amount of quantum information with a probability of 50%. In order to provide some quantum information, the eavesdropper is detected at 50% probability. Notice that the probability of detecting eavesdroppers is $1-(1/2)^n$ for bit quantity information.

8.6.3 QKD's SAFETY

We begin in this section by examining the quantum key distribution protocol in a noise-free channel to simulate real-world scenarios in the future internet. Additionally, we validate the protocol for noisy channel quantum key distribution. Table 8.1 details the quantic data encoding and measurement results for various measurement bases to assess the QKD protocol's security. Both sides agree in advance that the polarization is horizontal and obligation to downwards is "1," while the upward polarization in vertical and oblique is "0." The possibility of a QKD protocol involving an eavesdropper is as follows.

$$P_r = P_r \left\{ \text{Base}_A = \text{Base}_B \land \text{Measure}_A \neq \text{Measure}_B \right\}$$

The probability that a 1-bit quantum information eavesdropper is detected shall be determined as $1/2 \times 1/2 \times 1/2 = 1/8$ for 1-bit quantum information. The possibility of detecting eavesdroppers on a channel without noise will always be a challenging task. It has been seen that the eavesdropping odds are similar to 100% when the sum of transmissions exceeds 40 (Zhou *et al.* 2018).

When an eavesdropper sends a different chance over the channel, the recipient has a chance of failing. This means that without an eavesdropper, the receptor makes 25% of errors while making around 31% when the eavesdropper monitors 50% of the channel and about 37% when the eavesdropper observes the entire channel. It is discovered when the eavesdropper sends a different chance on the channel. Zhou *et al.* (2018) has represented the purple line, which indicates that the attacker monitors the channel continuously. In contrast, the green and red bars indicate that the attacker monitors the channel 50% and 20% of the time, respectively. These three curves demonstrate that regardless of the likelihood of canal monitoring eavesdropping, the number of transmitted bits will almost certainly increase. As a result of the preceding discussion, we can conclude that quantum cryptography offers complete protection and detection of sniffers for secure communication. In the future, such assets will ensure the internet's cyberspace security (Zhou *et al.* 2018).

8.7 CONCLUSION

This chapter has discussed about quantum cryptography. The image encryption and decryption is done through the quantum process. The chapter has covered the implementation details with the evaluation parameters that can measure the performance of the scheme. In this study, different types of images have been taken for the encryption purpose with approaches such as secret key rotation, encryption key, rotation matrices, and many more. The evaluation parameters used in this work are cipher randomity evaluation, pixel consistency, and correlation of pixels. The chapter discussed a novel method for encrypting data that makes use of quantum rotational operators. We used quantum halves pinning to introduce confusion and diffusion into this scheme. The key can be easily extended and compressed by multiplying each uninstalling matrix known to the cryptanalyst to send and receive to merge. Because no one knows which matrices from the set M, two or more matrices, are multiplied, Cryptanalyst would be nearly incapable of cracking the door (a challenge for crackers). The algorithm at issue is a half-spinning algorithm. According to statistical analysis, the algorithms should be a strong contender for image encryption. The work has shown that image encryption done through quantum cryptography scheme can provide fruitful results.

REFERENCES

Akl, Selim G., and Marius Nagy. 2009. "The future of parallel computation." In *Parallel Computing*, 471–510. Springer.

Aljawarneh, Shadi, Muneer Bani Yassein, and We'am Adel Talafha. 2017. "A resource-efficient encryption algorithm for multimedia big data." *Multimedia Tools and Applications* (Springer), vol 76: 22703–22724.

Anirudh, Rushil, Jayaraman J. Thiagarajan, Bhavya Kailkhura, and Peer-Timo Bremer. 2020. "Mimicgan: Robust projection onto image manifolds with corruption mimicking." *International Journal of Computer Vision* (Springer) 128: 2459–2477.

Azad, Saiful, and Al-Sakib Khan Pathan. 2014. *Practical Cryptography: Algorithms and Implementations using C++*. CRC Press.

Bastos, Daniel Chicayban, and Raphael C. S. Machado. 2020. "On pseudorandom number generators." *ACTA IMEKO* 9: 128–135.

Bedington, Robert, Juan Miguel Arrazola, and Alexander Ling. 2017. "Progress in satellite quantum key distribution. " *NPJ Quantum Information* (Nature Publishing Group) 3: 1–13.

Bhushan, S., Singh A. K., & Vij, S. 2019 "Comparative Study and Analysis of Wireless Mesh Networks on AODV and DSR," 2019 4th International Conference on Internet of Things: Smart Innovation and Usages (IoT-SIU), 2019, pp. 1–6, doi: 10.1109/IoT-SIU.2019.8777466.

Biryukov, Alex, and Christophe De Cannière. 2011. "Data encryption standard (DES)." *Encyclopedia of Cryptography and Security* (Springer): 295–301.

Butt, Khushbu Khalid, Guohui Li, Sajid Khan, and Sohaib Manzoor. 2020. "Fast and Efficient Image Encryption Algorithm Based on Modular Addition and SPD." *Entropy* (Multidisciplinary Digital Publishing Institute) 22: 112.

Chen, Sheng, Andreas Wolfgang, Chris J. Harris, and Lajos Hanzo. 2008. "Adaptive nonlinear least bit error-rate detection for symmetrical RBF beamforming." *Neural networks* (Elsevier) 21: 358–367.

Epping, Michael, Hermann Kampermann, Dagmar Bruß, and others. 2017. "Multi-partite entanglement can speed up quantum key distribution in networks." *New Journal of Physics* (IOP Publishing) 19: 093012.

Friggeri, Adrien, Guillaume Chelius, Eric Fleury, Antoine Fraboulet, France Mentré, and Jean-Christophe Lucet. 2011. "Reconstructing social interactions using an unreliable wireless sensor network." *Computer Communications* (Elsevier) 34: 609–618.

Gong, Li-Hua, Xiang-Tao He, Shan Cheng, Tian-Xiang Hua, and Nan-Run Zhou. 2016. "Quantum image encryption algorithm based on quantum image XOR operations." *International Journal of Theoretical Physics* (Springer) 55: 3234–3250.

Heron, Simon. 2009. "Advanced encryption standard (AES)." *Network Security* (Elsevier) 2009: 8–12.

Hoffman, Nick. 2007. "A simplified IDEA algorithm." *Cryptologia* (Taylor & Francis) 31: 143–151.

Horng, Ming-Huwi. 2012. "Vector quantization using the firefly algorithm for image compression." *Expert Systems with Applications* (Elsevier) 39: 1078–1091.

Jiang, Nan, Luo Wang, and Wen-Ya Wu. 2014a. "Quantum Hilbert image scrambling." *International Journal of Theoretical Physics* (Springer) 53: 2463–2484.

Jiang, Nan, Wen-Ya Wu, and Luo Wang. 2014b. "The quantum realization of Arnold and Fibonacci image scrambling." *Quantum information processing* (Springer) 13: 1223–1236.

Kapur, Jyotika. 2013. "Security using image processing." *International Journal of Managing Information Technology (IJMIT)* 5.

Khan, Majid, and Hafiz Muhammad Waseem. 2018. "A novel image encryption scheme based on quantum dynamical spinning and rotations." *PloS one* (Public Library of Science San Francisco, CA USA) 13: e0206460.

Khan, Muhammad Mubashir, Michael Murphy, and Almut Beige. 2009. "High error-rate quantum key distribution for long-distance communication." *New Journal of Physics* (IOP Publishing) 11: 063043.

Khan, Sajid, Han Lansheng, Yekui Qian, Hongwei Lu, and Shi Meng Jiao. 2021. "Security of multimedia communication with game trick based fast, efficient, and robust color-/grayscale image encryption algorithm." *Transactions on Emerging Telecommunications Technologies* (Wiley Online Library) 32: e4034.

Knill, Emanuel, Dietrich Leibfried, Rolf Reichle, Joe Britton, R. Brad Blakestad, John D. Jost, Chris Langer, Roee Ozeri, Signe Seidelin, and David J. Wineland. 2008. "Randomized benchmarking of quantum gates." *Physical Review A* (APS) 77: 012307.

Kour, Jasleen, Saboor Koul, and Prince Zahid. 2017. "A survey on quantum key distribution protocols." *International Journal on Computational Science & Applications (IJCSA)* 7.

Le, Phuc Q., Fangyan Dong, and Kaoru Hirota. 2011. "A flexible representation of quantum images for polynomial preparation, image compression, and processing operations." *Quantum Information Processing* (Springer) 10: 63–84.

Lee, Ya-Lin, and Wen-Hsiang Tsai. 2013. "A new secure image transmission technique via secret-fragment-visible mosaic images by nearly reversible color transformations." *IEEE Transactions on Circuits and Systems for Video Technology* (IEEE) 24: 695–703.

Li, Fei, Min Zhou, and Haibo Li. 2011. "A novel neural network optimized by quantum genetic algorithm for signal detection in MIMO-OFDM systems." *Computational Intelligence in Control and Automation (CICA)*. 170–177.

Lim, Yuan Liang, Almut Beige, and Leong Chuan Kwek. 2005. "Repeat-until-success linear optics distributed quantum computing." *Physical review letters* (APS) 95: 030505.

Liu, Hongjun, and Xingyuan Wang. 2010. "Color image encryption based on one-time keys and robust chaotic maps." *Computers & Mathematics with Applications* (Elsevier) 59: 3320–3327.

Liu, Yuxin, Chao Gao, Zili Zhang, Yuxiao Lu, Shi Chen, Mingxin Liang, and Li Tao. 2015. "Solving NP-hard problems with physarum-based ant colony system." *IEEE/ACM Transactions on Computational Biology and Bioinformatics* (IEEE) 14: 108–120.

Loebbecke, Claudia, and Arnold Picot. 2015. "Reflections on societal and business model transformation arising from digitization and big data analytics: A research agenda." *The Journal of Strategic Information Systems* (Elsevier) 24: 149–157.

Lv, Zefang, Lirong Wang, Zhitao Guan, Jun Wu, Xiaojiang Du, Hongtao Zhao, and Mohsen
    Guizani. 2019. "An optimizing and differentially private clustering algorithm for mixed
    data in SDN-based smart grid." *IEEE Access* (IEEE) 7: 45773–45782.

Majenz, Christian. 2018. *Entropy in Quantum Information Theory: Communication and
    Cryptography.* PhD Thesis, University of Copenhagen, Denmark. Faculty of Science,
    University of Copenhagen.

Mavroeidis, Vasileios, Kamer Vishi, Mateusz D. Zych, and Audun Jøsang. 2018. "The impact
    of quantum computing on present cryptography." *arXiv preprint arXiv:1804.00200.*

Meher, K., and D. Midhunchakkaravarthy. 2020. "Ntruencrypt – a Quantum Proof
    Replacement to RSA Cryptosystem." *International Journal of Advanced Trends in
    Computer Science and Engineering* 9: 7676–7679.

Moll, Florian, Thierry Botter, Christoph Marquardt, David Pusey, Amita Shrestha, Andrew
    Reeves, Kevin Jaksch, et al. 2019. "Stratospheric QKD: feasibility analysis and free-
    space optics system concept." *Quantum Technologies and Quantum Information
    Science* V: 111670H.

O'Malley, Sean. 2019. "Vulnerability of South Korea's Undersea Cable Communications
    Infrastructure: A Geopolitical Perspective." *Korea Observer* (Institute of Korean
    Studies) 50: 309–330.

Pang, Shanqi, and Yongmei Li. 2020. "Artificial Intelligence Techniques for Cyber Security
    Applications." *International Journal of Advanced Information and Communication
    Technology*: 89–94. doi:10.46532/ijaict-2020021.

Parkinson, John B., and Damian J. J. Farnell. 2010. "Quantum magnetism." In *An Introduction
    to Quantum Spin Systems*, 135–152. Springer.

Pirandola, S., U. L. Andersen, L. Banchi, M. Berta, D. Bunandar, R. Colbeck, D. Englund,
    et al. 1906. "Advances in quantum cryptography. arXiv 2019." *arXiv preprint
    arXiv:1906.01645.*

Planat, Michel, and Patrick Solé. 2008. "Clifford groups of quantum gates, BN-pairs and
    smooth cubic surfaces." *Journal of Physics A: Mathematical and Theoretical* (IOP
    Publishing) 42: 042003.

Pradhan, Pawan Kumar, Sayan Rakshit, and Sujoy Datta. 2019. "Lattice based cryptography:
    Its applications, areas of interest & future scope." *2019* 3rd International Conference on
    Computing Methodologies and Communication (ICCMC). 988–993.

Rahim, Robbi, Nuning Kurniasih, M. Mustamam, Liesna Andriany, Usman Nasution, and
    A. H. Mu. 2018. "Combination Vigenere Cipher and One Time Pad for Data Security."
    International Journal of Engineering Technol 7: 92–94.

Rawat, A., Gupta, A., Singh, A., & Bhushan, S. 2019. "Energy conservation and Missing
    value prediction model in Wireless Sensor Network," 2019 4th International Conference
    on Internet of Things: Smart Innovation and Usages (IoT-SIU), pp. 1–5, doi: 10.1109/
    IoT-SIU.2019.8777480.

Rusca, Davide, Alberto Boaron, Marcos Curty, Anthony Martin, and Hugo Zbinden. 2018.
    "Security proof for a simplified Bennett-Brassard 1984 quantum-key-distribution pro-
    tocol." *Physical Review A* (APS) 98: 052336.

Shao, Changpeng. 2017. "Generalization of Quantum Fourier Transformation." *arXiv pre-
    print arXiv:1712.01350.*

Shinozaki, Megumi, Masato Kusanagi, Kazunori Umeda, Guy Godin, and Marc Rioux.
    2009. "Correction of color information of a 3D model using a range intensity image."
    Computer Vision and Image Understanding (Elsevier) 113: 1170–1179.

Sidhu, Jasminder S., and Pieter Kok. 2020. "Geometric perspective on quantum parameter
    estimation." *AVS Quantum Science* (American Vacuum Society) 2: 014701.

Singh, A. K., Alshehri, M., Bhushan, S., Kumar, M., Alfarraj, O., & Pardarshani, K. R. 2021.
    Secure and Energy Efficient Data Transmission Model for WSN. *intelligent automa-
    tion and soft computing*, 27(3): 761–769.

Singh, H., D. L. Gupta, and A. K. Singh. 2014. "Quantum Key Distribution Protocols: A Review." *IOSR Journal of Computer Engineering (IOSR-JCE)*.

Splendiani, Andrea, Liang Sun, Yuanbo Zhang, Tianshu Li, Jonghwan Kim, Chi-Yung Chim, Giulia Galli, and Feng Wang. 2010. "Emerging photoluminescence in monolayer MoS2." *Nano Letters* (ACS Publications) 10: 1271–1275.

Tyo, J. Scott, and Andrey S. Alenin. 2015. "Fourier Transforming Properties of Lenses." In *Field guide to linear systems in optics*, by J Scott and Andrey S Tyo, Alenin, 102. English: SPIE Press.

Upadhyay, Lav. 2018. "Quantum Cryptography: A Survey." International Conference on Innovations in Bio-Inspired Computing and Applications. 20–35.

Van Der Walt, N. 2016. *The current state of quantum cryptography, QKD, and the future of information security.* Accessed June 20, 2016. https://labs.f-secure.com/archive/the-current-state-of-quantum-cryptography-qkd-and-the-future-of-information-security/.

Venegas-Andraca, Salvador E., and J. L. Ball. 2010. "Processing images in entangled quantum systems." *Quantum Information Processing* (Springer) 9: 1–11.

Venegas-Andraca, Salvador Elías, and Sougato Bose. 2003. "Quantum computation and image processing: New trends in artificial intelligence." *IJCAI* 1563.

Wan Ishak, W. I., and Khairuddin Abdul Rahman. 2010. "Software Development for Real-Time Weed Colour Analysis." *Pertanika Journal of Science & Technology* 18.

Wang, Shuang, De-Yong He, Zhen-Qiang Yin, Feng-Yu Lu, Chao-Han Cui, Wei Chen, Zheng Zhou, Guang-Can Guo, and Zheng-Fu Han. 2019. "Beating the fundamental rate-distance limit in a proof-of-principle quantum key distribution system." *Physical Review X* (APS) 9: 021046.

Wang, Yazhen. 2012. "Quantum computation and quantum information." *Statistical Science* (Institute of Mathematical Statistics) 27: 373–394.

Wang, Yufei, Zhe Lin, Xiaohui Shen, Scott Cohen, and Garrison W. Cottrell. 2017. "Skeleton key: Image captioning by skeleton-attribute decomposition." *Proceedings of the IEEE Conference on Computer Vision and Pattern Recognition*: 7272–7281.

Wootters, William K., and Wojciech H. Zurek. 1982. "A single quantum cannot be cloned." *Nature* (Nature Publishing Group) 299: 802–803.

Yan, Fei, Abdullah M. Iliyasu, Salvador E. Venegas-Andraca, and Huamin Yang. 2015. "Video encryption and decryption on quantum computers." *International Journal of Theoretical Physics* (Springer) 54: 2893–2904.

Yang, Bo, and Xiaofeng Liao. 2018. "A new color image encryption scheme based on logistic map over the finite field ZN." *Multimedia Tools and Applications* (Springer) 77: 21803–21821.

Yao, Xi-Wei, Hengyan Wang, Zeyang Liao, Ming-Cheng Chen, Jian Pan, Jun Li, Kechao Zhang, et al. 2017. "Quantum image processing and its application to edge detection: theory and experiment." *Physical Review X* (APS) 7: 031041.

Yin, Xiaoxia, Brian Wai-Him Ng, J. Axel Zeitler, Kieu Lien Nguyen, Lynn F. Gladden, and Derek Abbott. 2010. "Local computed tomography using a THz quantum cascade laser." *IEEE Sensors Journal* (IEEE) 10: 1718–1731.

Zhang, Yi, Kai Lu, Yinghui Gao, and Mo Wang. 2013. "NEQR: a novel enhanced quantum representation of digital images." *Quantum information processing* (Springer) 12: 2833–2860.

Zhou, Nan Run, Tian Xiang Hua, Li Hua Gong, Dong Ju Pei, and Qing Hong Liao. 2015. "Quantum image encryption based on generalized Arnold transform and double random-phase encoding." *Quantum Information Processing* (Springer) 14: 1193–1213.

Zhou, Ri-Gui, Xingao Liu, and Jia Luo. 2017. "Quantum circuit realization of the bilinear interpolation method for GQIR." *International Journal of Theoretical Physics* (Springer) 56: 2966–2980.

Zhou, Tianqi, Jian Shen, Xiong Li, Chen Wang, and Jun Shen. 2018. "Quantum cryptography for the future internet and the security analysis." *Security and Communication Networks* (Hindawi) 2018.

9 Cyber Security Techniques Management

Meenu Shukla, Fatima Ziya,
Sharmila Arun, and Suraj Pal Singh

CONTENTS

DOI: 10.1201/9781003296034-9

9.1   INTRODUCTION TO CYBER SECURITY

The internet is one of the most widespread and fastest-growing areas of technological development. In today's era, many organizations like business, distributed technologies, cloud computing, and next generation are periodically changing. In the latest survey 80% of total commercial transactions are done online, so this field requires well-developed and high-quality security services for transparent transactions. The extent of cyber security stretches out not exclusively to the security of IT but also maintain the more extensive computerized networks whereupon they depend including the actual internet and basic frameworks [1].Due to the development of information technology and internet services, cyber security plays an important role. The way of protecting information and information system,database,network,and applications is protected by cyber security management with the help of procedural and technological security. Some security measures are firewalls, antivirus software, and other technological solutions for preserving confidential data and computer networks. In the latest, it was predicted that almost 670,000 new malware threats are continuously growing on the internet every day [2]. This implies more than 45 new viruses, worms, spyware, and different threats were being made each moment—more than twofold the number from January 2009.To protect against these threats, various security agencies and technologies need to evolve even faster to stay ahead of these threats.

The world has been apparently increasingly more and more dependent on the internet since it was acquainted with the majority in the mid-1990s. Organizations have made huge organization frameworks to share and oversee information about their items, sellers, and representatives with other organization areas all throughout the planet. Enterprises have expanded their degree of awareness with respect to network protection and data security of the executives, as it has been expected that these are important issues with regard to intensity and endurance in worldwide business sectors. Organizations have made large network frameworks to share and manage information about their items, sellers, and workers with other organization areas all throughout the world. These equivalent frameworks are utilized to advertise their items to shoppers and offer them to these equivalent buyers by means of their organization site or outsider merchant. The COVID-19 pandemic has likewise had an adverse effect on online protection around the world, as more associates are telecommuting, which leads to speed up advanced change in endeavors [3]. Society has become reliant upon digital frameworks across the full scope of human activities, including business, finance, medical services, energy, amusement, correspondences, and public safeguard.

9.2   CYBER SECURITY AND INFORMATION SECURITY MANAGEMENT

These days, data security is a significant worry to all organizations, as they work in a worldwide market, are profoundly IT subordinate, and have a complete on the web and advanced presence. Data security is quite difficult for the organizations, as they intend to prevent and the openness to security and protection dangers to data frameworks and systems administration foundation. Cyber security management designs a model to define an organization's policies for information security. The relationship between the goals of information security is as follows: The model is based on three rules, i.e., Confidentiality, Integrity, and Availability commonly known as the CIA triad. Figure 9.1a shows the basic three principles of information security.

- Confidentiality:It refers to only the authorized person who can access the data, and the set of the rules and procedures in organizations is defined by only the authorized person. The most widely used example where confidentiality of information is used is the credit card transaction.
- Integrity: It ensures the accuracy of the data. Integrity means securing the data from an unauthorized modification.
- Availability: It defines that information must be presented only when it is needed. The information must be available on time, fair allocation of resources over the network, and also maintain the deadlock management in the database server.
- Integrity and availability of data ensure information's trustworthiness and accuracy accessed by authorized users. There are different types of cyber-attack security issues.

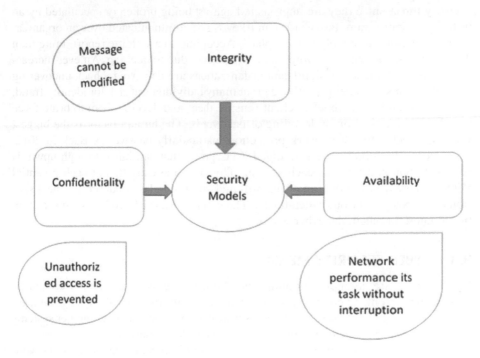

FIGURE 9.1A CIA model.

The objective of this chapter is to discuss some cyber security issues which commonly occur in the internet society. Spyware is one of the most common attacks. In these attacks, the hacker can use it to gain access to the network and confidential information. Basically, Spyware is a software program that collects information about a user without his/her knowledge. Attackers can also use this software to install other programs like keyloggers that can record user passwords and user record history. The variation of the data using a laptop or a personal computer is shown in Figure 9.1b The graph shows the percentage of PCs estimated to have spyware/adware and the percentage of PCs lacking data protection [2].

Worms are another cyber security issue. It is a self-replicating virus and spreading in a whole system. This type of virus consumes large memory as well as bandwidth. There are different types of worms like email worms, internet worms, message worms, file-sharing network worms, and computer worms exploiting the vulnerability of PC and mobile devices. Over the recent years, both worms and viruses have become a serious issue. The 1988 Morris worm helped the web local area to be industrious in looking for possible dangers of risky worms and has prompted a few kinds of safety hardware to be introduced from antivirus programming to interruption discovery frameworks. These viruses and worms are effective due to the security weaknesses that PCs and gadgets have that can be misused; the web is only a passage for a portion of this action.

Passwords are known as secret words or phrases used by different organizations and multiple sites to identify the users. Passwords are unfortunately an enormous security threat since they are unprotected against being broken or speculated by an individual or program. Passwords can likewise be communicated over an organization or put away unreliably in someplace. According to a Deloitte report, more than 90% of user-generated passwords will be insecure due to hacking. An ever-increasing number of frequently significant organizations are declaring a hack uncovering data of patients and clients putting a great many individuals at risk for identity fraud. Passwords can be secure when clients ensure them and develop them to brute force attack and investigation or decoding of passwords. The human factor is the biggest virus in practically all network protection, particularly passwords. Back in 2012, a secret key breaking master divulged a PC group that can burn through upwards of 350 billion speculations each second. This machine can attempt each potential Windows password in the run of the mill undertaking in less than 6 h.The next section describes the various cyberattacks. The graph in Figure 9.1a shows the variation of the latest threats in the cyber world.

9.3   CYBER SECURITY MEASURES

Cyberattacks are attempts to obtain unauthorized access to a personal computer, computing system, or computer system networks with the aim of causing damage. The attacker's goal is to disable, disrupt, destroy, or gain control of computer systems in order to change, delete, manipulate, or steal data/information stored on them.

Cyberattacks have grown increasingly common in recent years, coinciding with the digitalization of businesses and organizations.

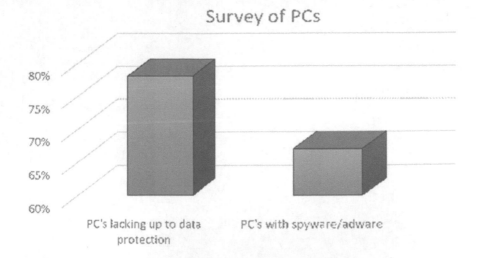

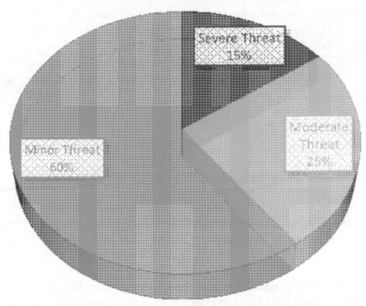

FIGURE 9.1B The latest threats.

Any individual or group of individuals can conduct a cyberattack from anywhere, employing one or more different attack techniques with the goal of destroying the target system. In most cases, an attacker assaults a system or a victim's computer, and after gaining access to the victim's computer, the attacker can either destroy or modify sensitive data/information. The majority of cyberattackers nowadays don't

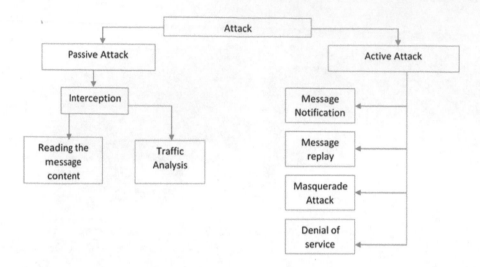

FIGURE 9.2   Various types of attacks.

want to harm your computer; instead of taking your money, they want access to your personal information or your login credentials. We may use a variety of innovative techniques or tools to prevent these types of assaults. [4]

In terms of concept, cybersecurity vulnerabilities may be split into two categories: passive attacks and active threats, as shown in Figure 9.2. The main differences between these two groups briefly, as well as how to characterize each of them briefly.

9.3.1 PASSIVE ATTACK

In a passive attack, an attacker monitors a system and scans for open ports vulnerabilities and other risks. The main objective of the attacker is to steal confidential information. The attacker has no authority to make any updating or changes in the particular data. The attacker can collect the information in a number of ways when it infiltrated the network. The attacker can use many techniques by which they can collect the data.

- In a *foot-printing* passive attack, the intruder will try to acquire a large set of data so that it can be used later to attack the target system. For Example when an intruder records network traffic using a packet analyzer tool, such as Wireshark for analyzing it later.
- Installing a *keylogger* is another sort of passive attack, where an intruder waits for the user to enter their credentials and after getting all the records the attacker will use those details in further possible ways.

The two most common use cases of passive attacks are:

9.3.1.1 Traffic Analysis

In this attack, an attacker analyzes the *traffic*, determines the location, identifies communicating hosts and observes the occurrence or frequency also analyses the length of the messages exchanged.

9.3.1.2 Release of Message Contents

In this type, an attacker monitors insecure communication, like data which is transferred through unencrypted channels also can intercept confidential information.

Another form of passive attacks includes "passive reconnaissance," in which an attacker wants to compromise the system or network where all the confidential information is gathered without directly sending any data packets that create network traffic. An attacker can fetch most of the sensitive data using this technique. An example of sensitive information includes Aadhar card details. Sometimes the hacker tries to compromise the security of the system's server by using passive reconnaissance techniques. This leads to exposure of sensitive details like Aadhar card, PAN card, etc. to the dark web. These details can further be used to extract information regarding a person's social networking accounts.

It is very difficult and sometimes becomes impossible to detect the passive attack because in any case it does not involve modification of the data. However, we can implement some protective counter measures to prevent it, including: We can use some encryption techniques to hide messages and make them in an unreadable form for unknown recipients. Some encryption techniques can be implemented in this case:

- Symmetric keys:
  The symmetric keys are still having a problem in exchanging the secret key confidentially. As these are the same key at both the ends;that is,the sender and the receiver are having the same secret key to exchange.
- Public-key encryption:
  In PKE each party involved in communication and they have two types of keys, one is *public key* which is known by both the users and another one is *private key* which is a secret key. An example of this type is using SSL certificates, SSL; more commonly called Transport Layer Security (TLS) is a protocol for encoding Internet traffic and verifying the server's identity. Any website with an HTTPS web address uses SSL/TLS certificates.

Figure 9.3 depicts the passive attack in which there are two people in the communication channel, Bob and Alice but due to this attack a hacker can steal the information and without any changes by the attacker the information loses its confidentiality.

9.3.2 ACTIVE ATTACK

An active attack involves using information gathered during a passive attack to compromise a user or network.In a two-way communication, data transmitted from one

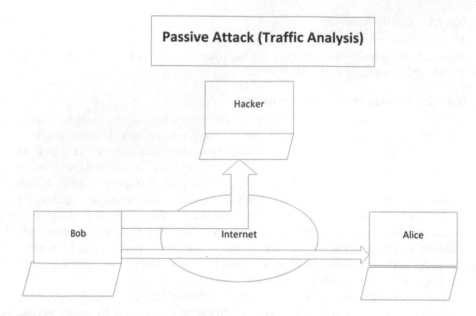

FIGURE 9.3　Passive attack.

end could be captured and altered; hence, the confidentiality, as well as integrity, could be compromised.

There are many types of active attacks.

- Denial of service (DoS)
- Distributed denial of service (DDoS)
- Session replay
- Masquerade

The *Denial-of-service* (*DoS*) and *Distributed denial-of-service* (*DDoS*) attacks are also examples of active attacks, both of which work by avoiding authorized users from retrieving a specific resource on a network (for example, flooding a web server with more traffic than it can handle). In a *session replay attack*, an attacker steals a valid session ID of a user and reuses it to impersonate an authorized user to perform fraudulent transactions/activities. In a *masquerade attack*, an intruder will pretend to be another user to gain access to the restricted area in the system. There are some protective measures against this type of attacks which are as follows:

1. A random session key can be generated which is only valid for one transaction at a time, this should effectively prevent a malicious user from re-transmitting the original message after the original session ends.
2. Using one-time passwords helps to authenticate transactions and sessions between communicating parties. This guarantees that even though an

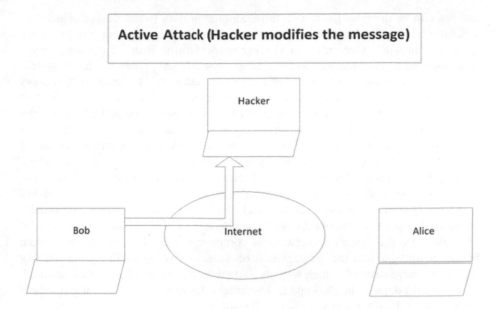

FIGURE 9.4 Active attack.

attacker was successful in recording and retransmitting the captured message again, the associated password will expire by that time.
3. Using Kerberos authentication protocol (usually used in Microsoft Windows
Active Directory) supports many countermeasures against different types
of replay attacks.

Figure 9.4 depicts the active attack in which there are two people in the communication channel, Bob and Alice, but due to an attack the hacker can steal the information
also can be able to do modifications and transmit the compromised and illegitimate
data to Alice. Here, in this sort of communication, Alice doesn't know the changes
that occurred by the attacker. So, in the active attack, the information loses its confidentiality and integrity too.

There are many more types of cyberattacks, which are as follows:

9.4   TYPES OF CYBER ATTACKS

There are different types of cyberattacks, which have occurred more frequently in
the cyber world. Some cyber threats are discussed below.

9.4.1   DoS AND DDoS ATTACKS

A denial-of-service (DoS) attack is a special kind of attack in which the perpetrator generates unusual traffic and tries to make the resources unavailable to intended
users. This will lead to either shut down a machine or crash the entire network. DoS

attacks can be done by flooding a large amount of data to the target computer or machine with traffic or directing the information which leads to crash of the entire system or network. Generally, an attacker renders traffic within a particular range as compared to the bandwidth of the target system [5,6]. When the target system overflows due to the consumption of maximum resources, the entire system slows down and thereafter the targeted system becomes insecure. The foremost reason of this kind of attack is to make the targeted system insecure first and then make the network slow down, which will ultimately lead toward crashing the whole network.

There is one more variant of denial-of-service attack that is *distributed denial of service attack (DDoS)*. The DDoS attack is a more advanced type of attack which generally executes at a large scale. In this attack, the perpetrator uses multiple compromised systems also known as Zombies or Bots to trigger the target system. DDoS is generally more dangerous than the DoS attack. These sorts of attacks are usually faced by big corporate networks with the intention to give the maximum financial loss. As once the system or network is compromised by the attacker, the system becomes unstable and the services will be unresponsive, this will lead to shutting down the entire network which will also affect the reputation of the organization.

Figure 9.5 depicts the DoS and DDos attacks. There are two different methods of DoS attacks: flooding services or crashing services.

The system is flooded with traffic on the server which results to slow down all the services rendered by the server to its users, and at last this will lead to discontinuing all the services. Popular DoS attacks include the following.

9.4.1.1   ICMP Flood

In this type of attack, the attacker spoofs an IP address of the system. Now, using the spoofed IP address, the attacker generates a large amount of PING requests to the targeted host. These requests are pretty much high in numbers and due to this the targeted host starts flooding during the PING replies. The replies are in big

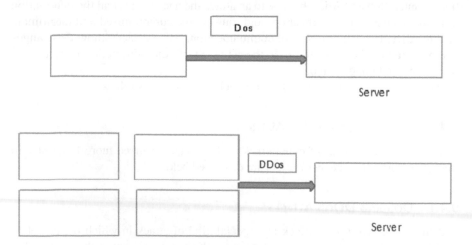

FIGURE 9.5   DoS and DDoS attack.

numbers so that the real requests are altered. This kind of DDoS attack is usually performed on a public network is known asa smurf attack.

9.4.1.2   Ping of Death

In a ping of death attack, an attacker sends the request of IP packets continuously to the targetcd system. Due to the surplus limit of the IP protocol, the targeted system overflows and is then not able to handle the load. As a result, this will leads to the failure of an operating system [7].

9.4.1.3   SYN Flood

Synchronize (SYN) flood is also known as Transmission Control Protocol (TCP) SYN flood attack. It is a type of distributed denial of service (DDoS) attack which affects the function of TCP three-way handshake in order to make the resources unavailable on the targeted server and rest it as idle mode. In this sort of attack, an attacker creates and sends a fake TCP SYN packet request to the targeted host. Now, the host issues those packets to the particular resources to establish the connection and complete the handshake procedure with those packets. Due to the high number of fake TCP SYN packets, the targeted system is unable to identify the difference between real and fake requests [8]. At last, the real packet request is altered and the fake packet request is processed. In this way, the targeted system completes its three-way handshake with fake TCP SYN packets and which ultimately exploits the handshake mechanism.

9.4.1.4   Buffer Overflow Attack

When an excessive amount of data is fed into the fixed-length buffer; the capacity of the memory buffer is overrun which is called buffer overflow attack. As a result, the excess information can overflow into contiguous memory space, which will corrupt or overwrite the data[9]. The buffer overflow attack will crash the system and also creates a way for the attacker to run the random code which leads to the malicious action. Many programming languages are also vulnerable to buffer overflow attacks.

9.4.2   MITM Attack

A man-in-the-middle (MITM) attack is a type of eavesdropping, when anattacker places himself in the existing conversation happening between the two parties with the intention to capture the information about one of the parties, pretending as if a normal communication. It looks like the information float as in their normal behavior. The main target of an attacker is to steal the financial credentials of the user such as login credentials, account details,and credit card numbers.

The attacker uses the captured information for many purposes, including identity theft, unapproved fund transfers, or an illegitimate password change. In effect on this, the attacker is just smurfing the communication between the two parties. It is the same as when an envelope comes for you and the delivery man or someone else already read the content and an open envelope is delivered to you.

Figure 9.6 depicts an MITM attack, where a perpetrator just establishes a new connection while discarding the old and spying on all conversations between the user and a web application.

There are many ways to prevent yourself and your system from MITM attacks. One of the ways to mitigate the MITM attacks is to usea strong encryption algorithm on your access points or to use a virtual private network (VPN).

9.4.3 PHISHING ATTACKS

Phishing starts with malicious or fraudulent emails that look like coming from an authentic source, with an intention to grab legitimate information from the target. It is just designed and prepared to lure a victim. The content and data sharing is made to look as it comes from a trusted sender. An attacker combines social engineering and technology to execute an attack. In maximum cases, the target may not understand that they have been compromised by someone, and by this the phisher can take the advantage of this attack. Figure 9.7 shows the phishing attack.

By carefully scrutinizing the emails, you open and the links you click on, you may prevent phishing attempts from succeeding. Pay attention to email headers and avoid clicking on anything that appears to be suspicious.

9.4.4 SPEAR-PHISHING ATTACKS

A spear-phishing assault employs email spoofing, which involves forging the information in the email's "From" section to make it appear as though it came from a legitimate sender. This may be someone the target knows and trusts, such as a friend from the same social circle, a close coworker, or a business associate. In this case, attackers may employ website cloning to make the message appear genuine.

The attacker uses website cloning to imitate a reputable website in order to deceive the victim. Because the target believes the website is legitimate, they are

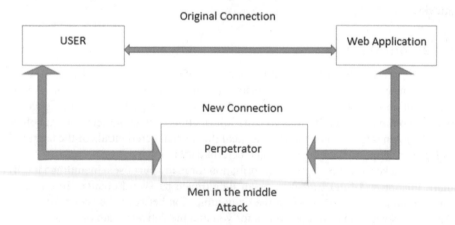

FIGURE 9.6 Man-in-the-middle attack.

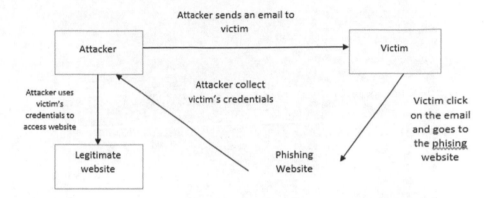

FIGURE 9.7 Phishing attack.

at ease while providing personal information. Spear-phishing attacks, like conventional phishing attempts, may be avoided by thoroughly verifying all fields of an email and ensuring that users do not click on any link whose destination cannot be verified as real.

9.4.5 RANSOM WARE

Until the victim agrees to pay some ransom to the attackers, their computers are captivated by the attacker. Only after receiving the payment by victim, they are given instructions to establish control of their computer by the attackers. As the ransom is demanded by the attacker from the victim in order to free their computer, hence it is named "ransom ware."

Generally the ransom software is downloaded by the target or victim from email attachment links or via an unknown or insecure website. These types of malwares are created so as to take the advantage of the flaws that cannot be rectified by the system manufacturer or by any IT staff. The victim's workstation is then encrypted by these malwares. The attack can also be utilized to target numerous groups of victims by limiting access to many machines or the central server that is critical to corporate operations.

In Figure 9.8, we can easily see the attacker demands some ransom from the target, and in order to take the data back with full of confidentiality, the victim's paysthe ransom amount to the attacker. One can also prevent many ransom ware attacks by inspecting the data packets deeply by using artificial intelligence.

9.4.6 PASSWORD ATTACK

The attacker can also attempt to interrupt the networks' traffic in order to obtain credentials that the network has not encrypted. Social engineering can be used by the attackers in order to convince the victim in entering their passwords to resolve the allegedly "critical" problem.

FIGURE 9.8   Ransom ware attack.

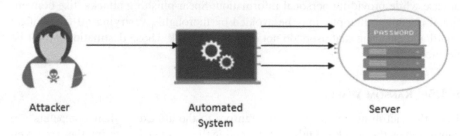

| Attacker | Automated System | Server |

FIGURE 9.9   Brute force attack.

In some circumstances, the password used by the user can be guessed by the attacker very easily, mainly when the user uses the default or the passwords like"87654321" that are easy to remember. Bruteforce methods are also frequently used by attackers to guess passwords. In order to gain the passwords, the attacker usually uses a combination of their personal details. To decrypt their password, for example, their names, birthday dates, anniversaries, or other private data could be assembled in numerous combinations.

A bruteforce password breach can take advantage of information that people provide on social media accounts. Passwords are sometimes formed using the individual's hobbies, particular hobbies, pet's name, and child's name, making them reasonably easy to guess for the attack. A *dictionary attack* can also be used by the attackers to figure out the password of the user. The dictionary attack is the method of guessing a target's password by using commonly used words and phrases, similarly the ones found in a dictionary.

As shown in Figure 9.9, the brute force attacks where an attacker tries to intercept the sequence of passwords using hit-and-trial concept and after entering multiple trials the attacker got the right password. There are many ways to avoid these sorts of attacks. Setting up a *lock-out policy* is an efficient way to prevent bruteforce and dictionary password attacks. After a specified number of failed tries, one is automatically locked out and cannot attempt again to access the device, applications, or website. With a lock-out policy, the attacker has only a few attempts before being denied access. The attackers can attempt only a few times before they are denied access with these lock-out policies.

9.4.7 SQL INJECTION ATTACK

The SQL injection attacks are the type of flaws in online security that let the attackers intervene in the database queries of the web-based application. Through this, the attackers can view the victim's data that is normally invisible to the outsiders.

The SQL attacks contain SQL queries that the user has sent to a database in the commands format on the server. The instruction is then inserted into the database replacing something else that would ordinarily be there, such as the passwords or the login. The command is then executed on the database server, and the systems are compromised. When the SQL injection is successful, it can lead to the exposure of personal and sensitive data, as well as change or loss of critical information. An attacker can also run administrator's commands such as the shutdown that can cause the termination of the database functioning.

In Figure 9.10, it shows the SQL injection attack. Use the least-privileged approach to protect yourself from a SQL injection attack. Only those who really require access to important databases are allowed in with the least-privileged architecture. Even if a user has power or influence inside the company, they may be denied access to certain network regions if their job does not need it.

9.4.8 DNS SPOOFING

The hackers redirect the traffic to a spoofed or false website by altering the Domain Name Server (DNS) records,it is domain name server spoofing. After the target is on the fake site, they may share their personal data which can be misused or traded by the hackers. They also try to make their opponents' company look bad by creating a low-level site with offensive and provocative content.

In Figure 9.11, it shows how the DNS spoofing attack works. While on that site, the user thinks that they are visiting a genuine site, and the attackers try to take the advantage of this fact and then attempt to commit crimes in the name of another company. We need to make sure that our DNS server is updated in order to prevent DNS spoofing. The main aim of attackers is to exploit the vulnerabilities in the DNS

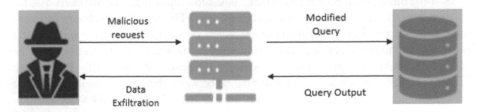

FIGURE 9.10 SQL injection attack.

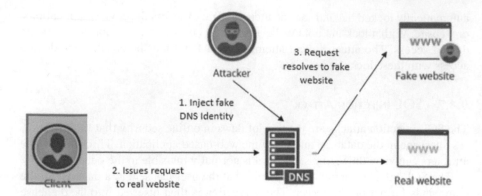

FIGURE 9.11   DNS spoofing attack.

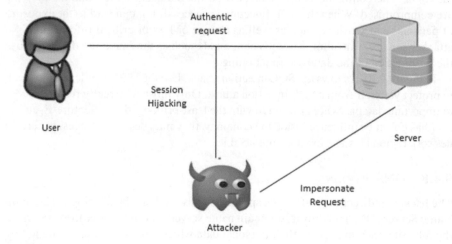

FIGURE 9.12   Session hijacking.

servers and the current version of the software contains the fix, which is the closer identified vulnerabilities.

9.4.9   SESSION HIJACKING

One of the most common MITM attacks is session hijacking. The attackers assume control over the session between client and server. The server is unable to differentiate between the attacker and the client as the attacker is using the same internet protocol (IP) address as the client without any suspicion. As the server is using the same IP address as clients' for their identity verification,it makes this attack more effective. Once the connection is established between the server and the client, the server will not be able to suspect even if the attackers' IP address ID added partly.

Figure 9.12 depicts a session hijacking attack, where all the messages are seen by the attacker and the innocent user even doesn't know about the suspicious activity done by an attacker. A VPN is used to access the servers that are business critical in order to avoid the session hijack. Thus, all communication is encrypted, and the attackers can't access the safe passage made by the VPN.

9.4.10 BRUTE FORCE ATTACK

The bruteforce attack is named after the word "brutish" or basic method used by the attacks. The login credentials of the person with access authority are guessed by the attackers. They are in, once they guessed it correct.

Bots are used by attackers for cracking the credential, which often takes time and is hard. The list of predicted or guessed credentials is provided to the bots to gain access. The attacker waits while the bots try each predicted credential. The attackers have access once the right credentials are cracked.

Figure 9.13 shows how an attacker tries multiple combinations of passwords for applying brute force attack. We should have lock-out policy as part of our authorization security architecture in order to prevent these attacks. The login credentials get locked after a certain number of failed attempts by the user. No one can evade this lockout even if they try it from another device with a different IP address, as the account is "freeze." Using random passwords is encouraged for prevention with no regular words, dates, or number sequence. Now, it may take attackers years to guess the correct password using the software, which makes it more effective and easy.

9.5 CYBER SECURITY RISK MANAGEMENT

Cyber risk management is the process of detecting, examining, assessing, and addressing cyber security threats. The term "cyber risk management" has been defined since the starting of the computer age in the name of computer security, information security, information security risk management, and cyber security. In 2013, Von Solms and Van Niekerk [10] defined the difference between cyber security and information security. Information security is the protection of information which is stored inside or outside cyberspace whereas cybersecurity is related to information within cyberspace. The term cyber risk management is a deal with the risk management process or steps utilized to manage cyber risk. Risk management is the process of recognizing the possibility of risk, assessing the impact of those risks, and making proper planning to mitigate the risk becomes reality [11]. Risk management plays significant for every organization, no matter the size of the industry to develop a plan for cybersecurity management.

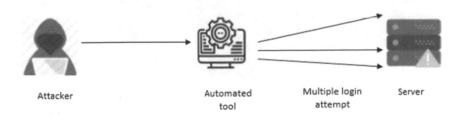

Attacker   Automated   Multiple login   Server
               tool   attempt

FIGURE 9.13 Brute force attack.

9.5.1 Cyber Security Risk Management Strategy

Cybersecurity risk management helps to mitigate cyber risk and preventattacks. It also increases the business reputation by preventing cyberattacks as well as reducing costs and protecting revenue [12]. (Figure 9.14 shows the different strategy of cyber risk management system)

9.5.2 Cyber Risk Management Process

The cyber risk management process has six different stages such as identify,analyze, evaluate, prioritize, treat, and monitor. (Figure 9.15 shows the different process of cyber risk management.)

The following steps are followed to manage the cyber risks [13]

1. **Environmental Scanning**
2. **Identification of Risk:** Identify the risk which compromises cyber security
3. **Analysis of Risk:** Analyze the severity of the risk by frequent assessing and its impact
4. **Evaluate:** Evaluate the risk level is acceptable or not
5. **Priorities:** Priorities the level of risk
6. **Risk Treatment:** Decide how to respond to each risk
7. **Risk Monitoring and Review process**

In this chapter, Steps 2–4 are mainly focused on managing cyber risk.Identification, analysis, and treatment of risk are the heart of the risk management process.

FIGURE 9.14   Cyber risk management strategy.

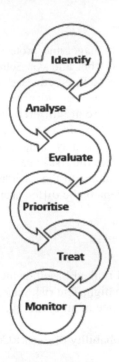

FIGURE 9.15 Cyber risk management process.

- **Risk Identification**

The cyber risk identification process researched initiated from the IT field.One method to detect cyberattack is whether they affect confidentiality, availability, or integrity of information or non-information system [7]. For example, the confidentiality of the message is affected by data breach; availability of the information is affected by denial of service and ransomware attacks, and integrity of the information is attacked by website defacement while confidentiality and integrity are affected by phishing attacks. In risk management, one of the biggest challenges is the identification of risk. Initially, identify the assets (data/information) and identify the threats to the data or information and vulnerabilities to the threats.

- **Identifying Threats**

The threats are everywhere, hacking, environmental flooding, business-related threat, insider threats, etc.

- **Identifying Vulnerabilities**

The next step after identified the threat is to identify the weakness of the overall cybersecurity environment which could be vulnerable to the threats.

9.5.3 RISK ANALYSIS

Risk analysis helps to identify, manage, and protect the data and assets that could be vulnerable to a cyberattack. Gerber and von Solms [14] addressed the difficulty of analyzing the risk with respect to three eras such as computercentric, IT centric, and information centric. Once the risks are identified,then the risk management process needs to be implemented. There are different strategies and are considered for different types of risks such as risk avoidance, risk reduction, risk sharing, and risk retaining [15]. The risk assessment is a systematic approach of risk analysis which identifies, quantifies, and prioritizes the risks against the criteria. Risk assessment is performed whenever there is a change in the environment, requirement of security, and risk situation. Figure 9.16 depicts the different approaches of risk management. (Figure 9.16).

9.5.4 RISK EVALUATE

Risk need to be prioritized and ranked based on the severity of the risk. The risks that are rated depends on low to high. The risk value can be estimated with the help of the probability of the occurrence of an event [14].

$$\text{Risk value} = \text{Probability of event} \times \text{Cost of the event}$$

ISO 31000:2009 is published in 2009 which provides standard guidelines for an effective risk management. This standard is used by different types of organizations to mitigate different types of risks such as financial, safety, any other project risks, etc.It defines risk as the effect of uncertainty on goals.

9.5.5 CYBERSECURITY RISK MANAGEMENT FOR APPLICATION MODEL

9.5.5.1 Cyber Security Risk Management for Internet of Things

A cyber physical system consists of many physical components which have cyber-capability with high interconnectivity. It is used in many critical national infrastructures such as communications, transportation, healthcare, and power system. One of

FIGURE 9.16 Risk management approaches.

the major threats for the physical system is cyber security threats due to complexity, communication system integration, computing, interdependencies among different systems, etc. Cyber security threat causes various risks which affect the infrastructure including performance and production degradation, unavailability of services, and violation of the regulations [15, 16, 17-21].

The internet of things (IoT) is an essential component for smart cities, smart grids, smart health, smart manufacturing, driverless car, drones, etc. A massive number of devices are connected into the IoT networks [9–11]. The hackers and attackers access the sensitive data and critical infrastructure from an IoT network due to a lack of security features. It could not be possible for an organization to take an effective decision about IoT cyber risk management without the IoT cyber security risk management framework. Lee [16] proposed four-layer IoT cyber risk management framework to a moderate cybersecurity risk for organizations and users for deploying secured IoT systems. The cybersecurity risk management framework layer has IoT cyber ecosystem, cyber infrastructure layer, risk assessment layer, and performance layer [22].

9.5.5.2   CyberSecurity Risk Management for Blockchain

Blockchain technology has become a paradigm shift in business revolution/ transaction. A blockchain is a data structure which records the transaction in the form of a chain and appended to every participant's ledger. Blockchain is a distributed digital ledger of transactions by removing centralized data management. Ituses a hash function to record the transactions with immutable cryptographic techniques. A substantial growth of the use of internet-based technologies have exposed to malicious attacks.In blockchain, the data are distributed throughout the entire computer network. Giscomo *et al.* [12] discussed the seriousness of the damage and the list of security breaches involving blockchain since 2011. Huru Hasanova *et al.* [11] described the classification of blockchain risks as double spending, 51% attack or gold finger, wallet security, flaw in PoS and DPoS, malleability attack, block producer collude, king of the ether throne, Blockchain 3.0 vulnerabilities, attacks against hyper ledger fabric, exploit law voter turnout, etc. The risk of blockchain is classified under three categories: smart contract risks, value transfer risks, and standard risks. Blockchain technology transforms human-based trust model into the algorithm-based trust model which leads to risks. In order to mitigate the risk, the organization should consider a risk management strategy and control framework [23]. Figure 9.17 shows the different components of risk managemen framework for vlockchain. (Figure 9.17).

9.5.5.3   CyberSecurity Risks in Health Facilities

The integration of digital technology in the health field increases the precision in healthcare data; still the advancement in cyber security measures is required. According to the report submitted by IBM in 2016, data breaches are increasing day by day in the healthcare industry since 2010. The patient private healthcare information in the individual medical file is blood group, name, date of birth, genetic information, past surgeries information, history of medical treatment, insurance, service

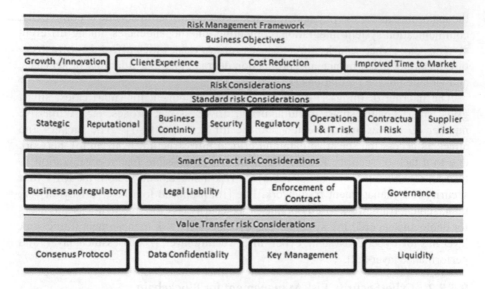

FIGURE 9.17   Components of risk management framework for block chain.

provider information, etc. The healthcare information accessed by the criminals is based on particular interests and compromises of the private data. In 2017, the United National Health System Hospital (UNHSH) reported the Wannacry ransomware attacks [13]. Due to this attack, all the treatment plans are delayed, rerouted the incoming ambulance because of lost information access from the hospitaland operation delays. The cyberattack affects the reputation and revenue of hospital and health facilities. Cybersecurity in the health field is very unique due to the sensitive patient's information at risk. John Riggi [24] suggested that toconsider cyber risk is enterprise risk. Cyber adversaries begin attack on a healthcare organization, which is not a technological hack, but rather than psychological harm when private informationis compromised.

The risk can be calculated based on quantitative and qualitative approaches. The quantitative risk management for healthcare cyber security report was published in 2020. The formula applied to calculate the risk is given by Bhushan *et al.* [13, 25].

$$RISK = (T + V + I) \times (P + V) \tag{9.2}$$

where T is the threat, V is the vulnerability, I is the impact, P is the probability, and V is the velocity.

Some of the ways to mitigate the cyberattacks are health workers need to understand the cyber hygiene as important as medical hygiene to protect patients; another way is enterprise cyber risk management is integrate and align with cyber risk management.To enhance the role of risk management, healthcare facilities need to adopt the enterprise risk management (ERM). ERM also follows the traditional aspects of risk management such as safety of patient and liability.

The key components of performance management of risk management in health-care is identify risk, quantify and prioritize risk, investigate and report sentinel events, perform compliance reporting, capture and learn from near misses and good catches, etc.

9.6 SUMMARY

In this chapter, we discussed different types of cyberattacks, their countermeasures, and the approaches to prevent these sorts of vulnerabilities. With the help of this chapter, we also get to know about many techniques to avoid the risk which is associated with cyberattacks. In future, many more digital attacks can take place and among those attacks some of them can be identified before it happens and can be controlled by the expert using advance techniques or encryption algorithms.

Risk which is associated with the digital transaction may be much more vulnerable to attacks. Various types of risk can affect a person in day-to-day life, like transactions through debit cards, credit cards, and internet banking. If these transactions did not perform through proper channels, their credentials may be compromised and can be used for any unauthenticated future transactions. To mitigate these risks, risk analysis is an important task in cyber or digital security.

REFERENCES

1. Nygard K.E., Rastogi A., Ahsan M., Satyal R. (2021) Dimensions of Cybersecurity Risk Management. In: Daimi K., Peoples C. (eds) *Advances in Cybersecurity Management.* Springer, Cham, doi: 10.1007/978-3-030-71381-2_17
2. A. Alahmari and B. Duncan (2020). Cybersecurity Risk Management in Small and Medium-Sized Enterprises: A Systematic Review of Recent Evidence. 2020 International Conference on Cyber Situational Awareness, Data Analytics and Assessment (CyberSA), pp. 1–5, doi: 10.1109/CyberSA49311.2020.9139638.
3. Kim-Kwang Raymond Choo, Keke Gai, Luca Chiaraviglio, Qing Yang. (2021). A multidisciplinary approach to Internet of Things (IoT) cybersecurity and risk management. *Computers & Security*, 102, 102136, ISSN 0167-4048, doi: 10.1016/j.cose.2020.102136.
4. Marotta, A., & McShane, M. (2018). Integrating a proactive technique into a holistic cyber risk management approach. *Risk Management and Insurance Review*, 21(3), 435–452.
5. S. K. Punia and F. Ziya (2019). Study on MAC Protocols and Attacks: A Review. 2019 6th International Conference on Computing for Sustainable Global Development (INDIACom), 2019, pp. 621–625.
6. Yong-Woon Kim. (2018). Trends in Research on the Security of Medical Information in Korea: Focused on Information Privacy Security in Hospitals. *Healthcare Information Research*, 24(1), 61–68. Published online January 31, 2018, doi: 10.4258/hir.2018.24.1.61
7. A. N. Jahromi, S. Hashemi, A. Dehghantanha, R. M. Parizi and K. -K. R. Choo. (Oct. 2020). An Enhanced Stacked LSTM Method With No Random Initialization for Malware Threat Hunting in Safety and Time-Critical Systems. *IEEE Transactions on Emerging Topics in Computational Intelligence*, 4(5), 630–640, doi: 10.1109/TETCI.2019.2910243.
8. Lilli, E. (2021). Redefining deterrence in cyberspace: Private sector contribution to national strategies of cyber deterrence. *Contemporary Security Policy*, 1–26.

9. Mazzoccoli, A., & Naldi, M. (2020). Robustness of optimal investment decisions in mixed insurance/investment cyber risk management. *Risk Analysis*, 40(3), 550–564.
10. Kamiya, S., Kang, J. K., Kim, J., Milidonis, A., & Stulz, R. M. (2020). Risk management, firm reputation, and the impact of successful cyberattacks on target firms. *Journal of Financial Economics*.
11. In Lee, Cybersecurity: Risk management framework and investment cost analysis. (2021). *Business Horizons*, 64(5), 659–671. ISSN 0007-6813, doi: 10.1016/j.bushor. 2021.02.022.
12. Martin Eling. (2021). Cyber Risk management: History and future research directions. *Risk Management and Insurance*, Wiley, 24, 93–125.
13. S. Bhushan, P. Kumar, A. Kumar and V. Sharma. (2016). Scantime antivirus evasion and malware deployment using silent-SFX. International Conference on Advances in Computing, Communication, & Automation (ICACCA) (Spring), 2016, pp. 1–4, doi: 10.1109/ICACCA.2016.7578894.
14. Ravi Sharma. (June-2012). Study of Latest Emerging Trends on Cyber Security and its challenges to Society. *International Journal of Scientific & Engineering Research*, 3(6). 1 ISSN 2229-5518 IJSER © 2012
15. Huru Hasanova (January 2019). A survey on blockchain cybersecurity vulnerabilities and possible countermeasures. *International Journal of Network Management*. https:// onlinelibrary.wiley.com/doi/10.1002/nem.2060
16. Lee, I. (2020). Internet of Things (IoT) Cybersecurity: Literature Review and IoT Cyber Risk Management. *Future Internet*, 12, 157, doi: 10.3390/fi12090157
17. Atul M. Tongel, Suraj S. Kasture, Surbhi, R. Chaudhari. (May–June2013). Cyber security: challenges for society- literature review. *IOSR Journal of Computer Engineering (IOSR-JCE)*, 12(2).
18. Rossouw von Solms, & Johan van Niekerk (2013). From information security to cyber security. *Computers & Security*, 38, 97–102, ISSN 0167-4048, doi: 10.1016/j. cose.2013.04.004.
19. Diwakar M., Singh P., Kumar P., Tiwari K., Bhushan S., Kaushik M. (2022) Secure Authentication in WLAN Using Modified Four-Way Handshake Protocol. In: Tomar A., Malik H., Kumar P., Iqbal A. (eds) *Machine Learning, Advances in Computing, Renewable Energy and Communication. Lecture Notes in Electrical Engineering*, vol 768. Springer, Singapore.
20. G. De Nicola (Jul2021). On the Intraday Behavior of Bitcoin. *Ledger*, 6.
21. Mohan V. Pawar, & J. Anuradha. (2015). Network Security and Types of Attacks in Network Procedia Computer Science. 48, 503–506, ISSN 1877-0509, doi: 10.1016/j. procs.2015.04.126.
22. Singh A.K., Bhushan S., Vij S. (2021) A Brief Analysis and Comparison of DCT- and DWT-Based Image Compression Techniques. In: Goyal D., Bălaş V.E., Mukherjee A., Hugo C.de Albuquerque V., Gupta A.K. (eds) Information Management and Machine Intelligence. ICIMMI 2019. Algorithms for Intelligent Systems.
23. Malhotra, A., & Kubowicz Malhotra, C. (2011). Evaluating customer information breaches as service failures: An event study approach. *Journal of Service Research*, 14(1), 44–59.
24. Garg, A.A.S., Kumar P., Madhukar M., Loyola-González O., Kumar M. Blockchain-based online education content ranking. Educ Inf Technol (Dordr). 2021 Nov 15:1–23. doi: 10.1007/o10639-021-10797-5. Epub ahead of print. PMID: 34803468; PMCID: PMC8591431.
25. Mariana Gerber. (February, 2005). Management of risk in the information age. *Computers and Security*, 24(1), pp. 16–30, doi: 10.1016/j.cose.2004.11.002

10 Quantum Cryptography and Quantum Key Distribution

Chindiyababy, Ramkumar Jayaraman, and Manoj Kumar

CONTENTS

10.1 INTRODUCTION

This chapter describes the concept of quantum cryptography and quantum key distribution by explaining their basic protocols. Generally, cryptography is a process of securing information and converting plaintext into ciphertext so that authorized one who has the right "key" can only read it. The basic cryptographic process is shown in Figure 10.1. It illustrates the basic cryptographic process. Initially, the plaintext (the original text from the sender which needs to be secured from the unreliable channel) is converted into ciphertext (unreadable until it is converted to plaintext) by the encryption algorithm using an encryption key. Further, it will be decrypted by the decryption algorithm using a decryption key. Finally, the receiver will get the original plaintext.

DOI: 10.1201/9781003296034-10

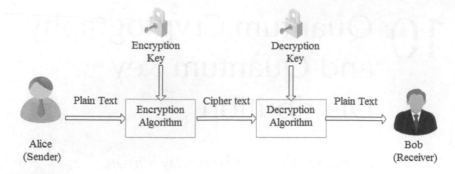

FIGURE 10.1   Basic cryptographic process.

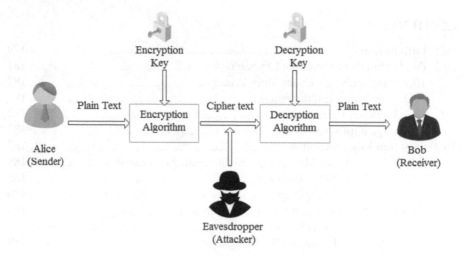

FIGURE 10.2   Basic model of cryptosystem.

Let us consider a simple cryptosystem model that ensures the confidentiality of transmitted information. The basic model of a cryptosystem is shown in Figure 10.2. It shows that a sender sends some secret data to a receiver. It will be converted into ciphertext. The eavesdropper may attempt to access the data, but it is difficult to extract the data on the communication channel. The main goal of this cryptographic system is that both the sender and the receiver only know the plaintext at the end of the process. In most classical cryptosystems, this is difficult to handle but it can be easily handled by a quantum cryptosystem.

When we come into quantum cryptography, it is a cryptographic technology that uses quantum physics to protect data resources secure. For example, the trust made by commercial enterprises and banks to hold our credit card details and other information secure while performing online business transactions. Encryption strategy: Can't you ensure the security of personal information? Of course, cybercriminals have been working hard to gain access to protected data, but hackers won't wait for the quantum system to initiate the process because they are collecting our encrypted data to decrypt it when the quantum system is ready. This will not happen when quantum encryption is used, because our data cannot be hacked (Rothe, 2002). Creating copies of unknown quantum states can be prevented by the quantum no-cloning theorem. In quantum computers, the information is stored in the form of qubits instead of classical bits (0s and 1s). Quantum computers are used to handle complex problems. It can be done with the help of the quantum superposition theorem. It states that exactly we don't know the position of an object. Quantum key distribution is used to distribute keys between two endpoints using a sequence of photons through a quantum channel (Wootters *et al.*, 1982). It is the first application to establish secure communication against eavesdropping attacks. This chapter gives an overview of the basic fundamental concepts of quantum cryptography and its various key distribution protocols.

10.2   FUNDAMENTALS OF QUANTUM CRYPTOGRAPHY

Quantum cryptography can be described using two parties called Alice and Bob (Gisin et al., 2002). Secure communication can be established between them using both classical communication channels and quantum communication channels. In a secure random key distribution process, firstly, the secret key can be distributed through the quantum channel, then the message can be exchanged through the classical channel (Christandl et al., 2004). During this process, an eavesdropper (Eve) can track this communication but cannot modify it. Quantum cryptography is shown in Figure 10.3 for better understanding.

In quantum cryptography, some major fundamental principles used are as follows:

1. Heisenberg's uncertainty principle
2. Quantum entanglement
3. Photon polarization
4. Quantum no-cloning theory

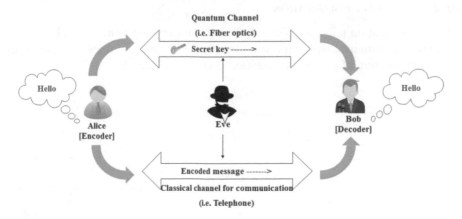

FIGURE 10.3   Quantum cryptography.

10.2.1 HEISENBERG'S UNCERTAINTY PRINCIPLE

It is one of the basic concepts of quantum mechanics. W. Heisenberg (1927) conducted an experiment to measure the electron's position by using a gamma-ray microscope. Based on this experiment, he came to the conclusion that we cannot measure more than one property simultaneously without disturbing its system (Ekert and Huttner, 1994). The polarized photon particles are known only when measured. For instance, consider that Alice (sender) and Bob (Receiver) want to share a secret key between them using quantum cryptography. The transmission can be done with the help of a quantum particle (photon) through a quantum channel. The basic communication can be done through the classical channel (Christandl et al., 2004). The uncertainty principle gives a guarantee that an attacker cannot measure the photon without disturbing its photon's states. So we can easily identify the attacks which are performed by attackers. This principle is the basis for most quantum-based applications.

10.2.2 QUANTUM ENTANGLEMENT

Quantum entanglement is generated by the process of splitting a single photon into two photons by firing a laser through the crystal. It is possible for two quantum particles to be entangled together and the particle's property is measured in one particle and it could be observed on another particle instantaneously. It can be represented as in Figure 10.4.

Here photon A is spinning up which represents the upper direction of measurement and photon B is spinning down which indicates the opposite direction of measurement to its entangled photon A. If we have the photon with vertical spin but we measure it in a horizontal direction, then the probability to get the spin up or down is of equal probability. Disturbing one quantum state will affect the other instantly. The communications between entangled states are done through a classical channel, which is also called quantum teleportation.

10.2.3 PHOTON POLARIZATION

Photon polarization plays a major role in quantum cryptography which is working based on quantum mechanics. It is used for generating an experimental quantum key. The representation of photon polarization is shown in Table 10.1.

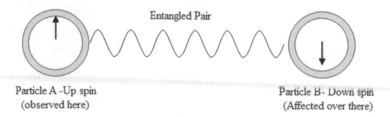

Entangled Pair

Particle A -Up spin
(observed here)

Particle B- Down spin
(Affected over there)

FIGURE 10.4 Quantum entanglement.

TABLE 10.1
Photons Representation

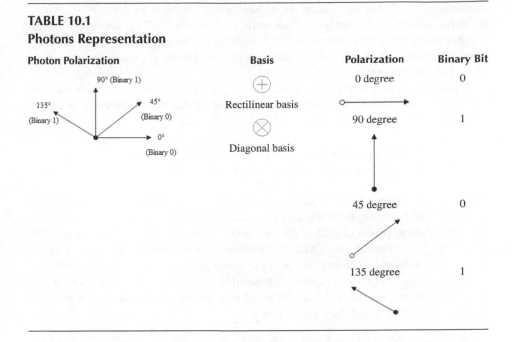

Photon Polarization	Basis	Polarization	Binary Bit
	Rectilinear basis	0 degree	0
		90 degree	1
	Diagonal basis	45 degree	0
		135 degree	1

It is a two-state quantum mechanical system. It has two types of basis called rectilinear polarization basis and diagonal polarization basis. The rectilinear polarization basis can be represented with 0 degree (horizontal) or 90 degree (vertical) quantum state, and the diagonal polarization basis can be represented with 45 degree or 135 degree direction. The polarization of a photon is known only at the time of measurement. It plays a major role in preventing eavesdropping attempts in cryptographic systems. The principle of photon polarization describes how photons are polarized in a particular direction.

10.2.4 QUANTUM NO-CLONING THEOREM

Quantum mechanics consists of the characteristics of linearity because of which an unknown quantum state cannot be cloned, which is called a no-cloning theorem. It works based on the principle of quantum mechanics. Initially, it was identified by Wooters, Zurek, and Deiks (1982). An eavesdropper cannot modify the information transmitted between a sender and a receiver. It also states that the encoded information in the quantum state is always being unique. The quantum bit information can't be amplified between a sender and a receiver.

10.3 QUANTUM KEY DISTRIBUTION

It is used to establish a secret key between two legitimate parties. The classical cryptographic applications could also be using this secret key to facilitate secure

communication. Military information, healthcare information, and all other confidential sectors need long-term security (Heisenberg, 1927). Current classical
cryptography could not guarantee that long-term security because if quantum computers come online, then the encrypted information can be recorded, further will be
decrypted as represented in Figure 10.5.

Quantum cryptography can provide long-term security. If we want to transmit
top secret information, then we need to go for quantum key distribution. It can be
categorized into two types based on their basic principles

1. An entanglement-based quantum key distribution
2. Prepare-and-measure-based quantum key distribution

Wiesner used the concept of quantum mechanics in the information security world
in the 1970s. In 1984, Benneth and Brassard (BB84 protocol) introduced the first
key distribution protocol called prepare-and-measure QKD. In 1991, Ekert (E91
protocol) (Gershenfeld and Chuang, 1998) introduces another protocol called an
entanglement-based protocol. After these basic protocols, a lot of protocols had
been introduced but they all are implemented based on either BB84 protocol or E91
protocol. Seven general steps are involved in a quantum key distribution protocol
(Lütkenhaus, 1999), and they are as follows:

1. Random number generation by the sender
2. Quantum communication
3. Key shifting
4. Reconciliation
5. Estimation of Eve's partial information gain
6. Privacy amplification
7. Key confirmation

Initially, the random number can be generated using a random generator by the sender,
then the quantum key distribution protocols are used to encode these random bits to the
sequence of signals, and further it will send through quantum channels to the receiver
(Gisin et al., 2002). The receivers measure those signals and then assign the bit values.
The measurement information can be discussed through the classical channel about

FIGURE 10.5   Quantum key distribution.

photon detection time slot details. The raw keys are identified if it measures the corresponding signals to its random bits. This raw key selection is made by public discussion between both the sender and the receiver. The random portions of these raw keys are selected separately which are called shifted keys. Generally, the sender and receiver's shifted key bits are correlated perfectly in an ideal system. If it is not perfectly correlated, then it has some transmission errors due to polarization imperfection. These errors should be corrected so that the receiver reconciles its shifted key using an error correction method. An eavesdropping estimation can be done based on transmission errors that are found in the receiver's shifted key. In some cases due to network noise, transmission errors may occur. In such cases, it can't be identified which error is caused by network noise or eavesdropper. The privacy amplification is used to distill a secret key from the reconciled key. An eavesdropper's gained information is easily identified, after this key filtration the final key will be confirmed.

10.3.1 PREPARE-AND-MEASURE-BASED QUANTUM KEY DISTRIBUTION

The first key distribution protocol called BB84 protocol was proposed by Bennett and Brassard in 1984, which uses quantum states for secure key distribution. It works based on Heisenberg's uncertainty principle. The basic idea of all other protocol implementations is based on this protocol. Heisenberg's uncertainty principle ensures that the eavesdropper can't measure any photons from Alice and send them to Bob without disturbing his photon's state so that the communication becomes more secure. If eavesdropper will do any modification, then it confirms its presence. It is based on the principles of Heisenberg's uncertainty principle and no-cloning theorem. In the prepare-and-measure-based protocol, first the quantum states are prepared and send through the quantum channel. Afterward, it could be measured. This protocol has done its work with the help of the polarization of photons to implement qubits.

10.3.1.1 BB84 Protocol

Classical cryptography has some key distribution problems that can be solved by quantum multiplexing channel theory (Bennett et al., 1992). This is the first quantum key distribution protocol. In this protocol, single-photon source is assumed to use. Every bit of information can be encoded with four polarization states. It contains two non-orthogonal rectilinear bases and two orthogonal diagonal bases. The rectilinear bases can be represented as binary 0 which is the polarization of 0 degrees (horizontal) and binary 1 which is the polarization of 90 degrees (vertical). The diagonal bases of binary 0 can be represented as the polarization of 45 degrees (diagonal) and binary 1, which is the polarization of 135 degrees (anti-diagonal). Alice records each photon and sends it to Bob. It was assumed that,

- Initially, no secret keys were shared between the sender and the receiver.
- The sender and the receiver use both classical and quantum channels. The basic communication can be done through a classical channel. A quantum channel is used for the key distribution.
- Eavesdropper was present and he was trying to access both channels.

In the first phase, Alice and Bob's communication can be established over a quantum channel. The sender initiates the process by selecting a random bit (A) and randomly chooses the basis (X) to encode the bit. She uses photon polarization to send a photon for each bit to Bob. Further, it will be measured by Bob. If Bob and Alice choose the same base for a particular photon, Bob needs to measure the same polarization, so he can guess exactly which bit Alice is trying to send. If Bob chooses the wrong basis, then the results will be random.

In the second stage, Bob advertises the criteria that Alice used to measure each photon over an unsecured channel. Alice reports to Bob whether Bob has chosen the correct criterion for each photon. In such a situation, the sender and the receiver discard bits corresponding to the photons that the receiver has measured according to different criteria. If no error occurs, or if no one manipulates the photon, then Bob and Alice both have the same bit. The following example shows the base on which Alice encoded bits selected by Bob, the basis used for measurements, and the final measurement results. Based on this measurement result (B), the unique key will be generated as represented in Table 10.2.

10.3.1.2 Other Prepare-and-Measure-based Protocols

In 1992 (Briege et al., 1988), Charles H. Bennet discussed a new protocol. In this protocol, two non-orthogonal quantum states are used to distribute keys. The main difference from the previous protocol (BB84) is that it only requires two polarization states instead of four states. The diagonal bases of binary 0 which is the polarization of 0 degrees in a rectilinear basis and binary 1 which is the polarization of 45 degrees in a diagonal basis. Alice records each photon and sends it to Bob. Like the BB84 protocol, Alice starts by selecting a random bit, and randomly chooses the basis to encode the bit. Alice and Bob's communication can be established over a quantum channel. Bob publically announces the bases which need to be chosen by Alice, then he randomly chooses the basis and makes a single measurement and keeps the results secret (Bruss and Macchiavello, 2002). If Bob measures the correct basis then, it will agree that and discard all other instances. Before using

---

TABLE 10.2

Measurement Result

Alice's Polarization Encoding			Bob's Projective Measurement		
Random Bit (A)	Encoding Basis (X)	Prepared Photon State	Detection Basis (Y)	Measured Photon State	Measurement Results (B)
0	$\oplus$	↔H	$\oplus$	↔H	0
1	$\oplus$	↕V	$\otimes$	↗D	Random
0	$\otimes$	↗D	$\oplus$	↕V	Random
1	$\otimes$	↘A	$\otimes$	↘A	1

it as a secret key, they will review and sacrifice certain parts of the keys to ensure that the keys received are completely related to each other and are not heard by eavesdroppers.

In 1999, Bechmann-Pasquinucci and Gisin introduced a new protocol called six-state protocol. It makes use of six polarization states on three orthogonal bases to encode the bits. In this protocol, additional two bases are used with the BB84 protocol. It gives three possibilities to the eavesdropper to choose the right basis among them and it leads to a higher error rate, thus becoming easier to detect the interrupt. Alice starts by generating a qubit string and encoded on a randomly chosen basis. It will be send through a quantum channel (Scarani et al., 2004). After receiving the encoded string, Bob measures it. Bob communicates over a classical authenticated channel to discard measurement if both of them use different bases. Brus and Micchiavello (2002) proved that a three-dimensional key distribution scheme provides more security than two-dimensional systems from eavesdropping.

In 2002, Inoue proposed a protocol called DPS02 protocol. Four fully non-orthogonal states are used for photon polarization. It gives more efficiency by increasing the number of paths in the sender's interferometer. In 2004, Valerio Scarani et al. introduced a new protocol called SARG04 protocol. It uses four non-orthogonal states. It provides security against PNS attacks in the communication channel for longer distances. The quantum level procedures are the same as the BB84 protocol. The classical shifting procedures only differ from the BB84 protocol. A more number of states are used to increase the distance limits. It is mainly implemented for increasing the robustness limits of the BB84 protocol.

In 2009, Khan et al. introduced a new protocol called KMB09 protocol. Both the sender and the receiver used the N-dimensional path-encoded state. It calculates and monitors the error bit rate to detect the eavesdropper. By using this protocol, it is easy to detect eavesdroppers and ensure robustness against photon-number-splitting attacks. In 2011, Zamani and Verma introduced a new protocol called ZV11 protocol. It uses two-way quantum channels for key shifting. In this protocol, the classical communication channel is not required for key shifting and key reconciliation. Initially, it assumes that the quantum channel is noiseless and the intruder is present in the channel.

In 2013, Serna introduces a new protocol called S13 protocol. This protocol was implemented for the purpose of sending secret keys with the same length of qubits and also reducing information losses. By using this protocol, we can achieve that there is no loss of information between the sender and the receiver. In 2013, Toshiba Research Europe Ltd introduced a new protocol called T13 protocol. It is analyzed and designed for improving the size of security efficiency of the BB84 protocol.

In 2015, Abushgra and Elleithy introduced a protocol called AK15 protocol. It reduces internal and external noise disturbances and also effectively detects an intercept-resend attack (IRA) compared to the BB84 protocol. In 2020, Djordjevic introduced the protocol called IB20 protocol. It provides higher secret key rates so that it can distribute the keys for a longer distance. It is one of the hybrid protocols which is implemented with the advantages of both discrete-variable and continuous-variable quantum key distributions.

10.3.2 An Entanglement-based Quantum Key Distribution

It is designed to provide security against physical side-channel attacks (Briegel et al., 1998). In an entanglement-based protocol, the information will exist only if the entangled quanta are measured so it doesn't have any information to eavesdrop. In some cases, extra quanta may be injected into the protocols at that time and those extra quanta will violate Bell's inequalities so that the presence of an eavesdropper can be detected. The basic system model of an entanglement-based QKD protocol is shown in Figure 10.6.

Figure 10.6 describes that the entangled photons are emitted from the photon source. One particle from each pair is received by either the sender or the receiver (Enzer et al., 2002). Initially, the sender (Alice) and the receiver (Bob) randomly choose the basis to encode the bit and the measurement results are discussed through the classical channel. If both use the same basis, then it gets opposite results. The eavesdropper can be detected by Bell's inequality test.

10.3.2.1 Ekert's Protocol

In 1991, Ekert introduced entanglement-based new quantum key distribution protocols that use pairs of entangled photons to design it. The principle of photon entanglement is used here. The photons' source is generated by either the sender or the receiver. It detects the eavesdropper by using the generalized Bell's theorem. This protocol can generate the random number by using Bohm's version of Einstein–Podolsky–Rosen (EPR) paradox as represented in Figure 10.7.

The EPR paradox shows that the photon source sends and emits entangled pairs of photons. The photons are entangled and then the spinning directions are not known until it is measured that means one particle is spinning in the up direction and another is spinning in the down direction but we don't know which particle is

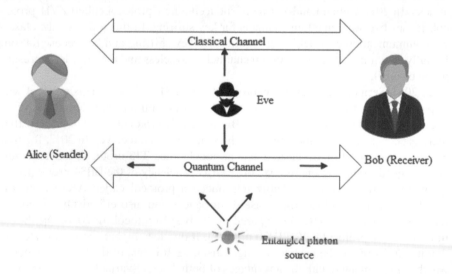

FIGURE 10.6 Basic system model of an entanglement-based QKD protocol.

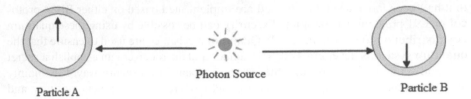

Photon Source

Particle A   Particle B

FIGURE 10.7 EPR paradox.

in which direction until it is measured (Enzer et al., 2002). If the sender and the receiver choose an incompatible basis, then there is a 50% probability to get the same measurement and a 50% probability to get the different measurement. If the sender and the receiver choose the compatible basis (30% possibility), then the measurement will be a deterministic one that means if one particle is in the up direction then another entangled particle should be spinning down.

Initially, the photon source emits two spins of photons: one spin of photons was send to the sender and the other was send to the receiver. After receiving these photon particles, the incoming particles will be measured by picks randomly from the three coplanar axes. The random measurement will be avoided by both the sender and the receiver discussing their bases publicly (Lucamarini et al., 2013). If both the sender and the receiver measure the particles in the same basis, the sender detects spin up and the receiver also detects spin up then it means an eavesdropper is present in the communication.

10.3.2.2 Entangled BB84 Variants

In 1992, Bennett et al. introduced a new entanglement-based protocol called BBM92 Protocol. This is the entangled version of the BB84 protocol. The basic concepts of key distribution, privacy amplification, and key shifting are all the same. The only difference is instead of a normal photon source, entanglement photon sources are used here. In 2002, Enzer et al. introduced the protocol called ESSP02 protocol. It is the implementation of an entangled version of the SSP99 protocol. The entangled photon pairs are used here and it provides a higher net yield of the secret key. In 2002, Bostrom and Felbinger introduced a protocol called KB02 protocol and are also called ping-pong protocol. Compared with the BB84 protocol, it provides a high probability of eavesdropping detection. The information can be accessed only if both the entangled photons are available.

10.4 CONCLUSION

This chapter gives an overview of quantum cryptography and its key distribution protocols. It is the first application to establish secure communication against eavesdropping attacks. BB84 was introduced as the first quantum key distribution protocol that works based on the principle of Heisenberg's uncertainty. After some years, another protocol called E91 protocol was implemented which works on the principle of quantum entanglement. After these basic protocols, there are a lot of protocols that had been introduced, but they all are implemented based on either BB84 protocol or E91 protocol. Unconditional security can be possible by using these quantum key distributions (Gisin et al., 2002). Quantum mechanics are used to ensure that the quantum system is never cracked. The sender and the receiver can establish a secret key and send messages through the insecure channel in a secure way. It is mainly aimed to implement this quantum cryptography where the government, military, and other high-security sectors needed confidential information transformation. It was proved theoretically as more secure.

REFERENCES

Abushgra A. and Elleithy, K. (2015). *Initiated decoy states in quantum key distribution protocol by 3 ways channel, Long Island Systems.* Applications and Technology, Farmingdale, NY, 1–5.

Bechmann-Pasquinucci, H. and Gisin, N. (1999). Incoherent and coherent eavesdropping in the six-state protocol of quantum cryptography. *Physical Review A*, 59: 4238–4248.

Bennett, C. H. and Brassard, G. (1984). Quantum cryptography: Public-key distribution and coin tossing. *Proceedings of the IEEE International Conference on Computers, Systems and Signal Processing*, Bangalore, India. New York: IEEE: 175–179.

Bennett, C. H., Brassard, G., and Mermin, N. D. (1992a). Quantum cryptography without Bell's theorem. *Physical Review Letters*, 68: 557–559.

Bennett, C. H. F. Bessette, G. Brassard, L. S., and Smolin, J. (1992b). Experimental quantum cryptography. *Journal of Cryptology*, 5(1): 3–28.

Bostrom, Kim and Felbinger, Timo. (2002). Deterministic secure direct communication using Entanglement. *Physical Review Letters*, 89(18).

Briegel, H.-J., Dur, W., Cirac, J. I., and Zoller, P. (1998). Quantum repeaters: The role of imperfect local operations in quantum communication. *Physical Review Letters*, 81: 5932–5935.

Bruss, D. and Macchiavello C. (2002). Optimal eavesdropping in cryptography with three-dimensional quantum states. *Physical Review Letters* 88: 127901(1)–127901(4).

Christandl, M., Renner, R., and Ekert, A. (2004). A generic security proof for quantum key distribution, quant-ph/0402131.

Djordjevic, I. B. (2020). Hybrid QKD protocol outperforming both DV- and CV-QKD protocols. *IEEE Photonics Journal*, 12(1): 1–8, doi: 10.1109/JPHOT.2019.2946910.

Ekert, A. K. (1991). Quantum cryptography based on Bell's theorem. *Physical Review Letters*, 67: 661–663.

Ekert A. K. and Huttner, B. (1994). Eavesdropping techniques in quantum cryptosystems. *Journal of Modern Optics*, 41: 2455–2466, Special Issue on Quantum Communication.

Enzer, D., Hadley, P., Gughes, R., Peterson, C., and Kwiat, P. (2002a). Entangled-photon six-state quantum cryptography. *New Journal of Physics*, 45.1–45.8.

Enzer, D. G., Hardley, P. G., Hughes, R. J., Peterson, C. G., and Kwiat, P. G. (2002b). Entangled-photon six-state quantum cryptography. *New Journal of Physics*, 4: 45.1–45.8.

Gershenfeld, N. and Chuang, I. L. (1998). Quantum computing with molecules. *Scientific American*, 66–71.

Gisin, N., Ribordy, G., Tittel, W., and Zbinden, H. (2002). Quantum cryptography. *Reviews of Modern Physics*, 74: 145–195.

Heisenberg, W. (1927). The physical content of quantum kinematics and mechanics. *Quantum Theory and Measurement*. Princeton, Princeton University Press, 62–84.

Inoue, K. (2002). Differential phase shift quantum key distribution. *Physical Review Letters*, 89(3).

Khan, M. M., Murphy, M., and Beige, A. (2009). High error-rate quantum key distribution for long-distance communication. *New Journal of Physics*, 11: 063043.

Lucamarini, M., Patel, K. A., Dynes, J. F., Fröhlich, B., Sharpe, A. W., Dixon, A. R., Yuan, Z. L., Penty, R. V., and Shields, A. J. (2013). Efficient decoy-state quantum key distribution with quantified security. *Optics Express*, 21(21): 24550–24565.

Lütkenhaus N. (1999). Estimates for practical quantum cryptography. *Physical Review A*, 59: 3301–3319.

Rothe, J. (2002). Some facets of complexity theory and cryptography. *A Five-lecture Tutorial*. *ACM Computing Surveys*, 34(4): 504–549.

Scarani, A., Acin, A., Ribordy, G., and Gisin, N. (2004). Quantum cryptography protocols robust against photon number splitting attacks. *Physical Review Letters*, 92.

Scarani, V., Acin, A., Ribordy, G., and Gisin, N. (2004). Quantum cryptography protocols robust against photon number splitting attacks for weak laser pulses implementation. *Physical Review Letters*, 92(5): 057901.

Serna, E. H. (2013). Quantum key distribution from a random seed, arXiv:1311.1582[quant-ph].

Wootters W. K. and Zurek, W. H. (1982). A single quantum cannot be cloned. *Nature*, 299: 802–803.

Wootters, W. K. and Zurek, W. H. (1982). A single quantum cannot be cloned. *Nature*, 299: 802–803, doi: 10.1038/299802a0.

Zamani F. and Verma, P. K. (2011). A QKD protocol with a two-way quantum channel. 5th IEEE International Conference on Advanced Telecommunication Systems and Networks (ANTS), Bangalore, 1–6.

11 Quantum Cryptography
Basics, Effects on Communication, and Data Management

Shashi Bhushan

CONTENTS

DOI: 10.1201/9781003296034-11

11.1   INTRODUCTION

The main objective of providing security is to restrict information and resource access to the authorized people who utilize the system. In general, a security breach can be classified into four categories: (a) interrupter, (b) interceptor, (c) modification, and (d) fabrication. Interruption implies the main core of the system which gets destroyed or becomes unavailable on unusable. Interceptor implies that an unauthorized party has hacked the service or data. Modification implies unauthorized alternator of data or service tempering such that it no longer adheres to its original specification, fabrication infers to the situation where additional data or activity gets generated that normally won't exist. Security is implemented in networks to give freedom risk or danger [1, 2]. In general, security prevents or protects against:

- Information access by unauthorized entities
- Destructions and alternation of information intentionally or unintentionally
- Security gives proper protection to information and system and resources

11.1.1   IMPORTANCE OF NETWORK SECURITY

Every network needs security against hackers and attackers. It includes two basic concepts: security of data and security of the system. Network security is not just restricted to a single network, rather it can be segregated into two major components: information security and data security [3]. Across the internet, huge chunks of data are exchanged on a daily basis, and this information could be misused by hackers and attackers. Information security is of utmost importance for the following reasons:

- To protect personal information from the user accessing the internet
- To protect information from being lost and ensure its delivery to the destination
- To ensure that acknowledgment is received for the message sent
- To ensure that message is protected in spite of unwanted time delay between transmitter and receiver

Firewalls also play a major component with regard to network security. Using firewalls, certain spams and phishing websites can be blocked from playing havoc on the system. By managing the operation of firewalls, the network downtime can be reduced, as well as threats and other security breaches [4]. When there is a discussion on network security, the most commonly used terminologies are vulnerability, threat, and attack. Vulnerability is basically a weakness that is present in every network and devices such as routers, switches, and desktops. Weakness or vulnerabilities can be classified as

- Vulnerabilities with respect to technology
- Vulnerabilities with respect to configuration
- Vulnerabilities with respect to security policy

11.2   CRYPTOGRAPHY IS CONVENTIONAL SENSE

This is a technique involving the usage of a mathematical formula to convert a plaintext to ciphertext and vice versa to ensure secure data transmission between transmitter and receiver. Encryption is a process that produces a ciphertext from a plaintext [5]. The reverse process is termed decryption. In this digital age, attackers and hackers are at large eavesdropping and performing cyber fraud, leading to the necessity of storing the information in a secure manner. This has also led to a massive awareness campaign for protecting digital assets from being disclosed, ensuring the authenticity of data and messages and also ensuring that the system is protected from network-based attacks on smartphones, ATM cards, and digital signatures, all employing cryptography in one form or other to ensure data protection.

11.3   BASIC SCHEMATIC OF QUANTUM CRYPTOSYSTEM

The schematic employs two important channels of communication. The first is the quantum channel that transmits and receives quantum bits and generates session keys. The second is the channel that forms the link between the sender and the receiver to compare whether the quantum bits are tapped [6, 7]. Encryption and decryption take place between the sender and the receiver, keeping the communication secure, the function of the eavesdropping detection block [8, 9] is to check whether a change in the quantum state occurs due to the eavesdropper obtaining the guarantee bits to compose a session key [10] thereby detecting the eavesdropper [11, 12]. Therefore, this scheme is more practical and efficient when compared to a conventional cryptographic system.

11.4   OBJECTIVE OF CRYPTOGRAPHIC SYSTEM

Any cryptosystem will not serve any purpose unless it satisfies the following major objectives:

- Confidentially
- Integrity
- Availability
- Accountability
- Authenticity

11.5   QUANTUM CRYPTOGRAPHY

Quantum cryptography involves the usage of quantum communication and quantum computation to perform various cryptographic tasks. The most important mathematical tools involved are (a) complex numbers, (b) vertical representation of function having infinite components, and (c) energy function and wave nature of the particle. Unlike conventional cryptographic tasks, where certain tasks are perceived to be impossible, quantum cryptography makes it possible by employing protocols such as

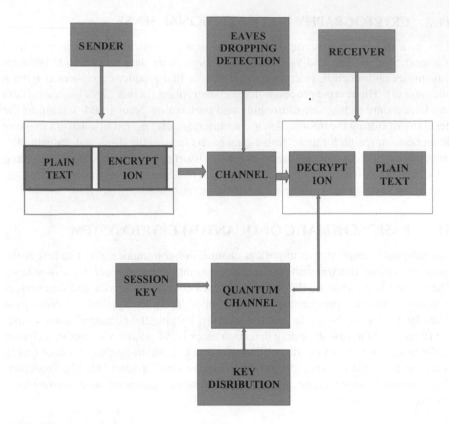

FIGURE 11.1 Quantum basic cryptosystems.

BB84 for a single photon and E91 for entangled particles in quantum cryptography. Quantum channels are employed generously for key distribution and the encoded messages are sent through public channels [13]. In conventional communication, the signal is split and amplified so the communication parties were completely unaware of whether eavesdropping has taken place or not, leading to jeopardizing the sharing of private keys [14]. The no-cloning theorem completely eliminates and duplicates the unknown state of a particle, thereby preventing the copies of the original particle.

11.6 SINGLE-PHOTON PROTOCOL

To encode information, single-photon or ensnared particles can be utilized. In this plan, the gathering keen on sending encoded information (regularly called Alice) sends single enraptured photons to the accepting party (Bob). On the communicating side, the polarization of these photons would be haphazardly chosen between one of two symmetrical expresses of photons. Alice sends in the premise (half of the photons), would be accurately estimated by Eve and sent onwards to Bob as though an estimation has not occurred [15]. Anyway, the remainder of the photons sent in the premise has an equivalent possibility of being estimated in every finder. The photons sent onwards to Bob subsequently are totally uncorrelated to the first ones and have a half possibility of enrolling an off-base outcome, regardless of whether Alice and Bob picked a similar basis. This sort of snooping endeavor would enroll a generally 25% mistake in the filtered key; this is the thing that Alice searches for in her examination of the subset of the moved key (Figure 11.2).

11.7 ENTANGLED PARTICLES (E91 PROTOCOL)

The plan for snared particles that cryptography utilizes a source produces two entrapped particles in the singlet state: One of which goes to Alice and the subsequent one to Bob (their course of movement is the z hub). The source doesn't need to be secure to achieve mystery and can even be in the ownership of Eve albeit then an outsider can just incapacitate correspondence (Figure 11.3).

11.8 LOSS OF DATA IN QUANTUM COMPUTING

Loss of data in quantum computing creates vulnerabilities in the system that implements quantum cryptographic techniques. One of the major threats in a quantum cryptographic system is the tampering of quantum key distributors, leading to the generation of duplicate keys due to random number generator attacks. The attacks can be classified into various categories: Trojan horse attack and time-shift attack [11]. Trojan horse attack can be detected to check the non-legitimate signal from entering the transmitter. Similarly, the time-shift attack can also be detected by modifying the implementation accordingly. Apart from these two attacks, there are

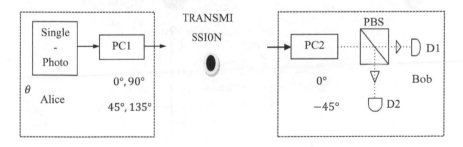

FIGURE 11.2 Single-photon protocol.

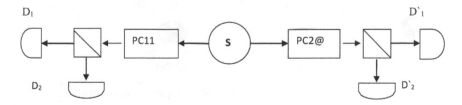

FIGURE 11.3 Entangled particle models.

many types like fake-state attacks, phase-remapping attacks, and time-shift attacks to name a few.

11.9   QUBIT

The unit of quantum information is the quantum bit or qubit. As its classical analog "bit," the qubit can be in two basic states which are symbolized as 0 and 1. The classical bit and qubit representation are shown in Figure 11.4.

11.10   SPEED AND ENERGY CONSUMPTION OF AN ENGINE

Conventional systems have heat dissipation proportional to the number of computing circuits or to the volume of the device (computer). The heat dissipation increases with an increase in thrice the radius of the device. To prevent the destruction of the system, the heat is removed from the surface surrounding the device. Henceforth, increasing heat is removed with an increase in twice the radius while the amount of heat increases with an increase in thrice the size of the computing engine. The speed versus energy consumption of an engine is shown in Figure 11.5.

11.11   ENTANGLEMENT

A solitary quantum framework in a superposition of similar potential states is called ensnarement pair. The ensnared state contains no data about the individual particles,

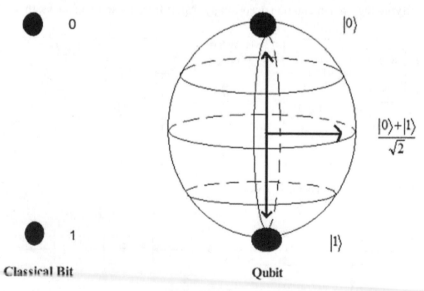

Classical bit and qubit representation

FIGURE 11.4   Classical bit and qubit representation.

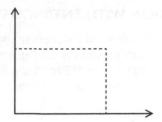

FIGURE 11.5 Speed versus energy consumption of an engine.

just that they are in inverse states. The significant property of a caught pair is that the estimation of one molecule impacts the condition of the other molecule. In this examination work, quantum entrapment is executed in QCL (Quantum Computer Language). The use of quantum trap and quantum teleportation circuit is executed in QCL.

11.12 LIGHT

Light is a type of electromagnetic radiation; the radiation frequency in the noticeable range changes from red to violet. Light is shifted by specifically engrossing some shading ranges and permitting through others. In this exploration work, polarization channel utilized as a part of the straightforward material that permits light of a specific polarization.

11.13 PHOTONS

Photons are very surprising from the twist 1/2 electrons due to their massless property and twist esteem. A photon is described by its vector energy (the vector force decides the recurrence) and polarization. In the old-style hypothesis, light is characterized as having an electric field which sways either vertically, the light is x-spellbound, or evenly, the light is y-captivated in a plane opposite to the course of engendering, the z-pivot. The two premise vectors are |h> and |v>. In this examination work, quantum cryptography is refined by misusing the properties of minute particles like photons. Photons are estimated to decide their direction compared with polarization at a time.

11.14 POLARIZATION FILTERS

A polarization filter (partially transparent material) is used to transmit the light of a particular polarization. In the horizontal (vertical) polarization filter, all photons in the vertical (horizontal) polarization state will be absorbed and only the photons in the horizontal (vertical) polarization state will pass through. When the polarization filter is set at an angle with respect to the coordinate system of the incoming beam of light, the emerging photons form a superposition state.

11.15   COMMUNICATION WITH ENTANGLED PARTICLES

Two entangled particles with anti-correlated state (spin up and spin down) are used in communication as they continue to interact with one another even after separation. Consider Particles 2 and 3 is an anti-correlated state. If Particle 2 is separated from Particle 3 and entangled with Particle 1, then the state of Particle 1 is the state of Particle 3.

11.16   QUANTUM CIRCUIT

Given a function $f(x)$, a reversible quantum circuit consisting of Fred king gate is constructed. The capability of transforming two qubits is shown in Figure 11.6.

11.17   QUANTUM PARALLELISM

The yield of the quantum circuit consists of data of both $f(0)$ and $f(1)$. This property of quantum circuits is called quantum parallelism. Quantum parallelism permits building the whole truth table of a quantum door cluster having $2n$ sections immediately. In an old-style framework, the reality table can register in a one-time venture with $2n$ entryway clusters running in equal, or $2n$ time steps needed for a solitary door exhibit. In a quantum circuit, with "n" qubits, each is in state l0> and a Welsh–Hadamard change is applied. This is shown in Figure 11.7.

11.18   STATE OF A TWO-QUBIT QUANTUM REGISTER

The condition of a quantum register is likewise a vector in a multidimensional Hilbert space and is given by the tensor result of the conditions of its qubits. On account of quantum register that involves two qubits $|q1\rangle$ and $|q0\rangle$ its state $|qR\rangle$ is given by equation 11.1:

$$| qR \rangle = | q1 \rangle | q0 \rangle = | q1 \rangle | q0 \rangle = | q1q0 \rangle \tag{11.1}$$

Where is the tensor item image?

Model: Condition of a four-qubit quantum register is shown in equation 11.2

$$| qR \rangle = C0 | 00 \rangle + C1 | 01 \rangle + C2 | 10 \rangle + C3 | 11 \rangle \tag{11.2}$$

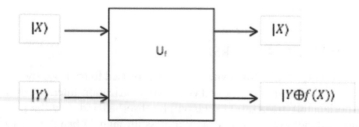

FIGURE 11.6   Quantum circuit.

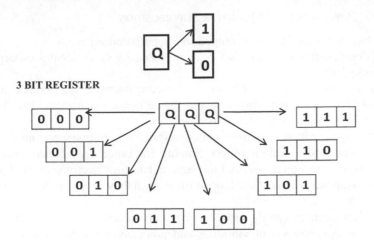

FIGURE 11.7 Qubit register.

Probability of estimating each state by equation 11.3

$$|C0|2+|C1|2+|C2|2+|C3|2=1 \tag{11.3}$$

11.19 SUPERPOSITION

The superposition standard, otherwise called superposition property, expresses that, for every direct framework, the net reaction at a given spot and time brought about by at least two improvements is the amount of the reactions which would have been brought about by every upgrade separately. So that whenever input produces reaction X and information B produces reaction Y at that point, the input (A+B) produces reaction (X+Y).

11.20 QUANTUM SUPERPOSITION

Quantum superposition is a key standard of quantum components that hold an actual framework existing incompletely in its whole specific hypothetically potential states (or, setup of its properties) at the same time; yet when estimated or noticed, it gives an outcome related to just one of the potential designs.

11.21 DOUBLE SLIT: AN EXAMPLE OF QUANTUM SUPERPOSITION

The double-slit experiment is a demonstration that light and matter can display the characteristics of both classically defined waves and particles. It displays the fundamentally probabilistic nature of quantum mechanical phenomena.

11.21.1 Application of Quantum Superposition

- A beryllium ion has been trapped in a superposed state.
- A double-slit experiment has been performed with molecules as large as Bucky balls.
- An experiment involving a superconducting quantum interference device ("SQUID") has been linked to the theme of the experiment. The A "cat state" has been achieved with photons.
- The superposition state does not correspond to a billion electrons flowing one way and a billion others flowing the other way. Superconducting electrons move en masse. All the superconducting electrons in the SQUID flow both ways around the loop at once when they are in the Schrodinger's cat state.
- A piezoelectric "tuning fork" has been constructed, which can be placed into a superposition of vibrating and non-vibrating states. The resonator comprises about 10 trillion atoms.

11.21.2 Quantum Superposition versus Quantum Entanglement

Quantum superposition is an expression that defines an event's final outcome as the combination of all possible outcomes. Quantum entanglement is the state of sub-atomic particles to come in pairs that complement each other so that if the state of one of the particles in the pair is known, then the state of the other is known without actually observing the state of the other particle.

11.21.3 Superposition Probability Rule

If an event may occur in two or more indistinguishable ways, then the probability amplitude of the event is the sum of the probability amplitudes of each case considered separately. This is called as superposition probability rule. A photon emitted by source S1 may take one of four different paths as shown in Table 11.1, depending on whether it is transmitted or reflected by each of the two beam splitters.

In this research work, quantum superposition is demonstrated in QCL using the "MIX" operator. The application of quantum superposition in a full binary adder is demonstrated in QCL.

TABLE 11.1
Different Paths of an Emitted Photon

Case	Probability of amplitude
Transmitter and transmitter (TT)	$(+q)(+q)$
Reflecter and reflecter (RR)	$(+q)(+q)$
Transmitter and reflecter	$(+q)(-q)$
Reflecter and transmitter	$(+q)(+q)$

11.21.4   MEASUREMENT OF SUPERPOSITION

The polarization of a photon is termed by a unit vector on a two-dimensional space with bases |0> and |1>. Measuring the polarization is the same as projecting the random vector onto one of the two basis vectors.

11.21.5   QUANTUM REGISTERS

A quantum register is the quantum mechanical equivalent of a conventional processor register. A group of qubits formed together is a qubit register. The calculations are performed by manipulating qubits within the register. Similar to a classical register, a quantum register stores data, i.e., if a quantum is designated as "N" bit, then it can have "N" bit and then it can have "N" quantum register. This is shown in Figure 11.7.

Unlike a conventional system, this can be overcome by quantum computing and it employs properties by using some parameters like uncertainty, interference, and entanglement so that extensive usage in computing and computation can be gained. The quantum state can be mathematically described as equation 11.4

$$|T\rangle = \alpha_0 |0\rangle + \alpha_1 |0\rangle \tag{11.4}$$

where $|\alpha_0 + \alpha_1|$ is the complex number and $|\alpha_0|^2 + |\alpha_1|^2 = 1$. $|\alpha_0|^2$ is the probability of observing the outcome "1." $|\alpha_1|^2$ is the probability of observing the outcome "0."

11.21.6   SUPERPOSITION AND UNCERTAINTY

Condition 1.1 is the superposition of two fundamental states, "0" and "1." The condition of the framework is obscure before the measurement interaction. After the measurement interaction, the condition of the framework is not at this point unsure, yet it is in one of the two fundamental states. In this examination work, in qcl "dump" order is used to quantify the current condition of the framework.

11.21.7   STATE SPACE DIMENSION OF CLASSICAL AND QUANTUM SYSTEMS

Singular state spaces of "n" particles consolidate quantum precisely through the tensor item. In the event that "**X**" and "**Y**" are vectors, their tensor item **X Y**, yet its measurement is faint (**X**) × faint (**Y**), while the vector item × **Y** has the measurement of faint (**X**) + faint (**Y**).

11.22   CONCLUSION

This section gives an outline of quantum cryptography and its key dissemination conventions. It is the principal application to set up the protected correspondence against snooping assaults. BB84 was presented as the first quantum key circulation convention which works depending on the rule of Heisenberg's vulnerability. After certain years of execution, another convention called E91 convention chips away at the guideline of a quantum trap. After these fundamental conventions, there are a parcel of conventions that had been presented, yet they all are executed depending on either BB84 convention or E91 convention. An unequivocal security can be conceivable by using these quantum key dispersions [14]. Quantum mechanics are used to guarantee the quantum framework that can never be broken. The sender and the collector can set up a mysterious key and send messages through unreliable diverts in a protected manner. For the most part, it intends to carry out this quantum cryptography where the public authority, military, and other high security required areas for private data change. It was demonstrated hypothetically as safer.

REFERENCES

1. W. Stallings, "Cryptography and network security principles and practice 2006", *J. Clerk Maxwell a Treatise on Electricity and Magnetism*, Clarendon, n.d., vol. 2, pp. 68–73.
2. B. Charles and H Gilles Brassard, *Quantum Cryptography: Public Key Distribution and Coin Tossing*, Elsevier B. V, 2014.
3. S. Bhushan, P. Kumar, A. Kumar and V. Sharma, "Scantime antivirus evasion and malware deployment using silent-SFX," in: 2016 International Conference on Advances in Computing, Communication, & Automation (ICACCA) (Spring), 2016, pp. 1–4, doi: 10.1109/ICACCA.2016.7578894.
4. N. Kaur, "Enhancement of network security techniques using quantum cryptography", *International Journal on Computer Science and Engineering (IJCSE)*, Vol 3, no. 5, 2011.
5. C. Guenther, *The Relevance of Quantum Cryptography in Modern Cryptographic Systems*, SANS Institute, 2004.
6. V. Ojha, A. Sharma, S. K. Lenka and S. R. Biradar, *Advantages of Classical Cryptography over the Quantum Cryptography*, World Applied Programming, 2012.
7. A.K. Singh, S. Bhushan and S. Vij. "A brief analysis and comparison of DCT- and DWT-based image compression techniques", in: Goyal D., Bălaş V.E., Mukherjee A., Hugo C. de Albuquerque V., Gupta A.K. (eds) Information Management and Machine Intelligence. ICIMMI 2019. Algorithms for Intelligent Systems, 2021.
8. P. Techateerawat, "A review on quantum cryptography technology", *International Transaction Journal of Engg Mangmt & Applied Sciences & Technologies*, vol. 1, 2010.
9. M. Elboukhari, M. Azizi and A. Azizi, "Quantum key distribution protocols: A survey", *International Journal of Universal Computer Sciences*, vol. 1, 2010.
10. M. Lopes and D. Sarwade, *On the Performance of Quantum Cryptographic Protocols SARG04 and KMB09*, IEEE, 2015.
11. A. Abushgra and K. Elleithy, *QKDP's Comparison Based upon Quantum Cryptography Rules*, IEEE, 2016.
12. M. Diwakar, P. Singh, P. Kumar, K. Tiwari, S. Bhushan and M. Kaushik, "Secure authentication in WLAN using modified four-way handshake protocol", in: Tomar A., Malik H., Kumar P., Iqbal A. (eds) *Machine Learning, Advances in Computing, Renewable Energy and Communication. Lecture Notes in Electrical Engineering.* Springer, vol 768, 2022.
13. L. O. Mailloux, C. D. Lewis, C. Riggs and M. R. Grimaila, "Post-quantum cryptography: What advancements in quantum computing mean for IT professionals", *IEEE Xplore*, vol. 18, no. 05, Sept.–Oct. 2016.

14. N. Gisin, G. Ribordy, W. Tittel and H. Zbinden, "Quantum cryptography", *Reviews of Modern Physics*, vol. 74, 2002.
15. M. P. P. Wasankar and P. P. D. Soni, "An invention of quantum cryptography over the classical cryptography for enhancing security", *International Journal of Application or Innovation in Engineering & Management (IJAIEM)*, vol. 2, 2013.
16. P. Curtacci, F. Garzia, R. Cusani and E. Baccarelli, *Performance Analysis of Different Multi-user Optical Passive Networks for Quantum Cryptography Applications*, SPIE Digital Library, 2006.

12 Quantum Number
Error Correction Circuits and Methods

Shashi Bhushan

CONTENTS

DOI: 10.1201/9781003296034-12

12.1 CLASSICAL ERROR CORRECTION CODE VERSUS QUANTUM ERROR CORRECTION CODE

Classical error correction method applies redundancy concept, that is, suppose the information is stored multiple items employing redundancy concept. In other words, suppose information is stored multiple times, and there is a mismatch in it, then the majority of things get hidden whereas in the case of quantum information copying is impossible due to the no-cloning theorem, thereby presenting a major challenge for formulating quantum error correction theory [1, 2]. In this regard, Peter Shor discovered the method of formulating a quantum error correction code by storing the information of one qubit on to a highly entangled state of nine qubits. Traditional mistake adjustment strategy applies a repetition concept. All in all, assume data is put away on numerous occasions, and there is a befuddle among them; at that point a greater part of option is performed whereas on account of quantum data duplicating is unthinkable because of the no-cloning hypothesis, thereby introducing a significant test for detailing quantum blunder amendment hypothesis in such a situation. Peter Shor found the technique for defining a quantum mistake revision code by putting away the data of one qubit on to a profoundly caught condition of nine qubits.

12.2 QUANTUM ERROR CORRECTION CIRCUIT

Overall quantum blunder follows up on a vector space, naming it as a super administrator. Touch flip, stage flip, total dephasing (decoherence), and pivot are a portion of the different sorts of single-qubit blunders [3] [4]. Irradiation procedure includes picking most of the pre-owned pieces of sorts of single-qubit blunders. In a customary strategy, if there is a solitary piece flip mistake, the blunder can be adjusted by picking the lion's share among the pre-owned pieces to address mistake including single piece flip blunder.

12.2.1 WORKING OF QUANTUM ERROR CORRECTION CODE

In this exploration work, a multi-qubit estimation is performed on encoded express that helps in recovering data about the mistake without upsetting the quantum data in the encoded express that helps in recovering data [6] [7] in the encoded state. Quantum mistake adjust the code and utilizes this estimation to check whether a qu-bit has been undermined, and assume that this is the case where results of the examination work showed about which physical qu-bit was influenced as well as the potential ways it was influenced.

In many situations, the mistake is because of touch flip, or a sign flip, or a blend of both. The explanation could be ascribed to the estimation that impacts quantum estimation. At the end of the day, if the blunder because of the commotion is subjective, then mistake can be communicated as a superposition of Pauli's framework and administrators can be recognized. The estimation of condition settles on the qubit to settle on the choice for explicit Pauli mistake [5] [9]. The Pauli administrator is followed up on the debased qubit to invert the impact of the blunder. The disorder estimation gives a great deal of data about the mistake happened, however gives little data about the worth that is put away in the consistent qubit with other qubits in the quantum PC [8].

12.3 TYPES OF BLUNDER IN QUANTUM COMPUTER

- Bit flip blunder
- Phase flip blunder
- Bit flip and stage flip blunder

12.3.1 BIT FLIP CODE

Touch flip code works in a reiteration code and is simple to gauge and to rehash.

12.3.1.1 Quantum Bit Flip Code

In the event of the redundancy code functions admirably in an old-style channel due to the instance of quantifiability and repeatability of traditional pieces (Figure 12.1). Anyway because of the use of no-cloning hypothesis [10] which doesn't permit the formation of copy duplicates of a vast quantum state, quantifiability and repeatability in a quantum channel turn into not, at this point achievable [11, 12]. It very well may be concluded that a solitary qubit can't be duplicated three times as its wave

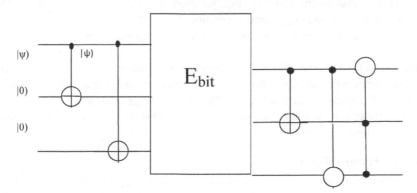

FIGURE 12.1 Quantum circuit of the bit flip code.

work will change radically because of the qubit estimation, to beat these difficulties, three-qubit bit flip code in utilized, which utilizes ensnarement and condition estimations and is on pair with redundancy code.

12.3.1.2 Flip Code Algorithm

Let $|f\rangle = \alpha_0|0\rangle + \alpha_1|1\rangle$ be a capricious qubit. The primary step involves entangling the qubit with two different qubits employing two CNOT gates with input $|0\rangle$. Leading to the result as $\vdash|f'\rangle = \alpha_0|000\rangle + \alpha_1|111\rangle$, which is nothing but a tensor product of three qubits, sent through channel E_bit leading to an assumption that at most one bit flip may occur. The situation, let as consider a scenario where the first qubit is flipped, leading to the result as $|f'\rangle = \alpha_0|100\rangle + \alpha_1|011\rangle$. To analyze bit flips in any three qubits, syndrome diagnosis is needed, which includes four projection operators:

$P_0 = |000\rangle\,(000| + |111\rangle\,(111|$
$P_1 = |100\rangle\,(100| + |011\rangle\,(011|$
$P_2 = |010\rangle\,(010| + |101\rangle\,(101|$
$P_3 = |001\rangle\,(001| + |110\rangle\,(110|$

Therefore, it is known that the error syndrome corresponds to p1. These three qubits' bit flip code corrects one error if at most one bit flip error has occurred in the channel.

12.3.2 STABILIZER ELEMENTS DETECT ERRORS

Assume M, S, and Pauli mistake E anticommutes with M. At that point, has eigenvalue -1 for M. On the other hand, if M and E drive for all, so has eigenvalue $+1$ for all M in the stabilizer. The eigenvalue of an administrator M from the stabilizer distinguishes blunders which anticommute with M.

12.3.3 BARRIERS IN EXISTING ERROR CORRECTION METHOD

- Error measurement destroys superposition
- No-cloning theorem prevents repetition
- Must correct multiple types of errors (e.g., bit flip and phase errors)

In this research work, the quantum error correction circuit is developed for continuous error correction and coherence, where it forms a basis for the code words and E. The matrix C_{ab} does not depend on i and j. As an example, consider $C_{ab} = T_{ab}$. Then a measurement can be made to determine the error [14]. If C_{ab} has rank < maximum, code is degenerate.

12.3.3.1 Erasure Error

Suppose the location of an error is known, but not its type (I, X, Y, or Z). This is called an erasure. By using QECC conditions: Corrections of "t" general error and "2t" erasures are possible in this research work. Tr_A does not depend on encoded state, where A is a set of qubits which are not erased. That is, erased qubits have no information about A.

12.3.3.2 Stabilizer Codes

For a properly encoded state 000 or 111, the first two would have an even count of 1's and the process is repeated for second and third bits for an incorrectly encoded state, the first two bits have an odd count 1's. In this research, rearrangement is performed by assuming b+1 as a Eigen value, For Y and for incorrectly encoded state, first or second bit has b−1 as a Eigen value J. For the measurement of the three-qubit phase error-correcting code, a code word has eigenvalue +1 for X, whereas a state of Y leads to detection of bit flip error and measuring X leads the detection of phase errors.

12.3.3.3 Error Detection Using Stabilizer Elements

Suppose we have A and S and Pauli error E does not support commutative property with M, then the condition can be termed as a leading to the conclusion that E has eigenvalue −1 for A. Conversely, if A and E satisfy the commutative property with M such that A and S lead to the conclusion that E has an eigenvalue of +1 for all A for a commutative property the stabilizer. The eigenvalue of an operator M from the stabilizer detects the errors which anticommutes with M.

12.3.3.4 Distance of a Stabilizer Cod

Let "S" be a stabilizer and let T(S) be denoted as quantum error correction code, we define B(S)={B, P_n s.t. AB=BA}. Then distance denoted by "d" of T(S) defined as the weight denoted by the smallest Pauli operator B in B(S) \S. The stabilizer code does not detect errors which satisfy the commutative property. Syndrome errors comprise the list of eigenvalue of s. The proposed quantum error correction code corrects errors by accumulating enough information about the error to determine which one occurred. The circuit correct errors for which $E^\dagger F$, B(S) \ S for all possible pairs of errors (E, F).

12.4 PHASE FLIP CODE (FIGURE 12.2)

12.4.1 QUANTUM CIRCUIT IMPLEMENTATION OF PHASE FLIP CODE

Flipped pieces are the solitary sort blunder which is experienced in an old-style PC. Although there is another danger of miscount with quantum PCs, the stages flip over the span of transmission along the channel with the sign somewhere in the range of $|0\rangle$ and $|1\rangle$ become transformed. For instance, a qubit in the state $|-\rangle = (|0\rangle - |1\rangle)/\sqrt{2}$ gets its sign changed to $|+\rangle = (|0\rangle + |1\rangle)/\sqrt{2}$. The qubit having its unique state $|f\rangle = \alpha \ 0|+\rangle + \alpha \ 1|-\rangle$ changes to $|f'\rangle = \alpha \ 0|+\rangle + \alpha \ 1|-\rangle$.

In the Hadamard premise, bit flips become sign flips and sign flips become bit flips. Let E_{Phase} be a quantum channel that can cause one stage flip. At that point, the piece flip code from above can recuperate $|f\rangle$ by changing into the Hadamard premise when transmits through E_{Phase}.

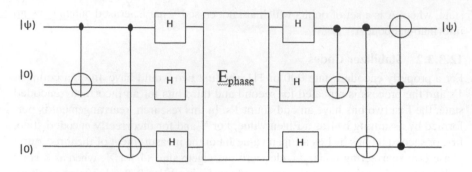

FIGURE 12.2   Quantum circuit of the phase flip code.

12.4.2   BIT FLIP AND PHASE FLIP CODE

A code that implements both bit flip code and phase flip code is described here (7-bit Steane code. The Steane code could be a perfect tool in quantum error correction. It was introduced by Andrew in 1996. It employs the classical binary self-dual programming code (x errors) and the turn of the programming code, along with phase flip errors. The Steane code has the ability to correct discretionally single-qubit error. Within the stabilizer formalin, the Steane code has six generators and therefore the check matrix in a standardized form. This representation gives us a compact illustration for a code. The generator represented here involved I's and X's as well as the I's and Z's. The pattern obtained from these operators follows the parity check matrix H of a classical linear code.

$$H = \begin{pmatrix} 0\,0 & 0\,1 & 1 & 1\,1 \\ 0\,1 & 1\,0 & 0 & 1\,1 \\ 1\,0 & 1\,0 & 1 & 0\,1 \end{pmatrix}$$

The above matrix is employed to correct each bit flip and phase flip errors. The Steane code applies the best features of both. The Hamming codes of |0⟩ and |1⟩ states for a seven-bit code are an even-weighed superposition of eight binary digits with all positive coefficients when measured. In the proposed research work, error propagation in q-bits is avoided while measuring.

The ancilla bits are those whose state is known in advance. In quantum computation, there is no methodology to predetermine the specific state without having the knowledge of the original state of the error in the ancilla bits and can be propagated to all these bits as shown in Figure 12.3.

Where |CAT⟩ is an equally weighed superposition of all even three piece strings (Figure 12.4):

$$|CAT\rangle = (|000\rangle + |011\rangle + |101\rangle + |110\rangle)/2$$

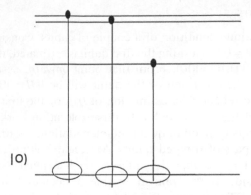

$|0\rangle$

FIGURE 12.3   Circuit diagram of parity check.

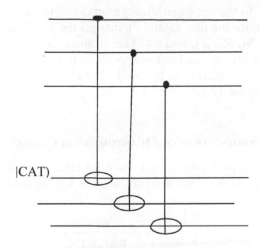

$|CAT\rangle$

FIGURE 12.4   Parity check circuit with CAT.

On the off chance that one of the three control pieces is in the |1) state, it will flip one of the three ancillas. This takes from a superposition of all even piece strings to a superposition of all odd piece strings:

$$|CAT'\rangle = (|001\rangle + |010\rangle + |100\rangle + |111\rangle)/2$$

Another piece flip will move back to the state |CAT). After each of the three CNOTs, the equality of three ancillas will be regardless of whether the three control bits had even equality, and odd if the three control bits had odd equality. At the point when the ancillas were measured, the equality of the string tells the equality of the three control bits; yet a blunder happening to one of the three ancillas will just proliferate up to a solitary control bit.

12.4.3 Bell States

Ringer state is a unique condition of a couple of qubits. Consider $\alpha\ 00 = \alpha\ 11 = 1$ and also $\alpha\ 01 = \alpha\ 01 = 0$. Assuming the first qubit is estimated, the condition of the qubit will be $|f\rangle = |11\rangle, |f\rangle = |00\rangle$. From that point onward, assuming the second qubit is estimated, the condition of the qubit will be $|fII\rangle = |00\rangle, |fII\rangle = |11\rangle$. The two estimations are related; the estimation of 0, 1 of the first qubit is the same as the estimation of the second qubit. In this exploration work, the quantum circuit of chime states is utilized in quantum teleportation. Assume Molecule 1 and Particle 2 are the pair of trapped qubits. Molecule 3 is utilized as the control qubit and Particle 1 is the objective qubit in the beneficiary side. Molecule 2 is in the beneficiary side. In the transmitter side, Molecules 1 and 3 are entrapped by utilizing the CNOT entryway [13]. The trapped state is sent to the beneficiary side through a quantum channel. Then the estimation of two particles (1 and 3) is done at the collector side and afterward the estimated values (00, 01, 10, and 11) are communicated to the recipient through an old-style esteem. In the recipient side, the estimation on the pair (1 and 3) changes the condition of Molecule 2 to one of four states: S1, S2, S3, and S4. The obtained estimated qualities like 00, 01, 10, and 11 separately applied to I-entryway, X-door, and Z-door. The acquired outcome converts the condition of Molecule 2 to a similar state as of Molecule 3. This is shown in Figure 12.5.

12.4.4 QCL Implementation of Quantum Error Correction Code

In this research work, bit flip error and phase flip error inserted for demonstration and then correcting an error are demonstrated. In this research work, 7-bit error

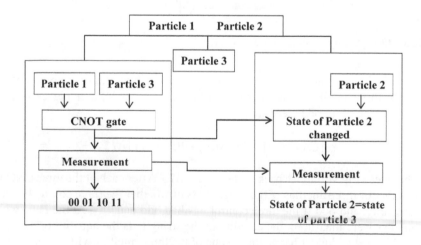

FIGURE 12.5 Quantum circuit of the Bell state.

correction code implemented based on the Steane code is done. The step–by-step procedure for the quantum error correction code is:

1	:	One qubit input register is declared.
2	:	According to the Steane algorithm, one-qubit input register is encoded into seven qubits.
3	:	The Hadamard gate is applied to seven-qubit encoded data to obtain superposition states.
4	:	Before inserting error bit and error correction, the initial state of seven-qubit encoded data measured by using the FT7 procedure and displayed.
5	:	Bit flip error or phase flip error inserted.
6	:	By using dump command state of quregister displayed.
7	:	FT7 procedure is used to measure, detect, and correct error.
8	:	Display the state of quregister after error correction.

The terms used in the quantum error correction code are shown in Table 12.1. The flow chart for quantum error correction code is implemented.

12.4.5 Applications of Quantum Error Correction Circuit

It is broadly acknowledged that a quantum PC will require some type of assurance against decoherence, and to date the lone device fit for giving adaptation to internal

TABLE 12.1
Terms Used in Quantum Error Correction Code

Terms	Description
Encode 7	To encode 1 qubit into 7 qubits
H7	To apply Hadamard transformation
FT7 (logical qubit, false)	To call FT7 function
qureg init[1]	Initiate "1" qubit register
qureg logicalqubit[7]	Initiate "7" qubit register
measure anc0[0],stabilizer	To measuring error in qubit
G0,G1,G2,G3,G4,G5,G6	Stabilizer used to detect position of error bit
IIIXXXX, IXXIIXX and XIXIXIX	Stabilizer for bit flip error
IIIZZZZ, IZZIIZZ, and ZIZIZIZ	Stabilizer for phase flip error
MakeCATstate	To generate superposition of qubit
dump logicalqubit	Display initial state of the encoded qubit
BitFlipError(int index)	To insert bitfliperror at required position
	Ex: BitFlipError (int 0) used to insert bitflip error at "0" th position
	If the state is "0", it is flip into 1
	If the state is "1", it is flip into 0
X(logicalqubit[index])	X-gate used to apply bitfliperror for correction
Z(logicalqubit[index])	Z-gate used to apply bitfliperror for correction
PhaseFlipError(int index)	To insert phasefliperror at required position
	It rotate the phase of the qubit by π radians (180^θ)

failure is quantum error correction (QEC). Constant variable quantum mistake remedying codes can be conjured to secure quantum entryways in superconducting circuits against warm and Hamiltonian clamor.

12.4.6 SIMULATION SETUP

In this research work, qcl simulator with 35-bit code is used. The code required atleast 32-bit code. "qcl -bits=35 –i Steane.qcl" command is used to run code in the terminal.

12.4.7 PROPOSED SYSTEM HARDWARE IMPLEMENTATION

Driven sources are arbitrarily spellbound. In the proposed framework, two sorts of polarization (set 0 and set 1) with two distinctive image sets utilized separately as additionally, Y, cross and square. The swaying point or plane of light from each point on the light source is time changing. Taken as a period normal, in this manner, arbitrarily energized light sources consistently yield different points of polarization. Polarizers ingest episode light swaying taking all things together yet one plane, its polarization hub, yielding direct polarization. Light that goes through two polarizers with symmetrical polarizing to Mohawk. Quantum encryption is accomplished to secure information correspondence. The connection between input/yield voltage and state is provided in Table 12.2.

In the receiver side of the proposed embedded system, encryption and polarization are carried out. In the receiver side of proposed embedded system, decryption and depolarization are carried out. Initially, data is encrypted into bits of 0's and 1's. Photons are used for the conversation of encrypted data into a polarized light between the transmitter and the receiver. Photon in the polarized light is used to denote a single bit of data. In the receiver side, the bit value (0 or 1) is decrypted by states of the photon such as polarization or spin. By using the proposed method, the receiver sends an encrypted data with photons to the receiver. The encryption and decryption are in the same arrangements that consist of two polarizing devices such as LED and LDR. This process is shown in Figure 12.6.

12.4.8 QUANTUM KEY DISTRIBUTION

In communication, data is encrypted for confidentiality. In conventional method, the existing encryption techniques depend on the encryption key (private key) and it is

TABLE 12.2
Input–Output Relation for Encryption Scheme

Symbol Set		Output Values (in Volts)	Minimum	Maximum
Zero	Plus	2.71, 2.72,...	2.70	3.2
	Y	2.75, 2.76, 2.77,...	2.75	3.3
One	Square	3.09, 3.1, 3.11,...	3.09	3.41
	Cross	3.66, 3.67, 3.68, 3.69,...	3.66	3.55

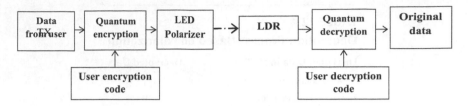

FIGURE 12.6 Block diagram of the proposed system.

TABLE 12.3

Encryption Process Based on Polarization

*i*th Bit of the String S_2	Polarization Type	Binary Form of Data in "S1" Encrypted into Photon Polarization	
		"1"	"0"
1	V/H polarization	Vertical polarization	Horizontal polarization
0	Diagonal polarization	Photon with "θ_1" polarization	Photon with "θ_2" polarization

used for one session only and then rejected. The need for reliable and effective methods for the distribution of the encryption keys is required in a conventional method. The secure and reliable methods for cryptographic key distribution are an active research area in communication. In this research work, polarization-based quantum key distribution is proposed. In this work, vertical/horizontal or diagonal polarized photons can be transmitted by the proposed system. If the photon with horizontal/vertical polarization is used in transmitter, then the photon with vertical polarization will transmit "1" and the photon with horizontal polarization will transmit "0." If the photon with diagonal polarization is used, then the photon with θ_1 degree is the encrypted form of "1" and photon with θ_2 degree is the encrypted form of "0." In the receiver side, photons are separated with different polarization. In the transmitter side, the encryption key is selected with the length of "*x*." In the transmitter side, two random strings (S_1 and S_2) are generated with the length of $(4+\delta)x$. By choosing "δ" sufficiently large transmitter and receiver ensure that the number of bits used is close to "$2x$" with a very high probability. A substring of length "*x*" of the bits in string "S_1" is used as the quantum encryption key and the bits in string "S_2" is used by the transmitter to select the (V/H) polarization or (DG) polarization for each photon: Transmit to receiver. The binary form of the data in string "S_1" is encrypted based on the corresponding values of the bits in string "S_2." The encryption process is shown in Table 12.3 and the decryption process is shown in Table 12.4. The original data is reconstructed by using Table 12.4 in the receiver side.

In this work, the inserted framework-based quantum encryption and decryption utilizing polarization is proposed. The data information and encryption code are taken care of into quantum encryption where the information is encoded. It is then passed to LED enraptured framework and the information is changed over as

TABLE 12.4

Decryption Process Based on Polarization

Encrypted Data in "S1"	Decrypted Data
Vertical polarization	1
Horizontal polarization	0
Photon with "θ_1" polarization	1
Photon with "θ_2" polarization	0

TABLE 12.5

Two Classes of Quantum Particles

Quantum Elements Based Classes	Description	Quantum Numbers
Baryon	Rotation half of the particles	$s = +1/2$ and $s = -1/2$
Bosons	Rotation one particles	$s = +1, s = 0$, and $s = -1$

photons and passed to the transmitter. At the recipient end, LDR is utilized as a locator for generation of electrical sign from light energy. LDR yield is decoded utilizing quantum unscrambling code and the first message is recovered in the recipient side. In the proposed framework, the polarization condition of a photon conveys quantum encryption key (private key of client) and the property of photons is utilized to blunder location.

12.5 SPIN OR POLARIZATION

In quantum mechanics, the characteristic rakish second is called as twist and its quantized qualities are products of the legitimized Planck consistent. The twist of a molecule or of a molecule is ordered by the twist quantum number "s," which might be whole number and half-number qualities. Two classes of quantum particles are appeared in Table 12.4. In this examination work, the scrambled estimation of the information, a "1" or "0," is controlled by both the conditions of the photon (twist or polarization) (Table 12.5).

12.5.1 QUANTUM CRYPTOGRAPHY USING XOR OPERATOR

Encryption and unscrambling are the cycles associated with the study of cryptography. In quantum encryption, plain content in message is scrambled and it can't be perceived besides by somebody having the decode key. Encode or unscramble a line of text to a series of characters depending on a client determined encryption key. In this examination work, bit-wise XOR correlations on the plain content are utilized for encryption with private key. By utilizing the proposed strategy, client can send delicate data to somebody, or need to store touchy data in a data set, and wish to utilize more security than the current cryptography techniques. In this work, the basic XOR figure is basic and is a sort of added substance figure utilized as an encryption calculation that works as per the standards:

- $A \wedge 0 = A$
- $A \wedge A = 0$
- $(A \wedge B) \wedge C = A \wedge (B \wedge C)$
- $(B \wedge A) \wedge A = B \wedge 0 = B$

Where "∧" signifies the selective disjunction (XOR) activity. This activity is at times called modulus 2 expansion (or deduction, which is indistinguishable). With this rationale, information is encoded by applying the bit-wise XOR administrator to each character utilizing a private key. The encoded information is unscrambled into plain content by reapplying the XOR work with the private key to eliminate the code. The XOR administrator is very normal as a segment in more perplexing codes. In remaining techniques, a consistent rehashing key was utilized and the code can inconsequentially be broken utilizing recurrence investigation. On the off chance that the substance of any message can be speculated or in any case known, the key can be uncovered. In this examination work, the XOR administrator encodes information by utilizing client's single private key. Its essential legitimacy is that it is easy to execute, and that the XOR activity is computationally reasonable. The proposed strategy conquers the issue of utilizing the existing technique for concealing data in situations where no specific security is required. In this work, the XOR figure secure level expanded by utilizing irregular private key of client in any event as long as the message. At the point when the keystream is produced by a pseudo-irregular number generator, the outcome is a stream figure.

12.5.2   PSEUDO CODE FOR THE PROPOSED QUANTUM CRYPTOGRAPHY

```
loop: xor operation data=plain text key=private key of user
enable empty string for dataout calculate the length of the
data display the length of data
for i to len dataout=cha(ord(data[i])^ord(key)) end for
return dataout
```

```
loop: encryption
open file in read mode
place original data in string1 get raw_input from user
if (raw_input value is '1') execute xor operation loop write
encrypted data into file else
close the file
```

```
loop: decryption
open file in read mode
place original data in string2 get raw_input from user
if (raw_input value is '2') execute xor operation loop write
encrypted data into file else
close the file
```

In this research work, encrypted and decrypted data using XOR algorithm with the use of the pseudo code is implemented in the Python code. The proposed method is hard to break through with the so-called "brute force" methods (i.e., using random encryption keys), and the pattern recognition is avoided by compressing the plain data before it is encrypted.

12.5.3 RANDOM SUBSTITUTION

In the existing technique, a computerized signature which is the opposite of public key encryption is utilized to demonstrate the character of the sender of a message. This can occur severally. The least complex is to send an irregular message as both plaintext and ciphertext. The beneficiary interprets the ciphertext variant utilizing the distributed public key, and if the two forms match it demonstrates the sender was in control of the private key. However, computerized mark is that it just confirms itself, no message to which it is appended. An elective structure utilizes a repetition or hash capacity to make a message digest from a message to confirm the source and dependability of the message. In this exploration work, a replacement figure is used to give incredible security. By making irregular replacements, the examples that make other replacement figures powerless are disposed of. The most straightforward type of arbitrary replacement is to break a message into squares of 4 bytes (4 ASCII characters) and add a pseudo-irregular number to each obstruct. To recuperate the plaintext (the info message) takes away a similar arrangement of pseudo-irregular numbers from the ciphertext (the encoded message). The key is basically the seed of an incentive for the pseudo-irregular number generator.

12.5.4 MAIN HIGHLIGHTS OF ARBITRARY REPLACEMENTS

*   Highly dependable
*   Simple
*   And it will overcome everything except the most decided and capable aggressors

12.5.5 KEY DEVELOPMENT CALCULATION IN XOR ENCRYPTION

Key development calculation is utilized to produce private key in non-key reiteration way. A plain book may contain not just ASCII console characters (ASCII esteem range 32–127) yet additionally extended ASCII characters (ASCII esteem range 128–255). Client indicated key isn't utilized for enciphering the entire record rather it is utilized as a contribution to initially impede of plain content to produce key utilizing the XOR-based key extension algorithm [15, 16]. Thus, another key is created for each ensuing square of plain text. This works like a scratch cushion

12.5.6   HYBRID REPLACEMENT

In this exploration work, the information to be encoded is given as a contribution to the scrambling calculation. The key extension calculation produces new key for each square and substitutes in a cross-breed way which incorporates both square code replacement followed by stream figure replacement. This methodology utilizes expanded altered Vignere's network. The segment record goes from 255 to 0. (initially it is 0–255). User enterable ASCII console characters range from 32 to 127 (for example, column file range from 0 to 95). The last framework size is of 96×256. This planning arrangement confounds the utilization of characters consequently reinforcing the proposed calculation.

12.5.7   ADVANTAGES OF PROPOSED QUANTUM CRYPTOGRAPHY

- The encryption and decoding are deliberation for client, for example, client envision as though interfacing with unique non-encoded data set, terminating the necessary inquiry.
- Sensitive data, of the put away report, is scrambled so that it isn't straightforwardly usable by the foe.
- The length of the encoded message doesn't surpass the first message.
- The strength of the calculation relies on the security of the key. The security of the key is kept up utilizing likelihood and replacement strategy. On the off chance that the quantity of replacement expands the security of key increments.
- No blunder proliferation.

12.5.8   ERROR DETECTION

Error detection is also possible by the proposed embedded system. In error detection, photon's state will be changed if any one tries to measure or to decrypt the data. This change confirms that the received polarized light will be changed. Both the sender and receiver detect that the message is interrupted.

12.5.9   HARDWARE SETUP

In hardware implementation, the positions of LED (T_X;) and LDR (Rx;) are shown in Tables 12.6 and 12.7.

12.6   PSEUDO CODE

Initialize serial port communication

TABLE 12.6

Position of LED in Hardware Setup

LED$_1$	LED$_2$	LED$_3$
LED$_4$	LED$_5$	LED$_6$
LED$_7$	LED$_8$	LED$_9$

TABLE 12.7

Position of LDR in Hardware Setup

LDR$_1$	LDR$_2$	LDR$_3$
LDR$_4$	LDR$_5$	LDR$_6$
LDR$_7$	LDR$_8$	LDR$_9$

```
Transmitter
execution calibration loop select polarization set enter the
data
encrypted data
x=length of data encrypted data=symbol set
```

```
Receiver
Select polarization set
if (received data length==x) receiver char is calculated
decrypt data
```

```
Loop: calibration
minimum value of plus maximum value of plus minimum value of Y
maximum value of Y minimum value of cross maximum value of
cross minimum value of square maximum value of square
```

12.6.1 RECEIVER CODE FLOW

The main menu of the receiver consists of four options, namely set voltage range, symbol set, receive data, and exit. The set voltage range is used for initial calibration. In calibration, the minimum and maximum values of various symbol sets are assigned. The symbol set is used for selecting the polarization type (0 or 1). The receive data is used to initiate the receiver. Exit is used to close the transmitter.

12.6.2 Transmitter Code Flow

The main menu of the transmitter consists of three options such as set symbol set, transmit data, and exit. The symbol set is used for selecting polarization type (0 or 1). The transmit data is used to transmit data by quantum cryptography. Exit is used to close the transmitter. The implemented hardware is shown in Figure 12.7.

12.7 SIMULATION SETUP

UART setup is used for interacting with the receiver, transmitter, and hyper terminal. USB address (for both transmitter and receiver) is found by using "dmesg" in the terminal window. Connect the circuit as per the connection diagram shown in Figure 12.8. The change corresponds to the USB address in minicom-s. To communicate on serial port in Linux, minicom is used. Minicom is a text-based serial port communications program. It is used to talk to external RS-232 devices such as mobile phones, routers, and serial console ports.

12.7.1 Receiver Setup

Initially, calibration is done for the corresponding polarization set. The receiver mode is enabled. The data is received through output voltage ranges.

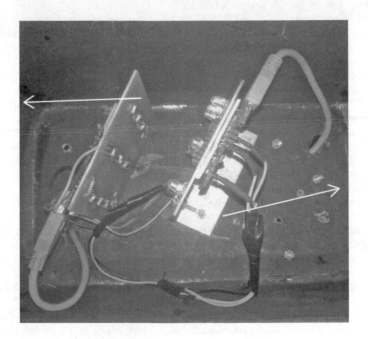

FIGURE 12.7   Implemented hardware.

12.7.2 Summary

In this chapter, a comparison between classical error correction code and quantum error correction code was performed and various types of errors like bit flip error, phase flip error, and combination of both were studied and analyzed. The novelty of this chapter is that hardware implementation is performed for all these types of errors.

REFERENCES

1. W. Stallings, "Cryptography and network security principles and practice 2006", *J. Clerk Maxwell a Treatise on Electricity and Magnetism*, Clarendon, n.d., vol. 2, pp. 68–73, 2006.
2. B. Charles and H Gilles Brassard, *Quantum Cryptography: Public Key Distribution and Coin Tossing*, Elsevier B. V, 2014.
3. N. Kaur, "Enhancement of network security techniques using quantum cryptography", *International Journal on Computer Science and Engineering (IJCSE)*, Vol 3, no 05, 2011.
4. C. Guenther, *The Relevance of Quantum Cryptography in Modern Cryptographic Systems*, SANS Institute, 2004.
5. V. Ojha, A. Sharma, S. K. Lenka and S. R. Biradar, *Advantages of Classical Cryptography over the Quantum Cryptography*, World Applied Programming, 2012.
6. L. O. Mailloux, C. D. Lewis, C. Riggs and M. R. Grimaila, "Post-quantum cryptography: What advancements in quantum computing mean for IT professionals", *IEEE Xplore*, vol. 18, no. 05, Sept.–Oct. 2016.
7. A.K. Singh, S. Bhushan and S. Vij. "A brief analysis and comparison of DCT- and DWT-based image compression techniques", in: Goyal D., Bălaş V.E., Mukherjee A., Hugo C. de Albuquerque V., Gupta A.K. (eds) Information Management and Machine Intelligence. ICIMMI 2019. Algorithms for Intelligent Systems, 2021.
8. P. Techateerawat, "A review on quantum cryptography technology", *International Transaction Journal of Engg Mangmt & Applied Sciences & Technologies*, vol. 1, 2010.
9. M. P. P. Wasankar and P. P. D. Soni, "An invention of quantum cryptography over the classical cryptography for enhancing security", *International Journal of Application or Innovation in Engineering & Management (IJAIEM)*, vol. 2, 2013.
10. S. Bhushan, P. Kumar, A. Kumar and V. Sharma, "Scantime antivirus evasion and malware deployment using silent-SFX," in: 2016 International Conference on Advances in Computing, Communication, & Automation (ICACCA) (Spring), 2016, pp. 1–4, doi: 10.1109/ICACCA.2016.7578894.
11. M. Elboukhari, M. Azizi and A. Azizi, "Quantum key distribution protocols: A survey", *International Journal of Universal Computer Sciences*, vol. 1, 2010.
12. M. Lopes and D. Sarwade, *On the Performance of Quantum Cryptographic Protocols SARG04 and KMB09*, IEEE, 2015.
13. A. Abushgra and K. Elleithy, *QKDP's Comparison Based upon Quantum Cryptography Rules*, IEEE, 2016.
14. M. Diwakar, P. Singh, P. Kumar, K. Tiwari, S. Bhushan and M. Kaushik, "Secure authentication in WLAN using modified four-way handshake protocol", in: Tomar A., Malik H., Kumar P., Iqbal A. (eds) *Machine Learning, Advances in Computing, Renewable Energy and Communication. Lecture Notes in Electrical Engineering.* Springer, vol 768, 2022.

15. P. Curtacci, F. Garzia, R. Cusani and E. Baccarelli, *Performance Analysis of Different Multi-user Optical Passive Networks for Quantum Cryptography Applications*, SPIE Digital Library, 2006.
16. N. Gisin, G. Ribordy, W. Tittel and H. Zbinden, "Quantum cryptography", *Reviews of Modern Physics*, vol. 74, 2002.

13 Risk Analysis Assessment of Interdependency of Vulnerabilities

In Cyber-Physical Systems

Shaurya Gupta, Manoj Kumar,
Shashi Bhushan, and Vinod Kumar Shukla

CONTENTS

13.1 INTRODUCTION

Cyber-physical systems (CPS) involve incorporations regarding calculations in addition to corporeal expansions. Entrenched processers and systems observe and govern corporeal practices that have an impact on calculations and vice versa [1]. Contemporarily, CPS is used extensively in acute nationwide structures like communication, electric power, and transference including energy businesses. Considering the scenario of a big gage overview in terms of IT expertise in various domains in addition to the programmed administration, any digital intimidations that may ascend will leave a concrete effect on the real world including its procedures also [2]. Possible network invasion by opponents leads to various significances while considering smart grid, ranging in terms of consumer inflow and outflow leading to a flow of catastrophes [3]. Preceding effort emphases on dependability—by defending CPSs contrary to any casual, autonomous, and benevolent errors besides fiascos of corporeal constituents—flop to discourse cyber security. Accordingly, the addressing of cyber security facets of CPS is quite imperative. Risk valuation plus investigation

DOI: 10.1201/9781003296034-13

has prospective to discourse the encounters. However, measurable hazard valuation procedures, like probabilistic risk assessment (PRA), are accomplished in CPS. A threat valuation method is based on the probabilistic risk assessment (PRA) for insolent grid structures [4]. Safety threat echelons are measured by the chances of incidence of cyber retreat proceedings. However, it has trouble in identifying the chances for possible security events, which have no existence in the database. The practice recommended by Xie *et al.* [5] delivers an operative means for modeling the outbreak backdrops besides enumerating the cyber security menace assessment in case of CPS. Roy *et al.* [6] discussed an outbreak countermeasure tree, permitting probabilistic analysis to be performed, which is centered, on a combinatorial model. The modeling of computer-generated corporeal security from a perspective of synchronized cyberattack is being discussed by Xu *et al.*[7], though it is quite problematic in identifying the ultimate objective of an aggressor. CPS security involves the security of discrete structure constituents also. An individual facet of the attack might not be of great danger to a consistent constituent, but a collective consequence can be shattering. Typically, current procedures are considering a single-stage attack. For resolving such issues, certain architectures of CPS are discussed with the interdependency of vulnerabilities. For the quantitative measuring of risk, a positive outbreak likelihood key and the outbreak effect key are discussed. Entrenched processers besides systems observe and also regulate corporeal procedures, thereby affecting computations [8]. Considering the case of large-scale information technology expertise in sectors besides involuntary administration, ordinal intimidations arise leaving perceptible impression in terms of an actual realm development [2]. Any kind of intrusion into a network leads to penalties of various sorts in a smart grid, which ranges from leakage of client information to a torrent of catastrophes [3]. The earlier study put emphasis on dependability by defending CPSs against unsystematic, self-determining responsibilities apart from mechanisms which failed to address the cyber security issue. Threat valuation besides exploration has an extraordinary opportunity in addressing encounters. A threat valuation technique, which is centered on probabilistic risk assessment (PRA) for smart grid systems, is being discussed by Kucuktezan *et al.* [9].

13.2 THREAT CONTROL PERSPECTIVE

The simple motive of retreat peril prevailing persists in susceptibilities of CPS. Possible aggressors interrupt the coordination of the overall system by exploiting its weaknesses besides the degree of destruction rests on the value of confronted multitudes.

The harshness of attacks is calculated which is centered on the information of cyberattacks besides outbreak attainment likelihood, which is also calculated and established on susceptibilities' data. Consequently, the hierarchical assessment model is used to estimate the threat of system's structure depending on the prominence of system nodes. Vulnerability scanning or penetration testing calculates data regarding susceptibilities. CPS threat control perspective is being depicted in Figure 13.1.

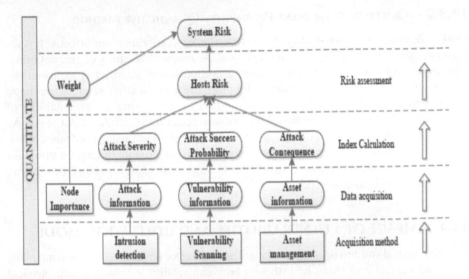

FIGURE 13.1 CPS threat control perspective.

13.3 METHODS FOR SCHEMING THE SEVERITY OF OUTBREAK

There are various methods that are very useful in calculating the intensity and severity of attacks. Two of the primarily used methods are being discussed.

13.3.1 OUTBREAK STERNNESS QUANTITATIVE METHOD

It inculcates the degree of cyberattack's intrinsic destruction limit besides being associated with rudiments like occurrence and strength in terms of cyberattacks. Taking CPS into consideration, the assailant can disable the controller and make him or her incapable of fetching information by aggressively confronting sensors. The assailant may adjust the regulator algorithm straightaway with the means of aggressively confronting the regulator. Various outbreak categories besides their significances are being showcased in Table 13.1.

TABLE 13.1
Strength of Mutual Attacks in CPS

Strength	Categories	Significances
5	Modify control algorithm	Control procedure executing error
4	Modify signals	Operatives involved in wrong decision making
3	Inject error signals	Actuators making incorrect achievement
2	Stop signal transmission	Operators incompetent in get system information
1	Steal cloistered information	Leaking of cloistered data

13.3.2 OUTBREAK ATTAINMENT PROBABILITY QUANTITATIVE METHOD

Outbreak attainment possibility states that the susceptibilities are effectively subjugated apart from signifying inherent besides essential features of susceptibility, which are persistent over phase. Attack accomplishment prospect is measured by exploitability of susceptibility depending on the complication level. A common vulnerability scoring system displays a method for calculating the exploitability of susceptibility. It describes exploitability of susceptibility as $V = Ac \times Au \times Av$. Ac defines how informal or challenging it will be in exploiting the exposed susceptibility. Au defines the number of times an aggressor must validate to target a threat for exploiting it. Av displays how a susceptibility can be subjugated and its types: Local, adjacent network, and network.

13.4 IMPACT OF VULNERABILITIES AND UTILIZATION MODE

Cyber-physical frameworks give another technique for partnering the existing plans with individuals and show how these plans can solidify estimations and physical exercises. These systems speak with the physical world utilizing the latest methodologies. Cyber-physical system (CPS) has the capacity to interrelate physical resources with the help of affiliation, assessment, and transmission. It is an essential factor for further developing future headways [9]. In a general sense, CPS executes certain strategies to change the way the framework acts on seeing the exercises the framework is performing. This is to fabricate a physical framework that should work appropriately in a further developed way. It may be perceived very well that the cyber framework is noticing the physical movement. Successively, various gadgets that can detect, impart remotely, and register are associated with this framework. In the physical area, the exercises are administered by standard occurrence, a human-made physical framework, or a dynamically bewildering blend of the two [9,10]. There is much headway in the PC programming dialects, techniques being utilized for calculation, origination or insight, design of compilers, frameworks for installed frameworks, and programming for framework programming with the assistance of novel methodology to get protected and reliable PC framework. Likewise, wide research in adaptation to non-critical failure and cyber security leads to numerous enhancements in these fields. CPSs merge the components of physical movement with transmission and programming. This merged framework outfits the thoughts that are shown close by the proposed and examination systems. Examination on CPSs plans to fuse information and make rules with the designing and assessed rules; for instance, regulate, code, balanced correspondence, the theory of learning, puts together comparably electrical, biomedical, mechanical and different rules to produce a novel CPS strategy through strong techniques. In various organizations, distinctive structure frameworks have been arranged by decoupling the control framework structure from the product data or shown equipment. This requires widespread reproduction to approve also, to determine vagueness in demonstrating and subjective contentions, ad-libbed guideline strategies are required. While keeping the framework workable and functional, a combination of various subsystems has been dreary and more costly. Government figuring assets screen and control the CPS, which are the physical structures that can be executed. CPSs just run any place that we could perceive. CPS assumes a critical part in ensuring the stateful organizations with the correspondence methodology. The correspondence holds a method of working with the innovations with successful improvements. The web which helps in conveying from anyplace to anyplace has changed the existence of human considerably less confusing than what might have been imagined. The impossible viewpoints are acknowledged as constant arrangements with the assistance of CPS as it made a recent fad in the correspondence framework. As time has progressed, modernized life scientist have begun the ways towards progressive substantial frameworks along with answers for varied works in fundamental systems. CPS has different and specific dissimilarities. Today is subsequently conceived in another grouping of frameworks that fundamentally installs possible cyber results in the physical world on either a nearby or base program. Because of the advancement made in the unpredictability of the parts and the utilization of significantly made developments for sensors and actuators, distant correspondence and multicore processors lead to a huge test for the design of state-of-the-art vehicle control frameworks. Both the seller and the integrator require an original framework which licenses a dependable and less costly blend of the parts that are set up autonomous to each other [9]. The design, assessment, and check of the modules at different phases of development are made with the assistance of apparatuses that are utilized to grow more affordable methods. The different phases of development contain item level, design level, assessment level, and acknowledgment of correspondence in the midst of the key framework and also its subparts to ensure security, immovability, and the conduct in spite of the truth that the costs are decreased for the client.

13.5 MODELING ATTACKS ON A CPS

In this we have to explore not many designated assault models utilizing control hypothesis and factual methods as clarified in Section 13.3. We utilize a contextual analysis on a standard four-tank framework. We foster a numerical model and reenact in recreation programming. The objective is in dissecting different CPS assault models as for state space conditions, furthermore, making a remedial move utilizing measurable methods as examined.

The fundamental commitments of this section are as per the following:

1. Grouping of different control mindful assaults (focused on assaults) utilizing state space conditions.
2. Reenactment of control mindful assaults on a four-tank model.
3. Identification of assault utilizing measurable strategies like SPRT, CUSUM, relationship, co-fluctuation, and so on: Consider a breeze power plant.

In the event that the speed of the rotor is expanded in mathematical movement, the plant will in any case stay functional until the information doesn't move it into a perilous zone. Essentially, if a forced-air system is constrained by a PLC exposed to a mathematical reduction in the temperature, then the room temperature will begin dropping gradually toward the start and afterward radically toward the end. This activity results in harms to the gadgets that were to work at a specific room temperature. In this section, we have recognized different designated control mindful digital assaults. We have ordered different control mindful assaults (focused on assaults) utilizing state space conditions.

1. The authors have likewise examined methods for getting control frameworks and showed the viability of the said procedures by fusing changes as expressed in the assault model.
2. Our work showed that the control assaults can be identified by development esteem change.
3. We have demonstrated different designated assaults utilizing control condition information from Section 13.3 utilizing a four-tank model.

We have stretched out the SPRT method further to plan security screens in the accompanying part. The proposed SPRT procedure anyway has a limit in separating framework disappointment because of inward shortcoming and assault. The SPRT technique is likewise not versatile to a huge disseminated control framework for which a definite state space model isn't accessible.

13.6   ONLINE MONITORING IN A CYBER-PHYSICAL SYSTEM

Measurable strategies like SPRT, CUSUM, and GLR which are talked about in the past part are helpful in the examination of little changes in regulator yield. In the current section, we expand the strategies utilizing a logical strategy dependent on regulator yield logs. Here we accept that regulators are acknowledged in programming-based frameworks with help of information chronicling. It is likewise accepted that enough information has been gathered so the measurements of its great presentation recorded over the long run are sufficient to arrange as typical activity and also conceivable unusual conduct.

For huge noteworthy or constant information, strategies, for example, SPRT, CUSUM, are not adequate, thus we need computational techniques that can deal with enormous log documents. The following segment clarifies the hypothesis of computational strategy that is helpful in planning a screen for investigation.

Different computational techniques accessible are

A. Euclidean distance
B. Mahalanobis distance
C. Pearson's connection coefficient
D. Rent square estimation (LSA)
E. Computational mathematical (convexity) technique least square estimation (LSA) and convexity (curved body) techniques are thought of for our examination.

13.7 CONCLUSION

The exploration work showed that designated digital assaults in charge frameworks are conceivable to be recognized utilizing measurable strategies. The theory has given a review on the attack models and we have recognized exploration challenges for getting control frameworks. We have executed measurable strategies to identify such commonplace digital assaults on programming executed regulators and showed the strategy utilizing a reproduction on the old-style four-tank model. We have examined different measurable strategies such as SPRT, CUSUM, and GLR for identifying digital assaults and calculations for getting control frameworks. We have moreover shown the viability of the strategies by fusing changes as expressed in an assault model, what's more, exhibited that these can be distinguished by advancement esteem change. Internet checking assumes a crucial part in noticing the control framework conduct and to distinguish irregular conduct. Computational calculation like LSA and mathematical strategies were planned and shown utilizing a recreated four-tank model. The adequacy of the curved body approach alongside LSA for peculiarity recognition is tried. Computational mathematical methodologies, for example, LSA and curved body techniques, enjoy the benefits in breaking down complex log information got from a SCADA worker and identifying abnormalities. Comprehend the troubles of how such screens can be integrated in lower-level regulators that would have the option to apply such calculations for the discovery of a node to run such complex calculations. An option in contrast to the web-based observing plan would be to utilize such calculations as disconnected screens. It is intriguing to perceive how the calculations could be acknowledged effectively.

REFERENCES

1. Hong, Seongsoo, Peter Puschner, and Luiz Bacellar, eds. Object-oriented Real-time Distributed Computing-ISORC 2002: Proceedings. IEEE Computer Society, 2002.
2. Chen, Thomas M., and Saeed Abu-Nimeh. "Lessons from stuxnet." *Computer* 44.4 (2011): 91–93.
3. Wang, Wenye, and Zhuo Lu. "Cyber security in the smart grid: Survey and challenges." *Computer Networks* 57.5 (2013): 1344–1371.
4. Kucuktezan, Cavit Fatih, and VM Istemihan Genc. "Dynamic security assessment of a power system based on probabilistic neural networks." 2010 IEEE PES Innovative Smart Grid Technologies Conference Europe (ISGT Europe). IEEE, 2010.
5. Xie, Feng, et al. "Security analysis on cyber-physical system using attack tree." 2013 9th International Conference on Intelligent Information Hiding and Multimedia Signal Processing. IEEE, 2013.
6. Roy, Arpan, Dong Seong Kim, and Kishor S. Trivedi. "Cyber security analysis using attack countermeasure trees." Proceedings of the 6th Annual Workshop on Cyber Security and Information Intelligence Research. 2010.
7. Xu, X., H. Q. Yu, and J. H. Huang. "Petri net based security quantitative analysis model for cyber-physical system." *Computer Engineering and Applications* 50.3 (2014): 82–88.

8. Lee, Edward A. "Cyber-physical systems: Design challenges." 2008 11th IEEE International Symposium on Object Oriented Real-Time Distributed Computing (ISORC). 2008.
9. Kucuktezan, Cavit Fatih, and VM Istemihan Genc. "Dynamic security assessment of a power system based on probabilistic neural networks." 2010 IEEE PES Innovative Smart Grid Technologies Conference Europe (ISGT Europe). IEEE, 2010.
10. Xie, Feng, et al. "Security analysis on cyber-physical system using attack tree." 2013 9th International Conference on Intelligent Information Hiding and Multimedia Signal Processing. IEEE, 2013.

Index

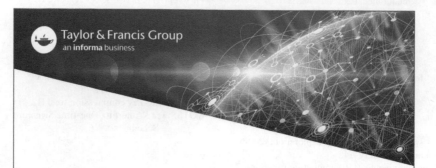